# Attitude Reports

Propositional attitude reports are sentences built around clause-embedding psychological verbs, like *Kim believes that it's raining* or *Kim wants it to rain*. These interact in many intricate ways with a wide variety of semantically relevant grammatical phenomena, and represent one of the most important topics at the interface of linguistics and philosophy, as their study provides insight into foundational questions about meaning. This book provides a bird's–eye overview of the grammar of propositional attitude reports, synthesizing the key facts, theories, and open problems in their analysis. Couched in the theoretical framework of generative grammar and compositional truth-conditional semantics, it places emphasis on points of intersection between propositional attitude reports and other important topics in semantic and syntactic theory. With discussion points, suggestions for further reading, and a useful guide to symbols and conventions, it will be welcomed by students and researchers wishing to explore this fertile area of study.

THOMAS GRANO is Associate Professor in the Department of Linguistics at Indiana University Bloomington. He is the author of *Control and Restructuring* (2015) and his work has appeared in numerous journals.

KEY TOPICS IN SEMANTICS AND PRAGMATICS

'Key Topics in Semantics and Pragmatics' focuses on the main topics of study in semantics and pragmatics today. It consists of accessible yet challenging accounts of the most important issues, concepts and phenomena to consider when examining meaning in language. Some topics have been the subject of semantic and pragmatic study for many years, and are re-examined in this series in light of new developments in the field; others are issues of growing importance that have not so far been given a sustained treatment. Written by leading experts and designed to bridge the gap between textbooks and primary literature, the books in this series can either be used on courses and seminars, or as one-stop, succinct guides to a particular topic for individual students and researchers. Each book includes useful suggestions for further reading, discussion questions and a helpful glossary.

Already published in the series:

*Meaning and Humour* by Andrew Goatly

*Metaphor* by L. David Ritchie

*Imperatives* by Mark Jary and Mikhail Kissine

*Modification* by Marcin Morzycki

*Semantics for Counting and Measuring* by Susan Rothstein

*Irony* by Joana Garmendia

*Implicatures* by Sandrine Zufferey, Jacques Moeschler and Anne Reboul

*The Semantics of Case* by Olga Kagan

Forthcoming titles:

*Frame Semantics* by Hans C. Boas

*Proper Names and Direct Reference* by Gregory Bochner

*Semantics and Pragmatics in Sign Languages* by Kathryn Davidson Zaremba

*Propositional Logic* by Allen Hazen and Jeffrey Pelletier

*Indirect Speech Acts* by Nicolas Ruytenbeek

# Attitude Reports

THOMAS GRANO
*Indiana University*

# CAMBRIDGE
UNIVERSITY PRESS

University Printing House, Cambridge CB2 8BS, United Kingdom

One Liberty Plaza, 20th Floor, New York, NY 10006, USA

477 Williamstown Road, Port Melbourne, VIC 3207, Australia

314–321, 3rd Floor, Plot 3, Splendor Forum, Jasola District Centre, New Delhi – 110025, India

79 Anson Road, #06–04/06, Singapore 079906

Cambridge University Press is part of the University of Cambridge.

It furthers the University's mission by disseminating knowledge in the pursuit of education, learning, and research at the highest international levels of excellence.

www.cambridge.org
Information on this title: www.cambridge.org/9781108423281
DOI: 10.1017/9781108525718

© Thomas Grano 2021

This publication is in copyright. Subject to statutory exception and to the provisions of relevant collective licensing agreements, no reproduction of any part may take place without the written permission of Cambridge University Press.

First published 2021

*A catalogue record for this publication is available from the British Library.*

*Library of Congress Cataloging-in-Publication Data*

Names: Grano, Thomas, author.
Title: Attitude reports / Thomas Grano.
Description: Cambridge ; New York, NY : Cambridge University Press, 2021 |
  Series: Key topics in semantics and pragmatics | Includes
  bibliographical references and index.
Identifiers: LCCN 2020049790 (print) | LCCN 2020049791 (ebook) | ISBN 9781108423281
  (hardback) | ISBN 9781108437202 (paperback) | ISBN 9781108525718 (epub)
Subjects: LCSH: Propositional attitudes. | Semantics. | Pragmatics. |
  Grammar, Comparative and general–Sentences. | Grammar, Comparative and
  general–Syntax. | Modality (Linguistics) | Intentionality (Philosophy) | Scope (Linguistics)
Classification: LCC P99.4.P72 G734 2021 (print) | LCC P99.4.P72 (ebook) |
  DDC 401/.45–dc23
LC record available at https://lccn.loc.gov/2020049790
LC ebook record available at https://lccn.loc.gov/2020049791

ISBN 978-1-108-42328-1 Hardback

Cambridge University Press has no responsibility for the persistence or accuracy of URLs for external or third-party internet websites referred to in this publication and does not guarantee that any content on such websites is, or will remain, accurate or appropriate.

For Amanda

# Contents

*Acknowledgments page xi*
*List of Abbreviations Used in Glosses xiii*

1. Introduction  1
   1.1 What Are Attitude Reports?  1
   1.2 Why a Book about Attitude Reports?  3
      1.2.1 Attitude Reports and Sentence Meaning  4
      1.2.2 Attitude Reports and Proper Names  6
      1.2.3 Attitude Reports and Grammar  7
   1.3 The Approach  8
   1.4 A Note on Readership and Topical Emphasis  9
   1.5 Guide to Logical Symbols and Notational Conventions  10
   1.6 Chapter Summaries  13
   1.7 Further Reading  14

2. Foundations  15
   2.1 Introduction  15
   2.2 Background on Possible Worlds Semantics  16
      2.2.1 Extensional Semantics and Its Limits  16
      2.2.2 Introducing Intensions  22
   2.3 Attitudes in Possible Worlds Semantics  26
      2.3.1 Logical Relations between Propositions  26
      2.3.2 The Hintikkan Approach to Attitude Semantics  29
      2.3.3 Predictions of the Hintikkan Approach  33
   2.4 The Problem of Logical Omniscience  36
      2.4.1 A Tension  36
      2.4.2 Strategy #1: Complicate the Hintikkan Semantics  39
      2.4.3 Strategy #2: Abandon the Hintikkan Semantics  41
   2.5 Hyperintensionality: Ways of Fine-Graining  42
      2.5.1 Motivation  42
      2.5.2 Propositional Concepts  47
      2.5.3 Impossible Worlds  49

vii

2.5.4 Situations  51
2.5.5 Structured Propositions  52
2.5.6 Sententialism  53
2.5.7 Interpreted Logical Forms  54
2.5.8 Taking Stock  55
2.6 Attitudes, Event Semantics, and Decomposition  55
2.7 Discussion Questions  63
2.8 Further Reading  65

3. Attitude Reports and Proper Names  66
3.1 Introduction  66
3.2 The Non-rigid Designator Approach  68
3.3 The Pragmatic Approach  71
3.4 The Hidden Indexicals Approach  75
3.5 Kripke's Puzzle  76
3.6 Substitution in Simple Sentences  79
3.7 Discussion Questions  80
3.8 Further Reading  80

4. The *de dicto/de re* Ambiguity  82
4.1 Introduction  82
4.2 The Scope Theory  84
4.3 Scope Mismatches  89
   4.3.1 Scope Islands  90
   4.3.2 Scope Paradoxes  93
   4.3.3 Third Readings  94
   4.3.4 Summary  96
4.4 Resolving the Mismatches  97
   4.4.1 World Pronouns  97
   4.4.2 Split Intensionality  102
   4.4.3 Presupposition Projection  105
4.5 Double Vision  106
   4.5.1 The Puzzle  107
   4.5.2 Acquaintance Relations  109
   4.5.3 The Shortest Spy  112
   4.5.4 *Res* Movement  115
   4.5.5 Concept Generators  117
4.6 Taking Stock  119
4.7 Discussion Questions  120
4.8 Further Reading  121

5. *De se* Attitude Reports   122
    5.1 Introduction   122
    5.2 Divorcing *de se* from Semantic Binding   125
    5.3 Properties and Centered Worlds   126
    5.4 PRO as Author-/Addressee- or Center-Denoting   132
    5.5 The *de re* Blocking Effect   137
    5.6 *De se* as a Special Case of *de re*?   140
        5.6.1 The Argument from Agreement   141
        5.6.2 The *de se* Generalization   142
    5.7 Expanding the Empirical Coverage   143
        5.7.1 Logophors   144
        5.7.2 Shifted Indexicals   146
        5.7.3 Long-Distance Reflexives   151
    5.8 Discussion Questions   152
    5.9 Further Reading   153

6. Desire Reports and Beyond   154
    6.1 Introduction   154
    6.2 Belief-Relativity   154
        6.2.1 The Better-Worlds Approach   155
        6.2.2 The Best-World Approach   159
        6.2.3 A Doxastic Presupposition   160
        6.2.4 Refining the Presupposition   162
    6.3 Monotonicity   164
    6.4 Conjunction Introduction and Conflicting Desires   168
    6.5 Gradability   172
    6.6 Focus-Sensitivity   174
    6.7 Presupposition Projection   176
    6.8 The Typology of Attitude Predicates   177
    6.9 Discussion Questions   182
    6.10 Further Reading   183

7. Other Topics   184
    7.1 Introduction   184
    7.2 Attitude Reports and Embedded Tense   184
        7.2.1 Introduction   184
        7.2.2 Tense Basics   185
        7.2.3 Tense Binding in Attitude Reports   186
        7.2.4 Past under Past: Sequence of Tense   188
        7.2.5 Present under Past: Double Access   192

- 7.3 Neg Raising  *193*
  - 7.3.1 Introduction  *193*
  - 7.3.2 In Favor of a Syntactic Approach  *194*
  - 7.3.3 Against a Syntactic Approach  *196*
- 7.4 Intensional Transitive Verbs  *198*
  - 7.4.1 Introduction  *198*
  - 7.4.2 Diagnosing Intensionality  *199*
  - 7.4.3 Propositionalism  *200*
  - 7.4.4 Intensionalism  *203*
- 7.5 Discussion Questions  *204*
- 7.6 Further Reading  *205*

*Glossary*  *207*
*Bibliography*  *213*
*Index*  *233*

# Acknowledgments

Many people helped make this book possible. First, I would like to thank (in alphabetical order) Alexander Williams, Ezra Keshet, Hazel Pearson, Kirk Ludwig, Larry Moss, Milo Phillips-Brown, Orin Percus, and Valentine Hacquard. Some of you offered concrete feedback on specific sections of this book. Some of you offered general advice and encouragement. All of you deserve some of the credit for the parts of this book that I got right. Of course, I assume 100% responsibility for those parts that – despite my best efforts – I inevitably got wrong.

I would like to thank Helen Barton at Cambridge University Press for her guidance, responsiveness, and encouragement throughout the preparation of this book, from the initial idea all the way through to the finished manuscript. I am also very grateful to two anonymous referees for their highly constructive feedback on the proposal and on the manuscript itself. Both of them helped improve the final product in important ways.

I would also like to thank my department colleagues and students at Indiana University for helping to create the kind of intellectually stimulating and collegial environment that makes writing a book like this possible. I wrote most of this book in my office at work, where you gave me the space that I needed, but also brought many forms of welcome relief that happily prevented this book from consuming my professional life for the past couple of years – even if world events compelled me to finish the book from home. At the time of this writing, I sorely miss your company, and hope that things get back to something like normal soon.

There is no way I can properly thank Amanda Grano, whose support (mental, emotional, and otherwise) since we met over twelve years ago goes beyond what words can express. (I know it's a cliché, but it's true.) It's been almost four years since I first had the idea for this book, and you've helped that time go by so quickly that it's hard to believe it represents almost a third of our lives together so far. At the time of this writing, our lives are about to take an exciting turn, and finishing this book seems an appropriate way for me to help mark that transition.

Finally, thanks go to my dog Beatrix (who's now been in our lives almost as long as this book project), my cat Maggie (who's old enough to remember keeping me company while I wrote my dissertation), and my cat Polly (short for Polysemy). I thank the three of you not only for your companionship throughout the years of working on this project, but also for your unwitting roles as protagonists in many of the example sentences featured in this book. Your names endowed these examples with a vividness (perhaps, in Kaplan's 1968 sense) that helped me approach them with a fresh mind, and with that said, I hope that readers will be charitable with some examples in understanding that these names refer to dogs and cats (e.g. *Beatrix chases Maggie*), while humoring me by pretending that they are people when the examples make much more sense that way (e.g. *Beatrix believes that she left her keys in the car.*) To what extent nonhuman animals have propositional attitudes that we can report on is a fascinating topic, but not one that I mean to stumble into in this book.

# List of Abbreviations Used in Glosses

- AREALS = areal subject (Navajo)
- COMPL = complementizer
- COP = copula
- FUT = future tense
- IMPF = imperfective aspect
- LOG = logophor
- NOM = nominative case
- NEG = negation
- OBL = oblique
- PERF = perfect aspect
- PFV = perfective aspect
- POSS = possessive
- PRES = present tense
- PST = past tense
- 1S = first-person singular
- 1sO = first-person singular object
- 3s = third-person singular
- 3SM = third-person singular masculine
- TOP = topic marker

# 1 Introduction

## 1.1 WHAT ARE ATTITUDE REPORTS?

Humans lead rich mental lives, and the languages that we speak afford us rich vocabularies for describing them. A sampling of some of that vocabulary as found in English (sorted into syntactically and semantically relevant groups) is shown in (1).

(1) a. think, believe, know, conclude, doubt, guess, understand, ...;
    b. dream, imagine, pretend, fantasize, ...;
    c. (be) happy, (be) sad, (be) mad, (be) surprised, ...;
    d. want, wish, hope, like, love, hate, fear, ...;
    e. intend, plan, decide, aim, try, ...

All of these verbs and adjectives share a syntactic behavior that has attracted a huge amount of attention from linguists and philosophers alike: they can embed sentences, or, in some cases, sentence-like constituents (in particular, infinitives, also known as nonfinite clauses). For example, all of the words in (1-a–c) and some of the words in (1-d–e) can embed the sentence in (2), yielding complex sentences like (3).

(2) It's raining.

(3) Beatrix thinks [it's raining].

Similarly, some of the words in (1-a–b) and all of the words in (1c–e) are able to embed some species or another of nonfinite clause, as illustrated in (4-a–b) for *want* and *intend*, respectively.

(4) a. Beatrix wants [it to rain].
    b. Beatrix intends [to buy an umbrella].

An important idea in generative grammar is that form does not always follow function; that is, not all syntactic behavior is explainable by appeal to semantic considerations. But *some* syntactic behavior is so explainable, and surely it is no accident that many of the verbs and adjectives we use for describing our mental lives have the ability to embed sentences or sentence-like constituents: it is emblematic of what philosophers of mind call INTENTIONALITY,[1] which is the capacity of the mind to represent mind-external objects.[2] Beliefs and desires, for example, have objects, and often those objects are of the sort that we can use sentences to name or describe. Perhaps not all of the mental states and actions described by the words in (1) work like this in every situation. Maybe, for example, I can have 'undirected' anger (ultimately, this is a question for psychologists or philosophers, not linguists). But I can also be angry *about something* or angry *that something is the case*.

In many theories of meaning, sentences denote PROPOSITIONS, which we might define, initially, as things that can be true or false. Accordingly, Russell (1940) coined the term PROPOSITIONAL ATTITUDE as a label for what we are talking about when we use sentences built around sentence-embedding psychological verbs like *believe*, *desire*, and *doubt*. In the meantime, it has become commonplace to use the term PROPOSITIONAL ATTITUDE REPORT as a label for the sentences themselves. For the sake of concision, I will often refer to these – as I do in the title of this book – simply as 'attitude reports.'

Let me now mention a couple of phenomena that – given what's just been said – one might be surprised to see included in this book, as well as one phenomenon that one might be surprised to see excluded.

First, I consider INDIRECT SPEECH REPORTS like (5) to be within the purview of this book.

(5)  Beatrix says [it's raining].

Although, strictly speaking, we would not want to consider sentences like this to be attitude reports in the narrow sense of naming a

---

[1] All small-capped terms in this book are listed alphabetically and defined in the Glossary at the end of the book, often with a cross-reference to the section of the book in which they are discussed. In general, I will use small caps for these terms only at their first occurrence in each chapter they appear in.

[2] Intentionality (with a 't') is not to be confused with INTENSIONALITY (with an 's'). The latter stands in opposition to EXTENSIONALITY, and has to do with the semantic machinery (often modeled using possible worlds) needed for model-theoretic analysis of expressions involving possibility and necessity, including not only attitude reports but also modal expressions more generally. (More on this in Chapter 2.) To make matters more confusing, both intentionality and intensionality stand in contrast with *intention*, which, just as in ordinary usage, names a particular kind of mental attitude that involves a commitment to perform an action, often expressed in English with the verb *intend*.

psychological state, indirect speech reports share so many semantic and syntactic properties with attitude reports in the narrow sense that it would be a mistake to ignore them entirely.

Second, I will also devote some discussion to sentences like (6), despite the fact that (at least superficially) they embed neither sentences nor sentence-like constituents; instead, they exemplify what are known as INTENSIONAL TRANSITIVE VERBS.

(6) a. Beatrix wants [a frisbee].
 b. Beatrix is looking for [a frisbee].

As we shall see, these sentences also share enough properties with overtly clause-embedding attitude reports that we would not want to exclude them on a superficial syntactic technicality. Not only that, we will see that foundational questions about the status of intensionality in natural language grammar turn in part on the analysis of sentences like (6).

As for what's not covered in this book: with the exception of some extremely brief comments in Section 2.6, I will have nothing to say about so-called PERCEPTUAL REPORTS like (7).

(7) Beatrix saw/heard/felt [the frisbee fly by].

Perceptual reports are centered around sense verbs like *see*, *hear*, and *feel*, and are syntactically distinguishable from most attitude reports in that they embed a so-called bare or naked infinitive (an infinitive that lacks the infinitival marker *to* ordinarily found in nonfinite clauses in English). In spite of their obvious connection to mental states, there are good reasons for isolating perceptual reports as a class of sentences that are in some ways distinct from attitude reports; see Barwise (1981), Higginbotham (1983) for two relevant classics. That being said, I think that a comprehensive picture of attitude reports will ultimately need to elucidate their similarities and differences with respect to perceptual reports. But that will have to wait for another occasion.

## 1.2 WHY A BOOK ABOUT ATTITUDE REPORTS?

So much for trying to define the object of study. Now on to a perhaps even more pressing question: why read (or for me, write) a book about attitude reports? In a nutshell, the answer is that attitude reports stand as one of the most central topics at the intersection between philosophy and linguistics. On the one hand, attitude reports bear on foundational questions about the nature of sentence meaning and about the nature of proper names. These questions are typically studied by philosophers of language. On the other hand, attitude reports also interact in intricate ways with a host of semantically relevant grammatical phenomena. This makes attitude reports a very fertile area of study for linguists interested in natural language semantics and its interface with syntax and pragmatics. And yet, despite all this, there exists to date no book-length resource surveying the major findings and open questions and helping one navigate the enormous scholarly literature that attitude reports have inspired (though see Section 1.7 for a list of relevant survey articles and book chapters). While no single book could hope to do full justice to all the dimensions of a topic as rich as attitude reports, we have to start somewhere, and this book is my modest attempt at beginning to fill this gap. Let me now elaborate on some of these themes in more detail.

### 1.2.1 Attitude Reports and Sentence Meaning

One central guiding idea behind formal semantics as ordinarily practiced is that sentences of natural language have meanings that are individuated by and statable in terms of TRUTH CONDITIONS. If I tell you that it is raining, you may not know whether I've spoken truthfully, but as a competent speaker of English, you know that what I've said is in principle either true or false, and you also have some idea of what the sentence's truth or falsity turns on. The predominant approach in formal semantics for modeling this property of sentences is to say that the meaning of a sentence is, on some level, a set of possible worlds, namely those worlds in which the sentence in question is true.[3] This approach is well suited for many natural language phenomena. But it threatens to break down for attitude reports, which seem to be sensitive, at least sometimes, to distinctions that are more finely grained than truth conditions.

To be sure, we already know, quite independently of attitude reports, that there are aspects of natural language meaning that are beyond the reach of truth conditionality. This is, after all, a cornerstone of speech act theory as first developed by Austin (1962), and similar themes continue to be explored today, sometimes under the label

---

[3] A variant of this approach is to say that the meaning of a sentence is a function from worlds to truth values, namely that function which returns the value true if and only if the world it applies to is one in which the sentence in question is true. The choice between the set approach and the function approach is irrelevant to the discussion here.

## 1.2 Why a Book about Attitude Reports?

USE-CONDITIONAL MEANING (see e.g. Gutzmann 2015). To take some extreme examples, it makes little sense to assign truth conditions to expressions like *Hello!* or *Ouch!* But the threat attitude reports pose to truth conditionality is an even more serious one. The reason is that when it comes to attitude reports, truth-conditional approaches seem to get the facts wrong on precisely the kinds of phenomena that they ordinarily excel at: accounting for logical inference patterns. To take one example from the literature (Kamp et al. 2011: 344), the two sentences in (8-a) and (8-b) are truth-conditionally equivalent, although it may take some mathematical sophistication to see this.

(8)    a. There are twice as many women in Bill's class as men.
       b. Any set containing the number of the men in Bill's class and closed under the operation of forming addition will contain the number of the women in his class. (Kamp et al. 2011: 344)

In spite of this truth-conditional equivalence, it is not difficult to imagine a scenario in which we would be prepared to accept the truth of (9-a) but not prepared to accept the truth of (9-b). This is the so-called PROBLEM OF LOGICAL EQUIVALENCE for attitude reports.

(9)    a. Bill believes that [there are twice as many women in his class as men].
       b. Bill believes that [any set containing the number of the men in his class and closed under the operation of forming addition will contain the number of the women in his class].

Considerations of this sort have led many scholars to hypothesize that the semantics of an attitude report sensitive in some way to the *form* that the embedded sentence takes, a sensitivity that discriminates even between differences in form that ordinarily do not engender differences in truth conditions. But if that's the case, then we are led to ask: does *any* difference in the form of the embedded sentence change the meaning of an attitude report? Consider another pair of truth-conditionally equivalent sentences, shown in (10). In contrast with the previous case, it is very difficult to imagine a scenario in which we would be prepared to accept the truth of (11-a) but not prepared to accept the truth of (11-b).

(10)    a. Beatrix is chasing Maggie.
        b. Maggie is being chased by Beatrix.

(11)    a. Polly believes that [Beatrix is chasing Maggie].
        b. Polly believes that [Maggie is being chased by Beatrix].

It should be intuitively clear why the two cases differ: recognizing the equivalence in (8) requires mathematical sophistication that Bill may not have, whereas the equivalence in (10) is something that we'd expect any competent speaker of English to acknowledge, even if only tacitly. But it is quite another matter to build a theory that draws a principled grammatical distinction between the two kinds of cases. Suppose no such distinction can be drawn. (Not that we should give up that easily – but suppose it, just so we can explore its consequences for a moment.) In that case, we are left with a choice. At one extreme, we might pursue a theory in which differences in the form of the embedded sentence always lead to differences in the meaning of the report, and explain away the perceived equivalence of (11) as something that is, strictly speaking, not a matter of semantics. At the other extreme, we might pursue a theory in which differences in the form of the embedded sentence that are not ordinarily truth-conditionally consequential never lead to differences in the meaning of the report, and explain away the perceived non-equivalence of (8) on pragmatic grounds: technically speaking, we would say, they are equivalent, but they give rise to different conversational implicatures that cloud this judgment.

In this way, attitude reports constitute a crucial testing ground for theories of sentence meaning. As things currently stand, there are a great many proposals on the market but nothing close to a consensus about which one is right. We will revisit this matter in Chapter 2.

### 1.2.2 Attitude Reports and Proper Names

Another important idea about natural language meaning – and, one could argue, a key explanandum of semantic theory – is that we can use language to refer to language-external objects. Proper names are a central example. I can utter the words *Stephen King* and thereby refer to a particular individual, namely the popular American horror writer who wrote *It* and other bestselling novels. And, according to the predominant view in formal semantics, the meaning of a proper name like *Stephen King* consists *solely* in its capacity to refer to the relevant individual. But if this is right, then two proper names that refer to the same individual should be semantically identical. Together with some other reasonable assumptions, this leads to the expectation that *Stephen King* and *Richard Bachman* (a pen name that Stephen King has occasionally used) should be interchangeable in all contexts without affecting the meaning of the sentence that they appear in. This expectation usually seems to hold up; for example, it seems intuitive that if Stephen King

## 1.2 Why a Book about Attitude Reports?

is Richard Bachman, then (12-a) is true if and only if (12-b) is true. But, in what has come to be known as FREGE'S PUZZLE (after Frege 1892), this expectation famously breaks down in attitude reports. Suppose that (13-a) is true and that Beatrix does not realize that Richard Bachman is Stephen King. Then, (13-b) might seem false.

(12)    a. **Richard Bachman** wrote *Thinner*.
        b. **Stephen King** wrote *Thinner*.

(13)    a. Beatrix thinks that [**Richard Bachman** wrote *Thinner*].
        b. Beatrix thinks that [**Stephen King** wrote *Thinner*].

If one accepts the thesis that proper names that refer to the same individual are semantically identical (although not everyone does), then Frege's puzzle is a special case of the problem of logical equivalence considered in the previous subsection, and some of the available solutions are similar: we could pursue a theory in which formal differences in the embedded sentence – even down to the difference between two co-referring expressions – lead to differences in the meaning of the report. Or we could pursue a theory in which, despite our intuitions, (13-a) and (13-b) really are equivalent; they only seem otherwise because our intuitions are clouded by pragmatic factors. Yet another kind of approach proceeds by complicating the semantics of attitude reports, in such a way that they are sensitive not just to the proposition encoded by the embedded sentence but also to contextual parameters that can be influenced by the choice of one proper name over another.

As is the case for the problem of logical equivalence, there are many proposals on the market for solving Frege's puzzle but no consensus about which one is right. This will be the focus of Chapter 3.

### 1.2.3 Attitude Reports and Grammar

Aside from bearing on foundational questions about meaning, attitude reports also interact nontrivially with many other independently interesting and important semantic phenomena. Often, they do so in ways that seem to be orthogonal to the foundational questions about sentence meaning and proper names. This is a good thing, because it means that one need not solve the problem of logical equivalence or Frege's puzzle in order to make progress on other puzzles. Some of the phenomena with which attitude reports interact include: scope and intensionality (see Chapter 4 on the DE DICTO/DE RE AMBIGUITY and Chapter 7 on intensional transitive verbs); INDEXICALity, LOGOPHORicity, and CONTROL (see Chapter 5 on DE SE ATTITUDE REPORTS);

MOOD, MODALITY, GRADABILITY, FOCUS, and PRESUPPOSITION PROJECTION (see Chapter 6 on the semantics of *want*); TENSE (see Chapter 7); and negation (see Chapter 7). These interactions, I would argue, constitute the primary attraction that attitude reports have to offer to linguists interested in semantics and the syntax–semantics interface.

## 1.3 THE APPROACH

Let me say something about how this book is organized and about the theoretical framework that it employs. As far as organization goes, the book takes a 'puzzle-driven' approach: a typical chapter begins by illustrating some phenomenon related to attitude reports that poses some puzzle or question for semantic theory. This then leads to a discussion of solutions that have been proposed in response and their theoretical implications. It also leads to further puzzles prompted by these solutions, which in turn spur refinements and alternative solutions. In recognition of the reality of the field, the point is never to come down firmly on any particular solution, but instead to illustrate as clearly as possible what is at stake in the choice between the various solutions. In this way, I hope to convey some of the richness of attitude reports as a topic of investigation.

Important work on attitude reports has been carried out within a number of different theoretical frameworks and intellectual traditions, and this of course poses a challenge for a book aiming to synthesize the important findings of these disparate sources. To the extent possible, I will cleave to the framework with which I am most familiar and in which much of the relevant work reviewed here has been carried out, namely that introduced and summarized by Heim and Kratzer (1998). More specifically, I assume that natural language grammar has two components relevant to the study of attitude reports: a generative (syntactic) component that assembles structures out of units drawn from a lexicon, and an interpretive (semantic) component that assigns denotations to those structures. I take the generative component to have a (broadly construed) Principles and Parameters architecture (see e.g. Chomsky and Lasnik 1993), but nothing in the book relies heavily on the details of any particular version of this theory. As for the interpretive component of the grammar, I assume as a working hypothesis that sentence meanings define truth conditions, derived compositionally via a small inventory of type-sensitive compositional rules (including at least Functional Application, Predicate

Modification, and Predicate Abstraction) that operate locally on sister constituents in the structure. I assume at the outset an ontology of semantic types that includes individuals and truth values as atomic types, and over the course of the book we will entertain a number of other atomic types that may prove useful, namely worlds, times, eventualities, and degrees.

## 1.4 A NOTE ON READERSHIP AND TOPICAL EMPHASIS

The primary target audience for this book is students or researchers of linguistics who have had at least one or two graduate-level courses in formal semantics. As already mentioned, the text that most closely matches the background theory of this book is Heim and Kratzer 1998, with augmentations developed by von Fintel and Heim 2011 for dealing with intensional phenomena. Some of the material we will be considering requires technology that goes beyond what is introduced in either of these texts, and I will do my best to explain that technology as lucidly as I can without derailing the discussion, with references to other relevant sources where I think that would be helpful. To get the most out of this book, it is therefore recommended that readers be at least somewhat familiar with a Heim and Kratzer 1998-style framework for investigating semantics. Also highly recommended is the first chapter of von Fintel and Heim 2011, which extends Heim and Kratzer's framework, in a very accessible and lucid way, to intensional semantics. Some of the relevant background from both of these works will be briefly covered in Section 2.2 of this book.

One of the challenges in surveying attitude reports is that it is a topic investigated both by philosophers and by linguists, but often with different emphases. As already touched on above, philosophers tend to be more concerned with how attitude reports bear on foundational issues such as the nature of sentence meaning and how proper names refer, whereas linguists tend to be more concerned with how the meanings of attitude reports are grammatically encoded and how they interact with semantically relevant grammatical phenomena such as scope, binding, tense, and presupposition. This book makes no secret about being written by a linguist for linguists, but I nonetheless include some material that is more traditionally in the domain of philosophy, especially some of Chapter 2's discussion of HYPERINTENSIONALITY, as well as pretty much all of Chapter 3 on attitude reports and proper names. These are topics that linguists working on attitude reports ought to know something about, even if they're not going to be engaging with them directly in their own work. The rest of the book, by contrast, including most of the material after Chapter 3, is more thoroughly grounded in the linguistics literature, even if much of it is ultimately traceable to important philosophical forebears, including especially Jaakko Hintikka, David Kaplan, Saul Kripke, David Lewis, W. V. O. Quine, and Robert Stalnaker.

Let me also say something about why so much of the book emphasizes belief reports as opposed to other kinds of attitude reports such as desire or intention reports. There are a couple of reasons for this. One is that belief reports are historically the variety that is best studied, and therefore the arena in which a lot of the core issues targeted by this book play out. Another is that it so happens that, for many of these core issues that we will be focusing on, the issue works the same way no matter whether we are looking at belief reports or some other kind of attitude report (though I will do my best to flag exceptions to this). But see Chapter 6 for a dedicated look at issues that come up when we turn our attention to other kinds of attitude reports. When we move beyond core issues, there is a great deal of richness to be found in exploring variation between different kinds of attitude reports, and there is still much work to be done in this area.

## 1.5 GUIDE TO LOGICAL SYMBOLS AND NOTATIONAL CONVENTIONS

In this section, I provide an informal key to the main logical symbols and related notational conventions that will come up over the course of this book. Let me begin by warning the reader that this guide will probably not be particularly helpful if this is your first exposure to these symbols and the concepts behind them; instead, this is intended as a refresher and quick reference guide. For a thorough, linguistically oriented introduction to these and other concepts from logic, see Partee et al. 1990.

First, from propositional logic, we borrow the concepts and corresponding symbols illustrated and informally defined in (14). Let $p$ and $q$ stand in for arbitrary propositions – each is either true (1) or false (0) – and 'iff' abbreviates 'if and only if.' Note also that the *ors* in the definitions of (14-b) and (14-c) are to be understand as *inclusive*: true even if *both* of the disjuncts are true.

(14) *propositional logic*
    a.   $\neg p = 1$ iff $p = 0$     *negation*
    b.   $p \wedge q = 1$ iff $p = 1$ and $q = 1$     *conjunction*

## 1.5 Guide to Logical Symbols and Notational Conventions

    c.  $p \vee q = 1$ iff $p = 1$ or $q = 1$         *disjunction*
    d.  $p \rightarrow q = 1$ iff $p = 0$ or $q = 1$     *material implication*

Next, from predicate logic, we borrow universal and existential quantification, as in (15-a–b), respectively, where $x$ is to be understood as a variable.

(15)   predicate logic
      a.  $\forall x[\ldots x \ldots] = 1$ iff $[\ldots x \ldots] = 1$ for all values of $x$
      b.  $\exists x[\ldots x \ldots] = 1$ iff $[\ldots x \ldots] = 1$ for at least one value of $x$

We also borrow some concepts and symbols from set theory. In that connection, it will be useful to be comfortable with notation like (16), where a set is defined by abstraction. Read it as in (16-a) or, even more succinctly, as in (16-b).

(16)   $\{x \mid x \text{ is a dog}\}$
      a.  'the set of all $x$ such that $x$ is a dog'
      b.  'the set of all dogs'

Beyond that, the following set-theoretic concepts and symbols will crop up over the course of this book (here, let A and B be arbitrary sets).

(17)   set theory
      a.  $\emptyset$ = the empty set (the set with no members)
      b.  *set membership:*
          $a \in A = 1$ iff $a$ is a member of A
      c.  *set non-membership:*
          $a \notin A = 1$ iff $a$ is not a member of A
      d.  *subset relation:*
          $A \subseteq B = 1$ iff every member of A is a member of B
      e.  *non-subset relation:*
          $A \nsubseteq B = 1$ iff not every member of A is a member of B
      f.  *set intersection:*
          $A \cap B$ = the set of all $x$ such that $x \in A$ and $x \in B$

In some places in this book you will see set-theoretic notation combined with predicate logic in the way illustrated in (18). The colon separates the quantifier's restriction from its nuclear scope, leading to paraphrases like (18-a) or, even more simply, (18-b).

(18)   $\forall x \in A: x$ is a dog
      a.  'For all $x$ such that $x$ is a member of A, $x$ is a dog.'
      b.  'Every member of A is a dog.'

We'll use lambda notation for writing out functions. The general anatomy of a function written out using lambda notation is as schematized in (19). Read it as a function looking for a particular input type that will then take that input and use it in a deterministic way to generate an output. For example, (20) is a function that inputs a positive integer and outputs the result of adding one to that positive integer.

(19)  [λ*variable*: *input.output*]

(20)  [λ*x*: *x* is a positive integer.*x* + 1]

In this book, though, we'll suppress the part of the function that specifies the input type, because we'll adopt variable naming conventions that make it clear what the input type is (see below). Many of the functions we'll be looking at have truth values as outputs and hence technically should start off '1 iff [truth conditions]' (i.e., true if and only if the specified truth conditions are met); frequently, though, we'll omit the '1 iff' when it's clear that we are looking at truth conditions. For example, (21) is a function that inputs an individual (*x* being, by convention, a variable that ranges over individuals) and outputs 1 iff that individual is a dog.

(21)  [λ*x*.*x* is a dog]

It will also be convenient to have names for various semantics types. As summarized in (22), the most important atomic semantic types in this book will be individuals (type *e*), truth values (type *t*) and possible worlds (type *s*). A few others will be introduced here and there on an ad hoc basis as needed. Functions built from these atomic types have types whose names follow the format ⟨*a,b*⟩, where *a* is the type of the function's input and *b* is the type of the function's output.

(22)  *semantic type naming conventions*

| | | |
|---|---|---:|
| a. | *e* | individual |
| b. | *t* | truth value |
| c. | *s* | possible world |
| d. | ⟨*a,b*⟩ | function from *a* to *b* |

For commonly recurring functions, I'll frequently omit the comma, as well as the surrounding angle brackets when that function is nested in a larger function. For example, ⟨*et*⟩ is the type of a function from individuals to truth values, and ⟨*et,st*⟩ is the type of a function that inputs a function from individuals to truth values and outputs a function from possible worlds to truth values.

Finally, let's turn to variable naming conventions. The most important ones are given in (23).

(23)   *variable naming conventions*
   a. $x, y, z, a$                                                                                 type $e$
   b. $p, q$                                        type $t$ or type $\langle st \rangle$
   c. $f, g$                                    type $\langle et \rangle$ or type $\langle s, et \rangle$
   d. $w, w', w''$                                                       type $s$

Others will be introduced as needed. Where there is any risk of confusion, such as in the case of $p$ and $q$ or $f$ and $g$, which stand for multiple types, I will subscript the variable with the type it ranges over, e.g. $p_{\langle st \rangle}$. I will also use subscripts for variables with types not listed in (23), e.g. $\phi_{\langle \langle e, \langle s, e \rangle \rangle, st \rangle}$. (Yes, that one will actually come up, in Section 4.5.5. Most of the types we encounter won't be that complex, though.)

## 1.6 CHAPTER SUMMARIES

Chapter 2 "Foundations" begins by reviewing extensional and intensional semantics and introducing Hintikka's (1969) highly influential approach to attitude reports couched in this framework. We then discuss the ensuing problems of logical omniscience and logical equivalence, and undertake a survey of various refinements and alternatives aimed at solving these problems. We also discuss a recently popular alternative to the traditional view regarding the relative contribution of the attitude verb and its complement clause in contributing to the meaning of an attitude report. We lay out this view and compare it to the more traditional approach, highlighting some of the pros and cons of each.

Chapter 3 "Attitude Reports and Proper Names" is concerned with Frege's puzzle and related problems such as KRIPKE'S PUZZLE. This leads to a survey of theories of proper names, attitude reports, and their interaction.

Chapter 4 "The *De Dicto/De Re* Ambiguity" is concerned with the well-known observation that, oftentimes, expressions (typically nominal expressions) in the embedded sentence of an attitude report can be interpreted either as part of the content of the attitude itself (the so-called *de dicto* reading) or as an attitude-external means of referring to or quantifying over some argument that figures into the content of the attitude (the so-called *de re* reading). We discuss the classic scope solution to the *de dicto/de re* ambiguity, as well as the various problems with that approach that have inspired other ways of handling the ambiguity and their implications for the grammar of attitude reports and of intensionality more generally.

Chapter 5 "*De Se* Attitude Reports" is concerned with a class of attitude reports that are, in some sense, first-personal from the attitude holder's perspective. Such sentences give rise to a mild version of the problem of logical equivalence, and this has inspired the view that at least some attitude reports involve quantification not over worlds simpliciter but instead over world-individual pairs. We discuss a number of variants of and alternatives to this approach, as well as their analytical connection to relevant cross-linguistic grammatical phenomena such as control, indexicality, logophoricity, and long-distance reflexives.

Chapter 6 "Desire Reports and Beyond" moves beyond belief reports to consider the semantics of desire reports (including especially sentences built around the verb *want*), which bring forth new puzzles that have inspired a literature of their own and that implicate attitude reports in grammatical phenomena such as mood, modality, gradability, focus, and presupposition projection. The chapter also scales out from belief and desire reports to consider broader points of similarity and divergence among different kinds of attitude reports.

Chapter 7 "Other Topics" rounds up three topics not covered elsewhere in the book, namely attitude reports and embedded tense, NEG RAISING, and intensional transitive verbs. The first two topics cover puzzling interactions that attitude reports give rise to with respect to tense and negation, respectively. The third topic has to do with attitude reports that involve ordinary direct objects rather than complement clauses, and we discuss the implications of such sentences for the status of intensionality in grammar.

## 1.7 FURTHER READING

Although the present volume is, to my knowledge, the first book-length survey of attitude reports, there are a number of relevant survey articles and book chapters on the market, from which I have profited greatly. These include: Ludlow 1997; Portner 2005: chapt. 9; Swanson 2011; von Fintel and Heim 2011: chapt. 2; Shier 2012; McKay and Nelson 2014; Pearson forthcoming. For books and articles on more specific topics related to attitude reports, see the suggestions for further reading found at the end of each subsequent chapter.

# 2 Foundations

## 2.1 INTRODUCTION

This chapter serves as a general introduction to attitude reports in possible worlds semantics, with attention not only to the motivation of such an approach but also to its main challenges and the major revisions and alternatives that such challenges have prompted. Major questions to be addressed include: Which of our intuitions about inference patterns involving attitude reports reflect semantic reasoning, and which reflect pragmatic or extra-linguistic reasoning? What do attitude reports tell us about what sentences denote? And what is the relative contribution of the attitude verb and the complement clause in contributing to the meaning of an attitude report?

The chapter is organized as follows. Section 2.2 provides a brief introduction to possible worlds semantics and situates it with respect to the more general background semantic theory assumed in this book. Against that backdrop, Section 2.3 sketches Hintikka's highly influential possible worlds-based approach to attitude reports and outlines the key predictions that it makes. Section 2.4 discusses the so-called PROBLEM OF LOGICAL OMNISCIENCE that Hintikka's approach faces and outlines two competing approaches for solving it. Section 2.5 is concerned with the more basic problem of logical equivalence that any approach to attitude reports in possible worlds semantics faces; we discuss several solution strategies on the market that broadly go under the name HYPERINTENSIONALITY in that they proffer ways of modeling PROPOSITIONS that achieve a finer grain than do possible worlds. Finally, in Section 2.6, we explore two competing hypotheses regarding the compositional semantics of attitude reports.

## 2.2 BACKGROUND ON POSSIBLE WORLDS SEMANTICS

### 2.2.1 Extensional Semantics and Its Limits

A foundational principle of formal semantics that will be assumed in this book is COMPOSITIONALITY, according to which the meaning of a complex constituent is a function of the meanings of its subconstituents and how they are arranged syntactically. Another is truth conditionality: the idea that sentence meanings determine TRUTH CONDITIONS (how the world must be in order for the sentence to be true). Taken together, this means that when faced with a syntactic structure like (1),[1] we want to ask: What are its truth conditions? And how are those truth conditions derived compositionally from the meanings of its parts and how they are put together?

(1) [Beatrix runs]

Some auxiliary assumptions help get this project off the ground. First, let's assume for now that a proper name like *Beatrix* has as its denotation the individual it refers to (type *e*). So if the word *Beatrix* refers to the individual Beatrix, then the following holds:[2]

(2)  [[Beatrix]] = Beatrix

Second, let's also assume for now that sentence meanings denote truth values (type *t*), of which there are just two: 1 (true) and 0 (false). Determining a sentence's truth value is a matter of comparing its truth conditions against the facts of the actual world. Since the facts of the actual world are beyond the purview of semantics, it will often be convenient to end the semantic analysis at the computation of truth conditions, which means that what we are after is something like (3), where the ellipsis is a placeholder for a statement of truth conditions.

(3)  [[ Beatrix runs ]] = 1 iff ...

---

[1] Unlike typical syntax texts, the trees that appear throughout this book lack syntactic category labels (TP, NP, VP, etc.). The reason for this is that, in the background theory assumed in this book, such labels are not relevant to semantic interpretation.

[2] Throughout this book, material found inside double brackets should be read as an expression of the object language (i.e., the language under analysis; in this case, English). The material on the right side of the equation in (2), on the other hand, is to be taken as an expression of the meta-language, which for convenience will often look quite a lot like English. The intention here is to specify that the English-language expression *Beatrix* has as its denotation the individual Beatrix.

## 2.2 Background on Possible Worlds Semantics

Third and finally, we'll assume that the main engine of semantic composition is Functional Application, which operates locally between sister constituents. In formal terms (cf. Heim and Kratzer 1998: 44):

(4) **Functional Application:** If $\alpha$ is a constituent with daughters $\beta$ and $\gamma$, and $[[\beta]]$ is a function whose domain contains $[[\gamma]]$, then $[[\alpha]] = [[\beta]]([[\gamma]])$.

Together, these assumptions imply that *runs* denotes a function from individuals to truth values (type $\langle e, t \rangle$). More specifically, it maps runners onto 1 and non-runners onto 0. In lambda notation, we can represent this function as follows, where $x$ is a variable ranging over individuals:

(5) $[[\text{runs}]] = [\lambda x.1 \text{ iff } x \text{ runs}]$

Now we can compute the truth conditions of *Beatrix runs* as in (6). (6-a) uses Functional Application (FA) to convert the input structure into a function applied to an argument. (6-b) converts the lexical items *runs* and *Beatrix* into their respective denotations. Finally, (6-c) uses lambda conversion ($\lambda$-Conv.) to simplify the resulting formula.[3]

(6) [[ /\ ]]
    Beatrix  runs

    a. $= [[\text{runs}]]([[\text{Beatrix}]])$     (FA)
    b. $= [\lambda x.1 \text{ iff } x \text{ runs}](\text{Beatrix})$     (Lexicon: *Beatrix, runs*)
    c. $= 1$ iff Beatrix runs     ($\lambda$-Conv.)

If all natural language sentences consisted of just two words, a proper name and an intransitive verb, then formal semantics would be a rather boring enterprise. What have we really done so far? We've made interesting though not obviously correct assumptions about the meanings of proper names and of sentences, and about how semantic composition works. We haven't said anything deeply insightful about the meaning of *runs*: it's some kind of function from individuals to truth values. But so are *jogs, jumps, sleeps,* and *snores*.

---

[3] We can define lambda conversion (sometimes also known as beta reduction) as follows:

(i)     **Lambda Conversion:** Rewrite $[\lambda v.\phi](\psi)$ as $\phi$, with all occurrences of $v$ replaced by $\psi$.

Lambda conversion should be thought of not as an independent rule of the grammar but rather simply as a way of spelling out what it means to apply a function to an argument.

But the program becomes more interesting when we see that the above concepts and fairly modest additions to them can be recruited to model the compositional derivation of truth conditions across a wide range of empirical territory. Using only individuals (e), truth values (t), and functions built from these atomic types, we can account not only for intransitive predication, but also for such phenomena as transitive predication, truth-functional connectives, intersective modification, quantification, and anaphora (also known as variable binding). These are exemplified in (7)–(12), respectively.

(7) Beatrix **runs**.  *intransitive predication*

(8) Beatrix **chases** Maggie.  *transitive predication*

(9) a. Beatrix runs **and** Polly runs.
    b. Beatrix does **not** run.  *truth-functional connectives*

(10) Polly is a **European philosopher**.  *intersective modification*

(11) **Most** dogs bark.  *quantification*

(12) Most cats admire **themselves**.  *anaphora/variable binding*

When paired with reasonable assumptions about the syntax and about the denotations of the lexical items involved, the phenomena above can be handled with only two additional composition rules, namely Predicate Modification (used for intersective modification), and Predicate Abstraction (used for anaphora/variable binding). For the reader's reference, I include here formulations of these two rules respectively in (13) (cf. Heim and Kratzer 1998: 65) and (14) (cf. Heim and Kratzer 1998: 186), but the reader is invited to refer to Heim and Kratzer 1998 chapters 1 through 7 for full explanations. In what follows, I assume basic familiarity with the syntax and semantics of the phenomena in (7)–(12).

(13) **Predicate Modification:** If $\alpha$ is a constituent with daughters $\beta$ and $\gamma$, and $[[\beta]] \in D_{\langle e,t \rangle}$[4] and $[[\gamma]] \in D_{\langle e,t \rangle}$, then $[[\alpha]] = [\lambda x.1$ iff $[[\beta]](x) = 1$ and $[[\gamma]](x) = 1]$.

(14) **Predicate Abstraction:** If $\alpha$ is a constituent with daughters $\beta$ and $\gamma$, where $\beta$ dominates only a numerical index $i$, then for any assignment function $a$, $[[\alpha]]^a = [\lambda x.[[\gamma]]^{a^{x/i}}]$.

---

[4] Read $D_{\langle e,t \rangle}$ as 'the set of all functions of type $\langle e,t \rangle$'.

## 2.2 Background on Possible Worlds Semantics

A crucial prediction of the program as sketched so far – and one that will ultimately move us to an intensional semantics and possibly beyond – is that if two expressions have the same denotation, then they should be interchangeable as subconstituents in a structure without having a truth-conditional effect on the denotation of the structure as a whole. For example, suppose Beatrix also goes by the name Trixie. Then, given our assumption that a proper name denotes the individual it refers to, *Beatrix* and *Trixie* share the same denotation, because they refer to the same individual. Then, the truth value of the sentence *Beatrix runs* should be identical to that of *Trixie runs*, as sketched in (15). And intuitively, this seems right: the prediction is accurate in the sense that it would be impossible to find a scenario where one of these sentences is true but the other false.

(15)  a.  If [[Beatrix]] = [[Trixie]] …

  b.  … then [[ Beatrix runs ]] = [[ Trixie runs ]]

Let's consider another case. To borrow an example from Quine (1951), suppose – possibly in line with reality – that all creatures that have hearts also have kidneys, and vice versa. Then, *creature with a kidney* and *creature with a heart* denote identical functions from individuals to truth values, and should also be intersubstitutable, as in (16). Intuitively, this also seems right: as long as we grant the premise that the relevant functions are identical, substitution works: the sentence *Beatrix is a creature with a kidney* denotes true if and only if the sentence *Beatrix is a creature with a heart* denotes true.

(16)  a.  If [[creature with a heart]] = [[creature with a kidney]] …

  b.  … then [[ Beatrix is a creature with a heart ]] = [[ Beatrix is a creature with a kidney ]]

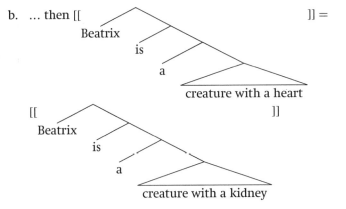

Finally, let's consider one more example involving substitution of entire sentences. Suppose that it is true that Polly runs and it is also true that Maggie sleeps. Then, the prediction is that in any sentence containing the smaller sentence *Polly runs* as a subconstituent, we should be able to swap in *Maggie sleeps* without affecting the truth of the sentence, as in the example in (17) involving coordination of two sentences via *and*. For this particular example, the prediction is accurate: when two sentences are coordinated with *and*, the resulting sentence is true if and only if each of the two coordinated sentences is true. So if it is true that Polly sleeps, substituting in any other true sentence has no effect on the truth of the coordination as a whole.

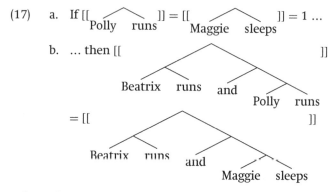

But when we move beyond truth-functional connectives like *and*, *or*, and *not*, sentence embedding presents the clearest case illustrating that a purely extensional semantics (which for our purposes here we can define for now as a semantics that recognizes only individuals and truth values as atomic types) is ultimately inadequate.[5] Take the examples in (18)–(19) and continue to suppose for the sake of illustration that it is true that Polly runs and that Maggie sleeps. Unlike the example involving coordination, in this case substitution fails. Beatrix could believe (correctly) that Polly runs, making (18) true, but at the same time believe (incorrectly) that Maggie does not sleep (or even just fail to believe that Maggie does sleep, perhaps having no opinion on the matter one way or the other), making (19) false.

---

[5] Whether sentence embedding is the *only* kind of syntactic configuration that spells trouble for extensional semantics is a source of some controversy. See Partee 1974, Larson 2002, and Section 7.4 below for relevant discussion.

## 2.2 Background on Possible Worlds Semantics

(18)

(19)

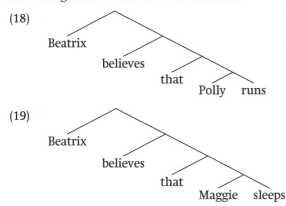

Put differently, the truth value of a belief report has no direct logical connection to the truth value of the believed proposition. I can believe true propositions and I can believe false propositions. I can also *fail* to believe true propositions and *fail* to believe false propositions. In this way, the move to an intensional semantics is motivated: sentence meanings must be more finely grained than truth values, to ensure that belief reports like (18)–(19) do not have identical truth conditions. And it is not just sentences embedded under *believe* that require moving to an intensional semantics. Using the substitution test, we find that attitude verbs in general, sampled in (20), create intensional contexts. And outside attitude reports, we also find that modal auxiliaries, modal adverbs, and conditional sentences require an intensional semantics. These are exemplified in (21)–(23), respectively; see von Fintel and Heim (2011) and references therein for more on these phenomena and their analysis.[6]

(20) a. Beatrix **believes** that Polly runs.
 b. Beatrix **hopes** that Polly runs.
 c. Beatrix **wants** to run.
 d. Beatrix **tries** to run. *attitude reports*

(21) a. Beatrix **must** be tired.
 b. Beatrix **might** be tired. *modal auxiliaries*

---

[6] More specifically, what we will see is that these phenomena motivate a model that includes as atomic types not just individuals and truth values but also possible worlds. It should be noted that other phenomena may call for yet more atomic types. Other atomic types that are often recognized include times (or time intervals), events (or eventualities), and degrees. Over the course of this book we will return to each of these types when relevant to the phenomenon at hand.

(22)  **Maybe** Beatrix is tired.  *modal adverbs*

(23)  **If** Beatrix ran, she would get tired.  *conditionals*

How can we modify our system of semantic interpretation so as to accommodate these phenomena? This is the question we turn to presently.

### 2.2.2 Introducing Intensions

One way of paraphrasing the point made at the end of the previous subsection is that truth values are insufficiently fine-grained to serve as objects of attitude predicates: depending on what the facts of the world are, they may fail to distinguish *Polly runs* from *Maggie sleeps*, and yet it is entirely possibly for Beatrix to believe that Polly runs while failing to believe that Maggie sleeps.

As an initial consideration in remedying this shortcoming, consider the fact that although *Polly runs* and *Maggie sleeps* may have identical truth *values*, they nonetheless have different truth *conditions*:

(24)  [[ Polly runs ]] = 1 iff Polly runs

(25)  [[ Maggie sleeps ]] = 1 iff Maggie sleeps

Truth conditions are much more finely grained than truth values and hence more appropriate as objects of attitude predicates and other modal expressions (though even truth conditions ultimately turn out to be not finely grained enough – see Section 2.5 below). But the problem is that as things stand so far, truth conditions are not built into the denotations themselves. They specify how we (as readers of semantic formulae) would go about determining whether a given sentence meaning is 1 or 0, but they are not part of the meaning of the sentence itself. If we want to move to a system in which truth conditions (or something like them) are themselves something that serve as semantic values, then we need to think more concretely about what truth conditions are. Here is a useful way of thinking about them: truth conditions are a specification of a way the world could be. Compare that to how we treat intransitive predicates like *runs*. This is a specification of how an individual could be, and we model this by treating *runs* as the set of individuals who run (or more technically, its characteristic function; i.e., the function that maps runners onto 1 and non-runners onto 0). If an individual is in that set, he or she runs; otherwise, not. In parallel fashion, we can think of a sentence's truth conditions as a set of possible worlds, namely

## 2.2 Background on Possible Worlds Semantics

those possible worlds in which the sentence in question is true. If the actual world is in that set, then the truth conditions are satisfied (and any sentence that has those truth conditions is therefore true); whereas if the actual world is not in that set, then the truth conditions are not satisfied (and any sentence that has those truth conditions is therefore false).

Going down this path requires expanding on our atomic semantic types, so that we now have not just individuals and truth values but also possible worlds. What are possible worlds? Taking a cue from Lewis (1986), a possible world is spatially and temporally all-inclusive. For example, the actual world (which is one member of the set of possible worlds) includes not just planet Earth but the entire universe. And it also includes the entire timeline of the universe, extending indefinitely into the past and indefinitely into the future. Furthermore, there are infinitely many possible worlds, each one representing a (spatially and temporally all-inclusive) way things could be.

Following a tradition that can be traced back to Carnap (1947), we will say that the EXTENSION of a sentence is its truth value, whereas its INTENSION is a proposition. Technically speaking, we will model a proposition not as a set of possible worlds but rather as the characteristic function of such a set, just like we model *runs* not as the set of runners but as the characteristic function of that set.

How to integrate this into our system?[7] The first step is to relativize denotations to possible worlds. Interpreting a sentence does not take place in a vacuum, but instead relative to certain parameters. This idea is already familiar from Heim and Kratzer's (1998) treatment of pronouns and traces, which involves relativizing denotations to an assignment function g that maps indices onto individuals, as in (26). The move now is to say that denotations are relativized also to an evaluation world w, as in (27): a sentence that is true in the actual world might be false in some other possible world, or vice versa.

(26)  $[[\ldots]]^g$

(27)  $[[\ldots]]^{w,g}$

Now, just as some expressions (namely pronouns and traces) have *assignment*-dependent denotations, some expressions will have *world*-dependent denotations. Take for example the intransitive verb *runs*.

---

[7] What follows is based roughly on von Fintel and Heim 2011: chapt. 1. The reader is referred to this work for a more thorough treatment of how to extend the system in Heim and Kratzer 1998 to integrate possible worlds semantics.

It should be fairly intuitive that the set of runners may vary from one world to the next: in the actual world, there is some particular set of runners, but in other worlds there will be different sets. So now the denotation for *runs* will be as in (28): it is still a function from individuals to truth values, but it is relativized to an evaluation world $w$ (here and in what follows, we will mostly suppress the assignment function $g$ when it is not relevant):

(28)    $[[\text{runs}]]^w = [\lambda x.x \text{ runs in } w]$

In general, verbs, adjectives, adverbs, common nouns, and (contentful) prepositions will all have world-dependent denotations because they name properties and relations that are contingent, i.e., that vary from one world to the next.

What expressions do not have world-dependent denotations? For now we will assume, following Kripke (1980), that proper names are RIGID DESIGNATORS, i.e., name the same individual regardless of the evaluation world, though we will revisit this assumption in Chapter 3. This means that when we write out the denotation for a proper name, the evaluation world will not figure anywhere in the right-hand side of the equation:

(29)    $[[\text{Polly}]]^w = \text{Polly}$

We will also assume that expressions whose meanings are purely logical, including quantificational determiners like *every* and truth-functional connectives like *and*, also have denotations that are not world-dependent. Again here, this means that the evaluation word will not appear in the right-hand side of the equation when we write out denotations for these items:

(30)    $[[\text{every}]]^w = [\lambda f.[\lambda g.\{x \mid f(x) = 1\} \subseteq \{y \mid g(y) = 1\}]]$

(31)    $[[\text{and}]]^w = [\lambda p.[\lambda q.p = 1 \wedge q = 1]]$

It will also be necessary to update our composition rules to accommodate the evaluation world parameter. Functional Application, for example, will now look like the following:

(32)    **Functional Application (revised)**: If $\alpha$ is a constituent with daughters $\beta$ and $\gamma$, then for any possible world $w$, if $[[\beta]]^w$ is a function whose domain contains $[[\gamma]]^w$, then $[[\alpha]]^w = [[\beta]]^w([[\gamma]]^w)$.

The revised version of Functional Application in (32) ensures that if we want to use Functional Application to calculate the semantic value of a branching constituent relative to some evaluation world $w$, then the

## 2.2 Background on Possible Worlds Semantics

semantic values of the immediate daughters are to be calculated relative to the same evaluation world $w$ as well. In this way, the evaluation world 'percolates down' the structure and we ensure consistency in the evaluation world throughout the derivation (unless something in the derivation triggers a shift in the evaluation world, which is exactly what we will pursue in a moment).

With this machinery in place, we now calculate semantic values for sentences relative to an evaluation world. For example, if we want to know whether the sentence *Polly runs* denotes 1 at some particular world – call it $w_7$ – we proceed as in (33):

(33) $[[\overset{\frown}{\text{Polly runs}}]]^{w_7}$

    a. $= [[\text{runs}]]^{w_7}([[\text{Polly}]]^{w_7})$     (FA)
    b. $= [\lambda x . 1 \text{ iff } x \text{ runs in } w_7](\text{Polly})$     (Lexicon: *Beatrix*, *runs*)
    c. $= 1$ iff Polly runs in $w_7$     ($\lambda$-Conv.)

So far, so good. The trick now is that when it comes to a verb like *believe* that triggers an intensional context, we want it to apply not to a sentence's extension but rather to its intension. And we now have the machinery in place to systematically relate an expression's extension to its intension, namely by taking the extension and abstracting over the evaluation world parameter:

(34) If an expression's extension relative to evaluation world $w$ is $[[ \ldots ]]^w$, then its INTENSION is $[\lambda w' . [[ \ldots ]]^{w'}]$.

So the intension of (33) is:

(35) $[\lambda w' . 1 \text{ iff Polly runs in } w']$

It is that function from worlds to truth values that inputs a world $w'$ and returns true if and only if Polly runs in $w'$. (We furthermore assume that complementizer *that* is semantically vacuous, or denotes the identity function, so that (35) is also the intension of *that Polly runs*. But see Section 2.6 below for a different possibility.)

Translating back and forth between an extension and its corresponding intension is completely mechanical: to go from extension to intension, abstract over the evaluation world parameter; to go from intension to extension, saturate the abstracted world argument with the desired evaluation world. But we do have to ask: Under what conditions does the interpretive system access an expression's extension and under what conditions does it access its intension? Here for now we will take a rather conservative approach: an expression's semantic value is *always* its extension. The only way intensions enter into the semantic computation is via a special composition rule, Intensional Functional Application (cf. Heim and Kratzer 1998: 308):[8]

(36) **Intensional Functional Application** (IFA): If $\alpha$ is a branching node with daughters $\beta$ and $\gamma$, then for any possible world $w$, if $[[\beta]]^w$ is a function whose domain contains $[\lambda w'.[[\gamma]]^{w'}]$, then $[[\alpha]] = [[\beta]]^w([\lambda w'.[[\gamma]]^{w'}])$.

The idea behind (36) is that when a function whose argument is an intensional type $\langle s, \tau \rangle$ (where $s$ is the type of possible worlds and $\tau$ is an arbitrary type) combines in the syntax with an expression whose type is $\tau$, IFA allows composition to proceed by letting the mother denote the result of applying the function to the intension of its sister, which is type $\langle s, \tau \rangle$.

So now, we can give an attitude verb like *believe* a denotation whereby its first argument is type $\langle s, t \rangle$:

(37)  $[[\text{believe}]]^w = [\lambda p_{\langle s,t \rangle}.[\lambda x. \ldots]]$

In the syntax, *believe* can combine with an expression of type $t$, and IFA will take care of the rest. But what should replace the ellipsis in (37)? What are the truth conditions of a belief report? This is what we turn to next.

## 2.3 ATTITUDES IN POSSIBLE WORLDS SEMANTICS

### 2.3.1 Logical Relations between Propositions

Although possible worlds semantics was developed as a way of capturing modal phenomena, the approach ends up having an interesting consequence as a general theory of sentence meaning: it reduces key logical relations between propositions to simple and familiar concepts from set theory. These relations are entailment, consistency, contradiction, and logical equivalence. Understanding these relations and their connection to possible worlds semantics is the key to grasping the vices and virtues of the highly influential Hintikkan approach to attitude reports, and so this is what we begin with here.

---

[8] Noteworthy alternatives to Intensional Functional Application include Keshet's (2011) SPLIT INTENSIONALITY theory, according to which expressions are intensionalized in the syntax via a special intensionalizing operator, and Percus's (2000) system in which world variables are pronouns in the syntax that can be bound and quantified over. These approaches will be reviewed in Chapter 4 below, where they will be relevant for understanding accounts of *de dicto/de re* phenomena.

## 2.3 Attitudes in Possible Worlds Semantics

A proposition *p entails* a proposition *q* if and only if it would be logically impossible for *p* to be true without *q* also being true. For example, (38-a) entails (38-b).

(38) entailment
   a. It's raining hard.
   b. It's raining.

In possible worlds semantics, entailment is the subset relation: if (38-a) denotes the set of worlds in which it is raining hard,[9] and (38-b) denotes the set of worlds in which it is raining, then to say that (38-a) entails (38-b) is to say that the denotation of (38-a) is a subset of the denotation of (38-b). In other words, every member of the former set is also a member of the latter set, as in (39).

(39) $\{w \mid \text{it's raining hard in } w\} \subseteq \{w \mid \text{it's raining in } w\}$

Since possible worlds are rather abstract objects, let's consider an analogy to a domain that affords more intuitive reasoning, namely the domain of individuals. For entailment, the corresponding relation for individuals is universal quantification, as expressed by determiners such as *all* and *every*. For example, the sentence in (40-a) can be modeled as (40-b), which is formally parallel to (39).

(40) a. All dogs are mammals.
   b. $\{x \mid x \text{ is a dog}\} \subseteq \{x \mid x \text{ is a mammal}\}$

Moving on, two propositions *p* and *q* are *consistent* if and only if it would be logically possible for both *p* and *q* to be true. This is a weaker notion than entailment in that neither *p* nor *q* needs to *guarantee* the other's truth but instead they must simply *not rule out* each other's truth. For example, (41-a) and (41-b) are consistent with each other because nothing logically precludes the co-occurrence of rain and wind.

(41) consistency
   a. It's raining.
   b. It's windy.

In possible worlds semantics, consistency is the non-empty intersection relation: there is at least one world that is both a member of the set of

---

[9] Strictly speaking, we are assuming that sentences denote not sets of worlds but rather the characteristic functions of such sets. For the sake of concision, though, I will frequently be loose about this distinction and speak of sentences as having sets of worlds as their denotations.

worlds in which it is raining and a member of the set of worlds in which it is windy.

(42)  $\{w \mid \text{it's raining in } w\} \cap \{w \mid \text{it's windy in } w\} \neq \emptyset$

Consistency is parallel to existential quantification over individuals, such as expressed by *some*. For example, the sentence in (43-a) can be modeled as (43-b), which is formally parallel to (42).

(43) a. Some dogs are brindle.
 b. $\{x \mid x \text{ is a dog}\} \cap \{x \mid x \text{ is brindle}\} \neq \emptyset$

Two propositions $p$ and $q$ *contradict* each other if and only if it would be logically impossible for both $p$ and $q$ to be true, such as is the case for (44-a) and (44-b). Contradiction is the opposite of consistency.

(44) *contradiction*
 a. It's raining.
 b. It's not raining.

In possible worlds semantics, contradiction is the empty intersection relation: there is no world that is both a member of the set of worlds in which it is raining and a member of the set of worlds in which it is not raining.

(45)  $\{w \mid \text{it's raining in } w\} \cap \{w \mid \text{it's not raining in } w\} - \emptyset$

The parallel to contradiction in the domain of individuals is expressed via the quantificational determiner *no*, as in (46), whose formula is formally parallel to (45).

(46) a. No dogs are cats.
 b. $\{x \mid x \text{ is a dog}\} \cap \{x \mid x \text{ is a cat}\} = \emptyset$

Finally, two propositions $p$ and $q$ are *logically equivalent* if and only if they entail each other, as for example (47-a) and (47-b) do.

(47) *logical equivalence*
 a. Beatrix chases Maggie.
 b. Maggie is chased by Beatrix.

In possible worlds semantics, logical equivalence is just set identity: the set of worlds in which Beatrix chases Maggie is identical to the set of worlds in which Maggie is chased by Beatrix, as in (48).

(48)  $\{w \mid \text{Beatrix chases Maggie in } w\} = \{w \mid \text{Maggie is chased by Beatrix in } w\}$

## 2.3 Attitudes in Possible Worlds Semantics

When it comes to the domain of individuals, there is no determiner syntactically parallel to *all*, *some*, or *no* that expresses set identity.[10] But we can get the effect in a roundabout way by conjoining two statements of universal quantification that have reciprocal restrictions and scopes:

(49) a. All dogs are canines and all canines are dogs.
b. $\{x \mid x \text{ is a dog}\} = \{x \mid x \text{ is a canine}\}$

### 2.3.2 The Hintikkan Approach to Attitude Semantics

The Hintikkan (1969) approach to attitude semantics, as applied to belief reports in particular, is based on two key ideas. The first is that, just as sentence meanings can be modeled as sets of possible worlds, so can the sum total of an individual's beliefs about the world she inhabits: for Hintikka, this is the set of possible worlds compatible with that individual's beliefs. The second key idea is that a belief report of the form *a believes p* is true if and only if the sum total of *a*'s beliefs *entail p*, or, more technically, if and only if the set of possible worlds compatible with *a*'s beliefs is a *subset* of the set of possible worlds defined by *p*.

Let's now unpack these two ideas in turn. First, what does it mean to say that an individual's beliefs define a set of possible worlds, namely all those worlds compatible with what the individual believes? Consider the set of all possible worlds. In order for me to be able to claim one of those worlds as the actual world, I would have to be infinitely opinionated; that is, I would have to have a belief about the precise arrangement of every atom and every subatomic particle in the universe, and not just as things stand now but more generally for every point in time from the indefinite past into the indefinite future. (Infinite opinionation is similar to but not quite the same as omniscience, because omniscience requires not just having a belief about everything but more strongly *knowing* – which requires, among other things, being *correct* – about everything. Infinite opinionation, by contrast, allows for mistakes.) At the other extreme, suppose I am totally devoid of any opinions: I have no beliefs about anything, so every possible world is, as far as I am concerned, a candidate for the actual one. Naturally, in practice, thinking beings reside somewhere in between these two logical extremes, having *some* beliefs that narrow

---

[10] This is not an accidental gap but instead reflects *conservativity*, a systematic constraint on possible meanings for quantificational determiners (Barwise and Cooper 1981). A quantificational determiner Q is conservative if and only if, for any sets A and B, Q(A)(B) = Q(A)(A∩B). Set identity is not conservative and hence by hypothesis not a possible quantificational determiner meaning.

down the set of possible worlds that we consider candidates for the actual world. Every time I form a new belief, the set of worlds compatible with what I believe shrinks accordingly to exclude those that are incompatible with my new belief; by the same token, every time I abandon a belief, the set expands accordingly (or if a new belief replaces the abandoned one, undergoes some kind of change in membership). A note on terminology: the set of possible worlds compatible with an individual's beliefs is known as his or her BELIEF SET or DOXASTIC ALTERNATIVES, but in what follows, for concision's sake, I will often simply refer to his or her *beliefs*.

Once this idea is adopted, then the sum total of an individual's beliefs becomes commensurate with propositions: both define sets of possible worlds. And we can explore logical relations that hold between them. To build up to the second key idea in the Hintikkan approach to belief reports, let's entertain the hypothesis that to assert that *a believes p* is to assert that the set of worlds compatible with *a*'s beliefs stands in some well-defined set-theoretic relationship with the set of worlds defined by *p*. What relation might that be? As outlined in the previous subsection, salient logical relations that hold between propositions and that can be captured in set-theoretic terms in possible worlds semantics are entailment, consistency, contradiction, and logical equivalence. It should be intuitively obvious that contradiction is not the right relation here: clearly, we would not want to characterize *a believes p* as being true when *a*'s beliefs *contradict p*. But for the remaining three relations – entailment, consistency, and logical equivalence – it takes some real linguistic argumentation to see that entailment is the most appropriate of the three. And this is what we now turn to. But let me be clear about what we are about to do: the argumentation that follows is intended to show that *if* we start by assuming that belief reports of the form *a believes p* are to be characterized as a logical relation holding between *a*'s beliefs and the worlds defined by *p*, *then* entailment is the right logical relation to use for this. But keep in mind that below we will question this starting assumption.

With that caveat out of the way, let's first entertain the hypothesis that *a believes p* means that *a*'s beliefs are *consistent* with *p*. Taking *Beatrix believes that it is raining* as an example to work with, this would amount to saying that if Beatrix believes that it is raining, then at least *some* worlds compatible with Beatrix's beliefs are worlds where it is raining, or in other words, Beatrix's beliefs are consistent with the proposition that it is raining. The problem with this approach is that it fails to rule out cases where there are some worlds compatible with Beatrix's beliefs where it is *not* raining. This leads to the prediction that (50) should be

## 2.3 Attitudes in Possible Worlds Semantics

coherent, contrary to initial impressions. And this then suggests that consistency is too weak a notion for characterizing belief reports.[11]

(50) #Beatrix believes that it is raining, but Beatrix also believes that it is not raining.

Suppose we were instead to entertain the view that *a believes p* means that *a*'s beliefs are *logically equivalent* with *p*, or in other words that the worlds compatible with Beatrix's beliefs are *set-theoretically identical* to the worlds in which it is raining. What would go wrong here is that if the set of worlds compatible with Beatrix's beliefs is *identical* to the set of worlds in which it is raining, then this would mean that the *only* thing Beatrix believes is that it is raining. In other words, the only factor constraining Beatrix's beliefs is that those worlds in which it is not raining are excluded. But this is clearly not right, as evidenced by the coherence of (51): we can perfectly well attribute to Beatrix the belief that it is raining and then in the same breath attribute to her some other belief. This is unexpected on the logical equivalence approach.

(51) Beatrix believes that it is raining, and Beatrix also believes that it is windy.

This just leaves entailment to consider. Unlike contradiction, consistency, and logical equivalence, the entailment relation is not symmetric: if *p* entails *q*, this does not imply that *q* also entails *p*. So there are two options to consider: first, that *a*'s beliefs *entail p*, and second, that *p entails a*'s beliefs. Applied to the example we've been working with, the latter approach amounts to saying that if Beatrix believes that it's raining, then all those worlds in which it is raining are worlds compatible with Beatrix's beliefs. This approach faces the same problem as the approach based on the consistency (non-empty overlap) relation: it allows for some of Beatrix's belief worlds to be worlds in which it is not raining and thereby erroneously predicts (50) to be coherent. Not only that, consider some of the bizarre goings-on within the space of possible worlds in which it is raining. Among them are

---

[11] Consistency may, however, be the right approach for characterizing belief reports that involve an embedded epistemic possibility modal, as evidenced by the coherence of (i).

(i) Beatrix believes that it **might** be raining, but Beatrix also believes that it **might** not be raining.

See Stephenson (2007a, b); Anand and Hacquard (2009, 2013).

worlds where it is raining and pigs fly. But to say that Beatrix believes it is raining is not to imply that porcine flight is compatible with Beatrix's beliefs, contrary to the expectations of this approach.

We are led, then, to the final possibility, that *a believes p* means that *a*'s beliefs entail *p*. This faces none of the aforementioned difficulties of the other approaches. It accounts for the incoherence of (50), as an instance of the same logic that renders (52) incoherent. It likewise accounts for the coherence of (51), as an instance of the same logic that renders (53) coherent.

(52) #Every dog is blue, and every dog is not blue.

(53) Every dog is blue, and every dog is also friendly.

We now turn to a formal, compositional implementation of this analysis. First, to carry out the idea that an individual's beliefs define a set of possible worlds, we define a function DOX (short for 'doxastic alternatives') that takes two arguments – an individual *x* and a world *w* – and returns the set of worlds compatible with *x*'s beliefs in *w*, as in (54). The rationale behind the world argument is that beliefs are contingent (vary from one world to the next): I have some set of beliefs, but if the facts of the world were different, I might have had some other set.

(54) $\text{DOX}_{x,w} = \{w' \mid w'$ is compatible with $x$'s beliefs in $w\}$

Then, we can equate (55-a) with (55-b) or, equivalently, (55-c) (abbreviating the denotation of *Beatrix* to simply *b*).

(55) a. $[[\text{Beatrix believes that it is raining}]]^w$
 b. $\text{DOX}_{b,w} \subseteq \{w' \mid \text{it is raining in } w'\}$
 c. $\forall w' \in \text{DOX}_{b,w}:$ it is raining in $w'$

How can this be carried out compositionally? Recall from before our idea that, schematically, the denotation for *believe* looks like (56): it is a relation between propositions and individuals. This can now be fleshed out as in (57) (adopting the notation from (55-c)).[12]

(56) $[[\text{believe}]]^w = [\lambda p.[\lambda x. \ldots ]]$

(57) $[[\text{believe}]]^w = [\lambda p.[\lambda x. \forall w' \in \text{DOX}_{x,w}: p(w')]]$

---

[12] For an alternative approach, in which the quantification over possible worlds in an attitude report is achieved by the complement clause rather than by the attitude verb itself, see Section 2.6.

## 2.3 Attitudes in Possible Worlds Semantics

With this denotation in place, *believe* can combine in the syntax with a complement clause like *that it is raining*, and the resulting complex will be interpreted via Intensional Functional Application to yield a denotation like (58).

(58) $[\![\text{believe that it is raining}]\!]^w = [\lambda x. \forall w' \in \text{DOX}_{x,w}: \text{it is raining in } w']$

This complex can then combine in the syntax with a subject like *Beatrix*, yielding, via Functional Application, the outcomes in (59), as desired.

(59) $[\![\text{Beatrix believes that it is raining}]\!]^w = \forall w' \in \text{DOX}_{b,w}: \text{it is raining in } w'$

### 2.3.3 Predictions of the Hintikkan Approach

Now that we've introduced the Hintikkan approach to belief reports and gotten a sense of the logic behind it, we consider in more detail the crucial predictions it makes. In particular, it predicts inference patterns in attitude reports according to which the set of propositions believed by an individual has the following properties:

(60)   a. closure under entailment
      b. closure under conjunction
      c. anti-closure under negation
      d. closure under logical equivalence

A note on terminology: following the standard definition, a set A is *closed* under an operation O if and only if applying O to any member (or members, plural, in case of multi-place operations like conjunction) of A always yields another member of A. It will also be convenient to have the concept *anti-closure*, which is not standard terminology but should be fairly transparent: a set A is *anti-closed* under an operation O if and only if applying O to any member (or members, plural, in case of multi-place operations) of A always yields a *non*-member of A.

The (anti-)closure properties in (60) have consequences for what we ought to be able to infer from a belief report – on the basis of its semantics alone – about other beliefs held by the same individual. In what follows, we review each of these properties in turn. Please note that, for now, we will refrain from passing judgment on whether these predictions are accurate. We will do this eventually, but it will require more sophisticated examples and argumentation. For now, the goal is just to be clear on what these predictions amount to and why they hold, and for that purpose we will restrict ourselves to extremely simple examples.

## Closure under Entailment

An elementary fact of set theory is that if A is a subset of B, and B is a subset of C, then A is a subset of C (the subset relation is transitive):

(61)  a. $A \subseteq B$
 b. $\underline{B \subseteq C}$
 c. $A \subseteq C$

Since, on the Hintikkan approach, *a believes p* means that *a*'s beliefs are a subset of *p*, it should follow that *a* also believes all entailments of *p*. For example, we predict that (62) is valid (given that *It's raining hard* entails *It's raining*).

(62)  a. Beatrix believes it's raining hard.
 b. Beatrix believes it's raining.

This is parallel to the following pattern in the domain of individuals (given that all big and blue things are necessarily blue):

(63)  a. All dogs are big and blue.
 b. All dogs are blue.

## Closure under Conjunction

Another basic fact of set theory is that if A is a subset of B, and A is a subset of C, then A is a subset of the intersection of B and C:

(64)  a. $A \subseteq B$
 b. $\underline{A \subseteq C}$
 c. $A \subseteq B \cap C$

This fact, coupled with the Hintikkan approach to belief reports, leads to the prediction that entailment patterns like (65) are valid.

(65)  a. Beatrix believes that it's raining.
 b. Beatrix believes that it's windy.
 c. Beatrix believes that it's raining and it's windy.

This is parallel to the following pattern in the domain of individuals:

(66)  a. All dogs are big.
 b. All dogs are blue.
 c. All dogs are big and blue.

## Anti-closure under Negation

The next relevant fact of set theory is that if A is a subset of B, and A is not the empty set, then it follows that A is not a subset of the

## 2.3 Attitudes in Possible Worlds Semantics

complement of B (where 'the complement of B' is the set of non-members of B):

(67) a. $A \subseteq B$
b. $A \neq \emptyset$
c. $\overline{A \not\subseteq \{x \mid x \notin B\}}$

This, coupled with the Hintikkan approach to belief reports, leads to the prediction that the entailment pattern in (68) is valid – provided that there is at least one world compatible with Beatrix's beliefs (if there are no worlds compatible with Beatrix's beliefs, then we would predict all sentences of the form *Beatrix believes p* to be trivially true, since the empty set is a subset of every set).

(68) a. Beatrix believes that it's raining.
b. Beatrix does not believe that it is not raining (i.e., It is not the case that Beatrix believes that it is not raining).

This is parallel to the following pattern of inference in the domain of individuals, which goes through as long as there is at least one dog:

(69) a. All dogs are blue.
b. Not all dogs are not blue.

*Closure under Logical Equivalence*

This final prediction is much more fundamental than the others, because it does not depend on any particular details of Hintikka's approach but instead is a consequence of a more basic architectural property of the system: in possible worlds semantics, sentences whose meanings are logically (truth-conditionally) equivalent have identical denotations, by virtue of picking out the same set of possible worlds. Hence, logically equivalent propositions should always be interchangeable, even when embedded under an attitude predicate like *believe*. For example:

(70) a. Beatrix believes that Maggie chased Polly.
b. Beatrix believes that Polly was chased by Maggie.

A parallel for individual quantification, trading on the synonymy of *dogs* and *canines*, would be:

(71) a. All of my pets are dogs.
b. All of my pets are canines.

*Stepping Back*

Now, finally, it's time to ask whether the predictions just outlined are accurate or not. In the next section, we focus on apparent problems for closure under entailment and closure under conjunction, and discuss two possible solution strategies, one that maintains the fundamental insights of the Hintikkan approach and one that abandons them in favor of a much weaker semantics. Then, in Section 2.5, we focus on problems for closure under logical equivalence, which will prompt a tour of various approaches to hyperintensionality.

## 2.4 THE PROBLEM OF LOGICAL OMNISCIENCE

### 2.4.1 A Tension

The predictions of the Hintikkan approach just outlined give rise to what is known as the problem of logical omniscience, i.e., the problem that any belief report – by virtue of its semantics alone – validates inferences that, taken together, endow the belief holder with omniscience with respect to all of the logical consequences of her beliefs. Before looking at some examples of the problem, let's consider two apparent selling points of the approach. Both are taken from Yalcin (2018). The first has to do with what Yalcin calls the 'holistic' nature of belief change. Here's Yalcin:

> First, it is constitutive of this model that beliefs do not come and go one at a time, and that belief change is holistic in nature. That seems to correspond with reality. When you form the belief that you left your keys in the car, you also come to believe that the car is where your keys are, that the keys are in a vehicle, that the keys are not in your pocket, that they are not in the room you are in, that to get your keys, you will have to go your car, that some keys are in some car, and so on. These are not discrete cognitive achievements. When the propositions we believe change, they change as a whole system, and in a way that tends to preserve overall coherence.
> 
> (Yalcin 2018: 25)

It is important to note that Yalcin is not talking about Hintikka's approach as a model of *belief reports* but rather as a model of *belief* itself. But sticking with Yalcin's example, in order to assess the plausibility of Hintikka's approach as a model of *belief reports*, what we need to do is ask whether the sentence in (72-a) entails the sentences in (72-b–f) (assuming, for the sake of argument, that the bracketed embedded clause in (72-a) does indeed entail the bracketed embedded clauses in (72-b–f)). Certainly, it is uncontroversial that if (72-a) is true, then we would *expect* (72-b–f) to be true as well. But the question to keep in mind as we proceed is whether this expectation is really underpinned by the *semantics* of belief reports, or whether it is instead underpinned

## 2.4 The Problem of Logical Omniscience

by world knowledge about how belief (typically) works in individuals who are at least moderately rational.

(72) a. Beatrix believes that [she left her keys in the car].
 b. Beatrix believes that [the car is where her keys are].
 c. Beatrix believes that [her keys are in a vehicle].
 d. Beatrix believes that [her keys are not in her pocket].
 e. Beatrix believes that [her keys are not in the room she is in].
 f. Beatrix believes that [to get her keys, she will have to go to her car].

The second apparent selling point of Hintikka's approach that Yalcin discusses has to do with implicit belief. Here's Yalcin again:

> Second, we are often comfortable attributing beliefs to agents whether or not the proposition said to be believed is one they have ever actively considered. Suppose you swerve to avoid hitting a stray moose on the highway. It seems true to say that you believe that the moose you just barely missed is larger than a golfball. This, even though no thoughts of golfballs need recently have crossed your mind. Our comfort with the ascription seems related to the fact that, had you not believed this, you wouldn't have swerved like that. The belief ascription seems appropriate because classifying the content of your state of belief with respect to this proposition does work explaining (inter alia) your failure to treat the moose as golfball-sized.
> (Yalcin 2018: 25)

As before, here Yalcin is talking about Hintikka's approach as a model of belief rather than as a model of belief reports. And this example is not as easy to translate into an idea about belief reports, because it has to do with an inference made on the basis of someone's actions rather than on the basis of a claim about someone's beliefs. But, tweaking the example just a little bit, suppose we are confronted with the belief report in (73-a). Does that belief report entail the belief report in (73-b) (assuming, for the sake of argument, that the bracketed embedded clause in (73-a) does indeed entail the bracketed embedded clause in (73-b))? It is tempting to say that it does. But the same disclaimer as above applies: surely it is reasonable to expect that if (73-a) is true, then (73-b) should also be true. But it is another thing to say that that expectation is underpinned by the semantics of the sentences alone.

(73) a. Beatrix believes that [the moose is normal in size for a moose].
 b. Beatrix believes that [the moose is larger than a golfball].

Now let's turn to some apparent problems. First up is a problem brought out by the following example from Braddon-Mitchell and Jackson (2007: 199), cited by Yalcin (2018: 27). As with the previous examples, suppose for the sake of argument that the bracketed embedded sentences in (74-a–c) jointly entail the bracketed embedded sentence in (74-d). Given this, does it then follow that the belief reports in (74-a–c) jointly entail the belief report in (74-d)? The intuition that Braddon-Mitchell and Jackson (2007) direct us toward is *no*: possibly, Jones has not reflected on the consequences of the beliefs reported in (74-a–c) and therefore has not formed the belief reported in (74-d). In contrast with the just-cited moose example, this seems to be a case where we are not necessarily comfortable attributing to Jones what should (assuming Jones is rational) be a belief of his, even if it is only an implicit belief.

(74)    a.   Jones believes that [Mary lives in New York].
       b.   Jones believes that [Fred lives in Boston].
       c.   Jones believes that [Boston is north of New York].
       d.   Jones believes that [Mary will have to travel north to visit Fred].

In a different but related vein, consider the following two apparent problem cases, both taken from Stalnaker 1984: 88 and cited by Yalcin 2018: 34:

> William III of England believed, in 1700, that England could avoid war with France. But avoiding a war with France entails avoiding a nuclear war with France. Did William III believe England could avoid a nuclear war? It would surely be strange to say that he did.
> (Stalnaker 1984: 88)

> The absentminded detective believes that the butler did it. There is no direct evidence of his guilt, but the detective has made what he thought was an exhaustive list of the possible suspects, investigated them one by one, and eliminated everyone except the butler. The problem is that he completely forgot about the chauffeur, who had both motive and opportunity. Would it be correct to say that the detective believes that the chauffeur did not do it? He does believe that no one other than the butler did it – that was essential to his reasoning – and this entails that the chauffeur did not do it. But it would be misleading to say that the detective had this belief, since that seems to suggest that the chauffeur was one of the suspects eliminated from his list.
> (Stalnaker 1984: 88)

## 2.4 The Problem of Logical Omniscience

Both of these are problematic for the closure under entailment prediction: the bracketed embedded clauses in (75-a) and (76-a) entail the bracketed embedded clauses in (75-b) and (76-b), respectively. And yet in the supplied contexts, we would be uncomfortable saying that (75-a) entails (75-b) or that (76-a) entails (76-b).

(75)   a.  William III of England believed that [England could avoid war with France].
     b.  William III of England believed that [England could avoid nuclear war with France].

(76)   a.  The absentminded detective believes that [the butler did it].
     b.  The absentminded detective believes that [the chauffeur did not do it].

Summing up, we have a tension: the 'key' and 'moose' examples seem to support the predictions of the Hintikkan approach, while the 'traveling north', 'nuclear war', and 'absentminded detective' examples militate against it. In general, there are two kinds of solution strategies that can be pursued for reconciling this tension. One is to maintain the basic Hintikkan architecture but to complicate it in ways that address the observed shortcomings. The other is to abandon the Hintikkan approach and instead relax the semantics so that the (anti-)closure properties catalogued above are no longer predicted (except for closure under logical equivalence, which is still predicted unless more radical revisions to the semantics are made; see Section 2.5 below). In what follows, we consider these two solution strategies in turn.

### 2.4.2  Strategy #1: Complicate the Hintikkan Semantics

First, let's reconsider the 'traveling north' example. This example is designed to guide us toward the idea that maybe it is an oversimplification to say that the semantics of a belief report makes reference to the sum total of an individual's beliefs. Maybe this needs to be more fine-grained in recognition of the fact that an individual can *compartmentalize* his or her beliefs into discrete systems that are internally coherent but that do not necessarily cohere with each other. This is an idea that Stalnaker (1984) proposes and Yalcin (2018) adopts.

The idea is very easy to implement in our setup. Whereas before, we had a function DOX from individuals and worlds to the set of worlds compatible with the relevant individual's beliefs at the relevant world, as in (77), we now redefine DOX as in (78), as a function from individuals, worlds, and states to the set of worlds compatible with the relevant individual's relevant belief state at the relevant world. (I use $e$ here as a variable over states or more generally over eventualities – see Section 2.6 below.)[13]

(77) $\text{DOX}_{x,w} = \{w' \mid w'$ is compatible with $x$'s beliefs in $w\}$

(78) $\text{DOX}_{x,w,e} = \{w' \mid w'$ is compatible with $x$'s belief state $e$ in $w\}$

Assuming existential closure over the state variable, we end up with truth conditions like (79) which can be derived by revising the denotation for *believe* as in (80).

(79) $[[\text{Beatrix believes that it is raining}]]^w = \exists e \forall w' \in \text{DOX}_{b,w,e}$: it is raining in $w'$

(80) $[[\text{believe}]]^w = [\lambda p.[\lambda x. \exists e \forall w' \in \text{DOX}_{x,w,e}: p(w')]]$

This modification to the semantics invalidates closure under conjunction and anti-closure under negation, because there is no guarantee that any two belief reports are verified relative to the same state of belief. But it leaves closure under entailment and closure under logical equivalence intact, because both of these kinds of inferences are made relative to just one state of belief.

What about Stalnaker's 'nuclear war' and 'absentminded detective' examples that are problematic for closure under entailment? Stalnaker's own conclusion from these examples is that perhaps belief reports of the form $a$ believes $p$ require more than just that $a$'s beliefs entail $p$; in particular, maybe they also require that $a$ "understand the proposition that" $p$ or that $a$ "have entertained the proposition that" $p$ (1948: 88). Then, the assertion that William III believed that England could avoid nuclear with France is invalidated given that William III would not have understood what nuclear war is and indeed never entertained its possibility; similarly, the assertion that the absentminded detective believes that the chauffeur did not do it would be invalidated by the fact that he never entertained this possibility. Yalcin (2018) develops a formal implementation of this idea. Yalcin proposes that beliefs are *question-sensitive*, achieved formally by treating

---

[13] The introduction of the state variable is highly reminiscent of the (neo-)Davidsonian approach to verb meaning – and in fact the approach suggested here may be taken as convergent with an independent line of argumentation in favor of including an eventuality variable in the semantics of attitude reports: see Hacquard 2006: 137–138, Hacquard 2010, Hegarty 2016, and Section 2.6 of this book. See also Blumberg and Holguín 2019 for the proposal that attitude alternatives need to be yet further restricted by a proposition that can be supplied by a conditional antecedent.

## 2.4 The Problem of Logical Omniscience

belief states not as sets of possible worlds simpliciter but rather as sets of possible worlds that are partitioned; in this way, "the cells of the [partition] represent ways the world might be, but they are not maximally specific in the manner typically assumed of possible worlds; they settle some but not all questions" (2018: 30; see Yalcin 2018 for the formal details of such an approach). On this approach, belief reports are relativized not only to a belief state (compartmentalization) but also to a partition (question-sensitivity). So, closure under entailment holds only relative to a particular partition, and the nuclear war and absentminded detective examples are thereby dealt with. The trade-off, though, is that now belief reports have a more complicated semantics, being not only state-sensitive but also question-sensitive. Is the trouble worth it, or is it instead a sign that we need to rethink the Hintikkan assumptions that we started with? In what follows, we have a look at the latter strategy.

### 2.4.3 Strategy #2: Abandon the Hintikkan Semantics

Another possible reaction to the 'traveling north', 'nuclear war', and 'absentminded detective' examples is to give up on the idea that a belief report is a report of what one's beliefs *entail*. Instead of defining a function DOX from individuals, worlds, and (if we adopt compartmentalization and question-sensitivity, respectively) states and partitions, let's define a function from an individual and a world to *the set of propositions (i.e., set of sets of possible worlds) that that individual believes*. This is sometimes called the Montague–Scott approach to belief (Sim 1997; Yalcin 2018: note 5), so let's call the function MS:

(81)  $\text{MS}_{x,w} = \{p \mid x \text{ believes } p \text{ in } w\}$

Then the idea would be that a belief report has truth conditions like (82), achieved compositionally via the denotation for *believe* illustrated in (83).

(82)  $[[\text{Beatrix believes that it is raining}]]^w = \lambda w'.[[\text{it is raining}]]^{w'} \in \text{MS}_{b,w}$

(83)  $[[\text{believe}]]^w = [\lambda p.[\lambda x. p \in \text{MS}_{x,w}]]$

This is the inferentially weakest possible approach to belief reports within the confines of possible worlds semantics, invalidating closure under conjunction, closure under entailment, and anti-closure under negation. On this approach, *believe* is logically no more interesting than an ordinary transitive verb like *kick*: *kick* can be modeled as a set of ordered pairs of kickers and things kicked, and *believe* is likewise on this approach modeled as a set of ordered pairs of believers and propositions believed. Just as a kick report of the form *a kicks b* leads to no entailments about anything else *a* does or does not kick, so a belief report on this approach makes no predictions about other propositions that the attitude holder does or does not believe. When faced with the apparent selling points of the Hintikkan approach described above, a proponent of this approach would have to say that the intuitions accessed there are actually not semantic intuitions but rather world knowledge intuitions about how belief typically works.[14] Conversely, a proponent of the Hintikkan approach may argue that the Montague–Scott approach throws the baby out with the bathwater, letting a couple of recalcitrant kinds of examples steer us to a semantics that is inferentially *too* weak.

My purpose here is not to defend forcefully either approach, though I will in the remaining chapters of this book use the Hintikkan approach as a baseline, because it is the one assumed as background in much of the literature to be reviewed and is often orthogonal to the kinds of questions that we will be dealing with anyway.

Anticipating the topic of the next section, it is noteworthy that even the inferentially weak Montague–Scott approach predicts closure under logical equivalence, since this follows simply from treating the complement to *believe* as a set of possible worlds. We now turn to some well-known problems for closure under logical equivalence, and take a tour of possible solutions.

## 2.5 HYPERINTENSIONALITY: WAYS OF FINE-GRAINING

### 2.5.1 Motivation

Regardless of whether one adopts the Hintikkan or the Montague–Scott approach to attitude reports, both approaches predict that attitude reports are closed under logical equivalence, because this is a direct consequence of treating the content of the attitude as a set of possible worlds.

As an aid in getting the empirical lay of the land to gauge how serious a problem this is, it will be convenient to distinguish a few different sources of logical equivalence. One potential source involves substitution of co-referential proper names. If, for example, *Superman*

---

[14] As Crimmins and Perry put it: "Such issues as logical and analytic closure of belief, explicit versus implicit belief, and inferential issues in belief change really belong to the logic of beliefs rather than to the logic of belief sentences" (1989: 711).

## 2.5 Hyperintensionality: Ways of Fine-Graining

and *Clark Kent* have the same intension (both rigidly designating a particular individual), then from the truth of (84-a) we should be able to guarantee the truth of (84-b) (and vice versa), contrary to initial impressions.

(84) a. Lois Lane believes that **Superman** can fly.
b. Lois Lane believes that **Clark Kent** can fly.

The status of cases like (84) and the relationship between attitude reports and proper names turns out to be a topic that is complex enough to deserve its own chapter, and so we will postpone further discussion of this kind of case until Chapter 3.

Another source of logical equivalence is lexical synonymy. For example, *woodchuck* and *groundhog* refer to exactly the same species of rodent, the one whose scientific name is *Marmota monax*. Given this, it is fairly intuitive that (85-a) and (85-b) are logically equivalent.

(85) a. The animal in the front yard is a **woodchuck**.
b. The animal in the front yard is a **groundhog**.

But when we embed those sentences into belief reports, as in (86), the intuition is less clear.

(86) a. Beatrix believes that the animal in the front yard is a **woodchuck**.
b. Beatrix believes that the animal in the front yard is a **groundhog**.

Do we need the semantics itself to encode a difference between (86-a) and (86-b), to allow for a situation where (for example) Beatrix recognizes the animal in question as a woodchuck (verifying (86-a)), but mistakenly believes that groundhogs are some other kind of animal (seemingly falsifying (86-b))? Or could the seemingly false nature of (86-b) in such a context instead be due to an interfering pragmatic inference? Potentially supporting a pragmatic approach, it should be noted that, sometimes, lexical synonymy seems not to lead to any intuitive difference in truth conditions. Consider the minimal pair in (87) from Pagin (2019), exploiting the synonymy of *rarely* and *seldom*. It is very difficult to imagine a situation where one would accept the truth of (87-a) but not (87-b), or vice versa.

(87) a. John believes that pelicans **rarely** fly.
b. John believes that pelicans **seldom** fly. (Pagin 2019: 246)

Yet a third source of logical equivalence involves what Partee calls "constructional synonymy" (1982: 94), i.e., synonymy between sentences that arises not by virtue of differing only in the choice between two synonymous words but rather by virtue of semantically inconsequential syntactic manipulations. For example, the bracketed embedded clauses in (88-a) and (88-b) are logically equivalent. Other examples of constructional synonymy include the active/passive voice alternation, as in (89), and variable particle placement in sentences with particle verbs, as in (90).

(88)     a.   Mary believes that [for John to leave now would be a mistake].
         b.   Mary believes that [it would be a mistake for John to leave now].

(Partee 1982: 94)

(89)     a.   Beatrix thinks [Maggie chased Polly].
         b.   Beatrix thinks [Polly was chased by Maggie].

(90)     a.   Beatrix thinks [Maggie turned the light on].
         b.   Beatrix thinks [Maggie turned on the light].

As observed by Partee (1982), belief reports involving constructional synonymy seem intuitively to preserve logical equivalence, unlike at least some cases of lexical synonymy. In other words, it is difficult to imagine a situation where (90-a) is true but (90-b) false, or vice versa. And indeed Partee even suggests that constructional synonymy may be a rare source of legitimate inferences among belief reports. That being said, it is possible to compromise intuitions even about cases like this by considering more sophisticated embeddings. Consider (91-a–b), based on a test for synonymy developed by Mates (1952) in his paper 'Synonymity'. (91-a) seems trivially true, but does it guarantee the truth of (91-b)? After all, all it would take would be for *one person* to have the doubt in question to (seemingly) falsify (91-b). This suggests that even an attitude semantics that predicts closure under constructional synonymy may be too strong – that is, unless we appeal to pragmatics to explain away apparent intuitions to the contrary.[15]

---

[15] Similar remarks apply to Pagin's *rarely/seldom* case considered above. It is not obvious that (i-a) and (i-b) are logically equivalent, despite differing only in the choice between *rarely* and *seldom*.

(i)     a.   Nobody doubts that whoever believes that pelicans **rarely** fly believes that pelicans **rarely** fly.
      b.   Nobody doubts that whoever believes that pelicans **rarely** fly believes that pelicans **seldom** fly.

## 2.5 Hyperintensionality: Ways of Fine-Graining

(91) a. Nobody doubts that whoever believes that Maggie **turned the light on**, believes that Maggie **turned the light on**.
   b. Nobody doubts that whoever believes that Maggie **turned the light on**, believes that Maggie **turned on the light**.

The fourth and final source of logical equivalence is what I will call – for lack of a better term – 'mathematical equivalence', reserved for cases of logical equivalence that cannot be subsumed under any of the prior three kinds but that are instead underpinned by logical or mathematical reasoning. Consider the examples in (92)–(93) culled from the literature. The bracketed embedded clauses in (92-a–b) are logically equivalent, as are those in (92-a–b), and yet it is not difficult to imagine a situation where one would be prepared to accept the truth of (92-a) or (93-a) while rejecting (92-b) or (93-b), respectively.

(92) a. Marian believes that [Robin will win].
   b. Marian believe that [everyone who does not compete, or loses, will have done something which Robin will not have done].

(Bigelow 1978: 103)

(93) a. Bill believes that [there are twice as many women in his class as men].
   b. Bill believes that [any set containing the number of the men in his class and closed under the operation of forming addition will contain the number of the women in his class].

(Kamp et al. 2011: 344)

Intuitively, what is going on in these cases is that it takes some real effort to discover that the bracketed embedded clauses are equivalent to each other. But then this would seem to imply that when we use a belief report, the embedded clause contributes more than just truth conditions (possible worlds) but also something about the means by which the attitude holder has encoded or conceptualized those truth conditions.

Now, conceivably, a possible worlds proponent could respond in the following way: strictly speaking, the truth of (92-a) does imply the truth of (92-b), and the truth of (93-a) does imply the truth of (93-b). But this judgment is clouded by pragmatics. (92-b) and (93-b) flout Grice's Manner maxim: Why report on the content of Marian's or Bill's beliefs in such an unnecessarily roundabout and logically complex way? This then triggers the conversational implicature that what is being reported on in (92-b) and (93-b) goes beyond its literal meaning to include also something about the complex way in which the attitude holder conceptualizes the relevant belief. Stalnaker argues for a view something like this, saying, "When a person believes that P but fails to realize that the *sentence* P is equivalent to the sentence Q, he may fail to realize that one of the propositions he believes is expressed by that sentence. In this case, he will still believe that Q, but will not himself put it that way. And it may be misleading for others to put it that way in attributing the belief to him" (1984: 72).

But now let's consider a more extreme case: mathematical truths and falsehoods. They are logically necessary and impossible, respectively. This means that in possible worlds semantics, all true mathematical statements denote the same proposition, namely the set of all possible worlds, and all false mathematical statements denote the same proposition, namely the empty set. But then this means that (94-a) and (94-b) should be equivalent (given that it is true that 59 is a prime number) and similarly for (95-a) and (95-b) (given that it is false that 87 is a prime number).

(94) a. Bill believes that [2 plus 2 equals 4].
b. Bill believes that [59 is a prime number].

(95) a. Bill believes that [2 plus 2 equals 5].
b. Bill believes that [87 is a prime number].

A pragmatic account of logical equivalences begins to look highly suspect here. It would be committed to the claim that (94-a–b) really are logically equivalent and so are (95-a–b), and that the perceived difference between them is just pragmatic. This is a virtual *reductio ad absurdum* of the pragmatic account. In fact, we can construct an even more extreme example. Any proposition $p$ is logically equivalent to the conjunction of $p$ with a logical necessity: true if $p$ is true and false if $q$ is false. So the prediction is that (96-a) and (96-b) are logically equivalent. And this seems flatly wrong.

(96) a. Bill believes that [it's raining].
b. Bill believes that [it's raining and 59 is a prime number].

If a pragmatic account is not available, is there any other way to reconcile intuitions about cases like (94)–(96) with the possible worlds approach to attitude semantics? In fact there is, but it involves complicating the relationship between a sentence and the set of possible worlds it picks out. In particular, one would have to come up with an account in which the bracketed embedded clauses in the pairs in (94)–(96) do *not* denote the same sets of possible worlds. This is the tack that Stalnaker takes, suggesting that mathematical statements

## 2.5 Hyperintensionality: Ways of Fine-Graining

are in a sense metalinguistic, denoting "propositions about the relation between expressions and the one necessary proposition" (1984: 74). In other words, "59 is a prime number" picks out that set of possible worlds in which that very sentence expresses the necessary proposition. It thereby becomes a contingent proposition, since it depends on details of the language. In the following subsection, we'll have a closer look at this style of analysis, applied to a non-mathematical example. Following that, in the remaining subsections, we'll consider various strategies that relax or even outright reject the hypothesis that sentences denote sets of possible worlds.

### 2.5.2 Propositional Concepts

As just mentioned, one strategy for reconciling possible worlds semantics with the problem of logical equivalence is to complicate the mapping between a sentence and the set of possible worlds that it picks out, in such a way that logically equivalent sentences do not necessarily pick out the same set of possible worlds. The example we'll work with here to illustrate this strategy is originally due to Burge (1979) and is further discussed by Stalnaker (1984). By way of background, consider that the term *arthritis* refers to inflammation of joints. Now imagine an individual (Stalnaker calls her Mabel) who has arthritis. Recently, her thigh has become inflamed, and she has formed the belief that she has arthritis in her thigh. Since, by definition, arthritis cannot occur in the thigh, Mabel's belief is necessarily false. But in possible worlds semantics, there is only one necessarily false proposition, namely the empty set. So we should be able to take (97-a) and replace the bracketed embedded clause with any other necessarily false statement and still get a true report, as in (97-b), for example. This is obviously a bad result.

(97)    a.   Mabel believes that [she has arthritis in her thigh].
        b.   Mabel believes that [married men are bachelors].

Stalnaker suggests the following approach. (The sketch that follows is based in part on Stalnaker 1984 – where the arthritis example is discussed – and in part on Stalnaker 1987, where the approach is fleshed out in more detail, although with different examples.) Intuitively, what goes wrong in this example is that Mabel is mistaken about the meaning of the term *arthritis*. In general, two factors go into determining the truth of a proposition: the rules for determining what truth conditions the proposition has, and the facts of the world. Both are contingent. Just as we can imagine some worlds where Mabel's thigh is inflamed and some worlds where it is not, we can imagine some worlds where *arthritis* refers to joint inflammation and some worlds where *arthritis* refers to inflammation more generally. For concreteness, imagine the following four worlds:

(98)     a.   $w_1$: Mabel has inflammation in her thigh; *arthritis* means 'joint inflammation'
        b.   $w_2$: Mabel has inflammation in her thigh; *arthritis* means 'inflammation'
        c.   $w_3$: Mabel has no inflammation in her thigh; *arthritis* means 'joint inflammation'
        d.   $w_4$: Mabel has no inflammation in her thigh; *arthritis* means 'inflammation'

Now consider the following sentence evaluated in a possible worlds semantics that has only the worlds in (98).

(99)     Mabel has arthritis in her thigh.

We still want to be able to encode the fact that, on some level, (99) is a contradiction. We do this by holding constant the facts about the rules for determining truth conditions – in particular, we hold them constant to those of the actual world, where *arthritis* means 'joint inflammation'. Considered from that perspective, (99) denotes the empty set, because there is no world where Mabel has *joint* inflammation in her thigh. But we can also use (98) to construct what Stalnaker (1987) calls a PROPOSITIONAL CONCEPT, where we cross the facts at each world with the rules for determining truth conditions at each world, yielding the result in Table 2.1, where, as usual, 1 is 'true' and 0 is 'false'.

A few general remarks on propositional concepts: just like an INDIVIDUAL CONCEPT is a function from possible worlds to individuals, a propositional concept is a function from possible worlds to propositions. Since Stalnaker assumes that propositions are sets of possible worlds, this means that propositional concepts are functions from possible worlds to sets of possible worlds. For Stalnaker, propositional concepts are not determined by the grammar of a

Table 2.1 Propositional concept for *Mabel has arthritis in her thigh*.

|  | $w_1$ | $w_2$ | $w_3$ | $w_4$ |
|---|---|---|---|---|
| $w_1$: | 0 | 1 | 0 | 1 |
| $w_2$: | 0 | 1 | 0 | 1 |
| $w_3$: | 0 | 0 | 0 | 0 |
| $w_4$: | 0 | 0 | 0 | 0 |

## 2.5 Hyperintensionality: Ways of Fine-Graining

sentence but rather by "particular utterance *tokens* and their contexts" (1987: 182). To be able to get from the utterance of a sentence to its associated propositional concept involves knowing not only what that sentence means at the actual world but also what it means in the other possible worlds in which the utterance takes place.

The contradictory status of (99) – relative to the *linguistic* rules of $w_1$ and $w_3$ – is reflected in the fact that the first and third columns of this table are both 0s all the way down. But in the second and fourth columns – where the linguistic rules are different – the proposition is contingent. When we report someone's beliefs, ordinarily we use (what we take to be) the linguistic rules of the actual world to evaluate the truth conditions of the believed proposition. But – Stalnaker suggests – under some conditions, for Gricean pragmatic reasons, we take the *diagonal* of the propositional concept; that is, at each world, we evaluate the truth of the proposition relative to the linguistic rules *at that world*.[16] In this case at hand, this gives us the truth profile {0, 1, 0, 0}: Mabel believes that the actual world is one in which she has inflammation in her thigh *and* in which *arthritis* means inflammation. So for Mabel, $w_2$ is a candidate for the actual world, while the other three are not.

This concludes our brief introduction to propositional concepts, which I include here to give you a taste of the kind of work one has to do if one is committed to possible worlds semantics at all costs. The alternative to propositional concepts is to hypothesize that sets of possible worlds are too coarse-grained to serve as objects of attitude verbs, and to seek instead a more finely grained replacement. Broadly speaking, any approach or procedure for yielding objects that are finer-grained than sets of possible worlds (intensions) can be called a HYPERINTENSIONAL approach. There are many ways to go about this – many more, in fact, than we can do justice to here. But in what follows, we will have a look at a few.

### 2.5.3 Impossible Worlds

One way to achieve hyperintensionality is to generalize out from possible worlds so as to include impossible worlds as well. Whereas possible worlds encompass only logically possible ways things could be, impossible worlds incorporate logical impossibilities. While two logically equivalent statements pick out identical sets of *possible* worlds, maybe – so the idea goes – they do not necessarily pick out identical

---

[16] The concept of diagonalization grew out of Kaplan's work on INDEXICALS, though Stalnaker is careful to distinguish the notions. See Stalnaker 2004 for points of connection to other work in so-called two-dimensional semantics.

sets of *possible and impossible* worlds, since there could be an impossible world at which (for example) $p$ is true but not $q$, even though $p$ and $q$ are logically equivalent. Early suggestions along these lines include Cresswell (1973) and Hintikka (1975), and the idea is further developed by Rantala (1982).

A potential piece of independent support for admitting impossible worlds into semantic theory comes from so-called counterpossible conditionals: conditionals with impossible antecedents. At first blush, it would seem that (100-a) is true whereas (100-b) is false.

(100) a. If Hobbes had squared the circle, then all mathematicians would have been amazed.
b. If Hobbes had squared the circle, then Kennedy would not have been killed. (Berto 2013)

But if we restrict ourselves to possible worlds only, both should come out trivially true. Impossible worlds, on the other hand, enable us to model (100-a) as true but (100-b) false: in the relevant impossible worlds where Hobbes had squared the circle, it is the case that all mathematicians were amazed, but it is not the case that Kennedy was not killed.

Fleshing out a theory of impossible worlds involves addressing two related questions, one more conceptual and the other more empirical. On the conceptual end, the question is: What kind of ontological status do impossible worlds have? Are they on a par with possible worlds in having a primitive status in the theory, or are they derived somehow? For example, Berto (2010) develops the view that whereas possible worlds are ontologically basic, impossible worlds are modeled as sets of inconsistent sets of possible worlds. On the more empirical end, the question is whether there are *any* logical limitations on what can constitute an impossible world. The reason this latter question is at least partly empirical is that it has to do with whether attitude reports validate any kinds of inferences at all. Take (101). Does (101-a) entail (101-b)?

(101) a. Beatrix believes that Maggie chased Polly
b. Beatrix believes that Polly was chased by Maggie.

This reasoning seems valid. But if it is genuinely valid, and if belief reports quantify over worlds that are not restricted to the possible, then there must be some constraints on what the impossible worlds are; otherwise, the inference would be blocked by the existence of impossible worlds in which Maggie chased Polly but Polly was not chased by Maggie. But it turns out to be very difficult to constrain

## 2.5 Hyperintensionality: Ways of Fine-Graining

impossible worlds so as to rule out the 'trivially' impossible but let in the 'subtly' impossible: see Bjerring 2013. The other option, then, is to reject the idea that (101) is valid. That option comes with the obligation to explain why (101) seems valid. Perhaps, one could respond, it seems valid because of assumptions that we as interpreters bring in about the reasoning powers of the agent whose beliefs are being reported, as discussed earlier in connection with the problem of logical omniscience. But there is no consensus on what the right approach to impossible worlds is, or even on whether impossible worlds – in any form – are on the right track at all.

### 2.5.4 Situations

Another approach to modeling sentence meanings that makes distinctions that are finer-grained than possible worlds is known as SITUATION SEMANTICS, as developed by Barwise (1981) and Barwise and Perry (1983) (see also Barwise and Perry 1985 and Cooper and Ginzburg 1996), according to which sentence meanings are sets of situations. In a sense, situations collapse the distinction between possible worlds and Davidsonian eventualities (on which see Section 2.6 below), although situations encompass more than just eventualities. Any world, or any spatio-temporal chunk of a world, defines a situation.[17] Barwise and Perry (1983) illustrate how situations lead to a finer grain than possible worlds with the following pair of examples.

(102) Joe is eating.

(103) Joe is eating and Sarah is sleeping or Sarah isn't sleeping.

As Barwise and Perry (1983) point out, (102) and (103) are logically equivalent: every possible world in which (102) is true is also a world in which (103) is true, and vice versa. But in situation semantics, they nonetheless have distinct meanings: (102) denotes the set of situations in which Joe is eating; (103), in contrast, denotes the set of situations in which Joe is eating and Sarah is sleeping or in which Joe is eating and Sarah is not sleeping. Since Sarah is necessarily present in all of the latter set of situations but not in the former, the two sets are distinct. So if attitudes are relations to sets of situations, it is conceivable that one could, for example, believe (102) but not (103), or vice versa.

How well does situation semantics fare when it comes to tautologies (necessary truths) and contradictions (necessary falsehoods)? The same

---

[17] This characterization of situations is based in part on Kratzer's influential work on the topic. See Kratzer 2019 for an overview.

reasoning applied to (102)–(103) will show that (104)–(105), despite both being tautologous, are nonetheless distinct: (104) picks out a set of situations that all necessarily involve Sarah, whereas (105) picks out a set of situations that all necessarily involve Joe.

(104)   Sarah is sleeping or Sarah isn't sleeping.

(105)   Joe is eating or Joe isn't eating.

Contradictions, on the other hand, are not so easy: (106) and (107) both pick out the same set of situations, namely the empty set.

(106)   Sarah is sleeping and Sarah isn't sleeping.

(107)   Joe is eating and Joe isn't eating.

With this kind of problem in mind, Barwise and Perry (1983: 95–96) decide to admit what they call "incoherent situations," which is very reminiscent of impossible worlds, as reviewed in the previous subsection. It seems, then, that situations do not have any advantage over worlds in being able to distinguish logically equivalent propositions, insofar as both end up needing to admit representations of the impossible. Consequently, the choice between worlds and situations needs to be assessed in other ways. If it turns out that some version of situation semantics is correct, then a side effect will be the ability to distinguish among logically equivalent, non-contradictory propositions without resorting to impossible worlds or situations. But impossible worlds or situations will still be needed to distinguish contradictions.

### 2.5.5 Structured Propositions

In contrast with the view that propositions are reducible to sets of objects of the appropriate sort (whether that be possible worlds, possible and impossible worlds, or possible and impossible situations), another view, popular especially among some philosophers of language, is that propositions are *structured* in some way that mirrors the structures of the sentences that represent them. On such theories, the problem of logical equivalence is avoided, because two sentences that are logically equivalent may nonetheless be structurally quite different, thereby blocking the inference that belief in one should entail belief in the other. The idea has roots in the work of Bertrand Russell (see e.g. Russell 1903; contemporary work in this vein includes Soames 1985, 1987; Salmon 1986; Richard 1990; Crimmins 1992; King 1995, 1996, 2007; Moltmann 2003; Hanks 2011; Pickel 2017).[18]

---

[18] See also Kamp 1990 on Discourse Representation Theory. As described by Geurts et al. (2016), in this theory, "the logic of belief and other attitudes must involve

## 2.5 Hyperintensionality: Ways of Fine-Graining

One of the main criticisms leveled against structured propositions is what is known as the problem of the unity of propositions (see e.g. Pagin 2019; Moltmann forthcoming for recent discussion): in a nutshell, the criticism is that there is no natural, non-arbitrary way of associating structures with truth conditions; instead, this has to be stipulated. A set of possible worlds, by contrast, is naturally associated with truth conditions, since it picks out that set of worlds where the relevant truth conditions are satisfied.

Also on the market are theories that use STRUCTURED INTENSIONS, marrying structured propositions with possible worlds semantics. Cresswell and von Stechow (1982), in particular, develop an approach that builds on structured propositions as well as Kaplan's (1968) approach to *de re* attitude reports. Now is not the time to review their approach in detail, because it relies on ideas that we won't be getting into until Section 4.5 of this book. But the interested reader is invited to refer to Cresswell and von Stechow 1982 after reading that discussion. See also Section 2.8 below for pointers to other relevant readings.

### 2.5.6 Sententialism

It should be clear from the foregoing that there is no consensus on how to properly characterize propositions. There is another kind of approach that sidesteps this question altogether by arguing that propositions need not play any role in the semantics of attitude reports at all. According to this approach, complements to attitude predicates do not denote propositions but instead denote sentences. Following Schiffer (1987) and others, I will call this view SENTENTIALISM. Since complements to attitude predicates (often) *are* sentences, this view can also be described, as Higginbotham (2006) does, as one in which complements to attitude predicates refer to themselves. The prospect of freeing oneself of the burden of having to properly characterize propositions is rather enticing, and hence worth careful consideration.

Sententialism, broadly construed, can be traced back as far as Carnap (1947: 53–64), who proposes (simplifying slightly) that a sentence of the form *a believes S* is true if and only if there is some sentence $S'$ such that *a* "is disposed to an affirmative response to" $S'$ and $S'$ is "intensionally isomorphic to" $S$, where two sentences are intensionally isomorphic if and only if they are composed out of intensionally equivalent items structured in the same way (this appeal to structure also brings in

structured mental representations. The problem of logical omniscience is then resolved in terms of the failure of human agents to perform logically complete computations over these representations."

some aspects of structured propositions, discussed above; see also early discussion by Church 1950, 1954; Mates 1952; Putnam 1954; Scheffler 1955).

An important later landmark for sententialism is Davidson (1968), who proposes a paratactic account of INDIRECT SPEECH REPORTS according to which a sentence like (108-a) has a logical form suggested by (108-b), wherein *that* is analyzed as a demonstrative that refers to the utterance that follows it.

(108)   a.   Galileo said that the earth moves.
        b.   Galileo said that. The earth moves.

Of course, *my* utterance of the sentence *The earth moves* cannot literally be taken as the utterance of Galileo's that guarantees the truth of (108-a) (for starters, the utterances differ in author, language, time, and place); so Davidson introduces the notion of *samesaying*: "Galileo uttered a sentence that meant in his mouth what 'The earth moves' means now in mine," which according to Davidson involves "a judgment of synonymy between utterances, but not as the foundation of a theory of language, merely as an unanalyzed part of the content of the familiar idiom of indirect discourse" (1968: 140).

A thorough evaluation of sententialism is beyond the scope of this book, but see Section 2.8 below for some relevant pointers to further reading in this area.

### 2.5.7 Interpreted Logical Forms

Larson and Ludlow (1993) – building on Harman (1972); Burge (1978); Higginbotham (1986, 1991); Segal (1989) (cf. also Bigelow 1978) – develop the proposal that attitude predicates denote relations between individuals and INTERPRETED LOGICAL FORMS (ILFs), where an ILF is a syntactic structure whose terminal and nonterminal nodes are each paired with a semantic value. Thus a change in either the syntax (form) or the semantics (interpretation) (or both) of a complement clause can potentially produce attitude reports with distinct truth conditions.[19] The central case of a change in form but not meaning is substitution of co-referring names, as in (109), on the assumption that proper names are rigid designators and that sentences pairs like (109-a) and (109-b) are truth-conditionally distinct (FREGE'S PUZZLE, revisited in Chapter 3).

---

[19] A precursor to this approach can be found in Lewis (1970), who writes, "Only when we come to non-compound, lexical constituents can we take sameness of intension as a sufficient condition of synonymy ... It is natural, therefore, to identify meanings with semantically interpreted phrase markers minus their terminal nodes: finite ordered trees having at each note [sic] a category and an appropriate intension" (1970: 31).

(109)  a.  Kelly believes **St. Petersburg** swings.
       b.  Kelly believes **Leningrad** swings.
                                            (Larson and Ludlow 1993: 316)

By the same token, differing truth conditions as a result of change in semantics but not syntax is evident from examples like (110).

(110)  a.  Hans is brawny. Arnold believes **he** works out. (*he* refers to Hans)
       b.  Franz is brawny. Arnold believes **he** works out. (*he* refers to Franz)                    (Larson and Ludlow 1993: 320)

As was the case for sententialism, a thorough evaluation of interpreted logical forms is beyond the scope of this book, but see Section 2.8 below for some relevant pointers to further reading in this area.

### 2.5.8 Taking Stock

In the foregoing subsections, we've reviewed several strategies for circumventing the problem of logical equivalence engendered by the possible worlds framework for attitude reports: we can complicate the mapping between a sentence and the set of possible worlds it encodes (propositional concepts); we can augment possible worlds with impossible worlds or replace them with (possible and impossible) situations; we can enrich intensions with structure; or we can eschew intensions altogether and pursue approaches based directly on sentences or on Interpreted Logical Forms. Rather than adopting one strategy or another, I will for the remainder of this book continue to work in the possible worlds framework, with the understanding that it will ultimately need to be enriched by or replaced with something else that responds to the challenges outlined above. The reason is a practical one: in spite of its known limitations, the possible worlds framework is, for better or worse, the one used by much of the linguistics literature that I will be reviewing below, and this is in part because the problem of logical equivalence is to a large degree orthogonal to the other puzzles surrounding attitude reports that will take up the rest of this book.

## 2.6 ATTITUDES, EVENT SEMANTICS, AND DECOMPOSITION

The last thing that I want to do before closing this chapter is revisit our assumptions from Section 2.3.2 above about the relative role of the attitude verb and the complement clause in contributing to the truth conditions of an attitude report. For this purpose, we'll revert – as we essentially will for the remainder of this book – to the assumption that the Hintikkan approach to attitude reports is basically correct. The reason that I want to take some space to explore this alternative compositional setup is because it links up with some highly interesting recent work on attitude reports that identifies important connections to event semantics and modal semantics, and it also anticipates some of the interesting features that distinguish different varieties of attitude reports (e.g. belief reports vs. desire reports) that we will be revisiting in Chapter 6.

As discussed above in Section 2.3.2, the usual way of compositionally implementing a Hintikkan semantics for an attitude report like (111) is to treat the attitude predicate as naming a relation between propositions and individuals that effects quantification over possible worlds, as in (112).

(111)   [[Beatrix believes it's raining]]$^w$ = $\forall w' \in \text{DOX}_{b,w}$: rain($w'$)

(112)   [[believe]]$^w$ = [$\lambda p.[\lambda x.\forall w' \in \text{DOX}_{x,w}: p(w')$]]

On this view, attitude verbs are formally quite similar to modal auxiliaries like *can* and *must*, the main difference being that whereas modal auxiliaries quantify over worlds restricted by a contextually supplied MODAL BASE and ORDERING SOURCE (see von Fintel and Heim 2011: chapts. 3–5), attitude verbs quantify over worlds in a way that is not context-sensitive but is instead determined by the attitude verb, the subject, and the evaluation world.

One immediate shortcoming of this setup is that, unlike modal auxiliaries, attitude verbs are full-fledged verbs. As such, they can be modified by adverbs, as in (113), and they can also combine with aspectual auxiliaries, as in (114).

(113)   Beatrix **firmly/half-heartedly** believes it's raining.

(114)   a.   Beatrix **is** hop**ing** that it will rain.
        b.   Beatrix **had** believ**ed** that it would rain.

In the tradition of Davidson (1967), we can integrate adverbial modification into semantic representations by adding an eventuality argument to the verb, so that the modifier can be treated as a predicate of eventualities.[20] (Integrating aspect is likewise usually achieved with

---

[20] Following standard practice, I use the term 'eventuality' to encompass both events and states. Whereas Davidson's work concerned *event* descriptions in particular, some of its descendants in the linguistics literature have generalized it to encompass state descriptions as well, and we will have to follow that trend if we want to go down the path explored in this section, because some of the most

## 2.6 Attitudes, Event Semantics, and Decomposition

the help of an eventuality argument, though this is not illustrated here because it would take us too far afield.) For example, the sentence in (115) would have the representation in (116).[21]

(115) Beatrix suddenly chased Maggie.

(116) $\exists e[\text{chase}(e) \land \text{Ag}(e,b) \land \text{Pt}(e,m) \land \text{sudden}(e)]$

How to integrate a Davidsonian event semantics with a Hintikkan attitude semantics? Note first that (117) will *not* do.[22]

(117) $[[\text{Beatrix firmly believes it's raining}]]^w =$
$\exists e[\text{believe}(e,w) \land \text{Exp}(e,b) \land \text{firm}(e) \land \forall w' \in \text{DOX}_{b,w}: \text{rain}(w')]$

The problem with (117) is that nothing links together Beatrix's belief state $e$ with the status of her doxastic alternatives as entailing that it is raining. This leads to erroneous predictions, such as (118-a) and (118-b) together implying (118-c), which is intuitively not valid reasoning.

(118) a. Beatrix firmly believes that it's raining.
 b. Beatrix half-heartedly believes that it's windy.
 c. Beatrix firmly believes that it's raining.

The solution, following Hacquard (2006: 137–138), is to adopt the idea that some eventualities – namely speech and attitude eventualities – are special in that they have propositional content, i.e., define sets of possible worlds. Then we can define a function CON(tent) from eventualities to the set of worlds compatible with the content of that eventuality. With that in place, (117) is replaced by (119). (See also Hegarty 2016 for a variation on this idea, one difference being that, for Hegarty, belief ascriptions sometimes but do not always incorporate an eventuality argument.)

(119) $[[\text{Beatrix firmly believes it's raining}]]^w =$
$\exists e[\text{believe}(e,w) \land \text{Exp}(e,b) \land \text{firm}(e) \land \forall w' \in \text{CON}_{e,w}: \text{rain}(w')]$

What consequences does this have for the composition of attitude reports? The gentlest way of revising the compositional implementation

---

central attitude verbs (e.g. *believe* and *want*) are stative rather than eventive. For a recent overview of the ontological status of states, see Baglini 2015.

[21] This representation is not just Davidsonian but rather *neo*-Davidsonian in that the arguments of the verb (in this case *Beatrix* and *Maggie*) are introduced via thematic relations (Ag [Agent] and Pt [Patient], respectively) rather than treated as arguments of the predicate *chase*. While this extra move is not needed if the goal is simply to add an eventuality argument to handle adverbial modification, the neo-Davidsonian move will be a better fit for us once we apply it attitude reports.

[22] Exp abbreviates the thematic relation 'Experiencer'.

would simply be to add an eventuality argument to *believe*; this is, for example, the route taken by Hacquard (2010: 101):

(120)  $[[\text{believe}]]^w = [\lambda p.[\lambda x.[\lambda e.\text{believe}(e) \wedge \text{Exp}(e,x) \wedge \forall w' \in \text{CON}_{e,w}: p(w')]]]$

But the inclusion of the eventuality argument now enables a neo-Davidsonian analysis of attitude reports with full thematic separation, as pursued by Kratzer (2006), Moulton (2009), Bogal-Allbritten (2016), and others. We begin by assuming that *believe* is just a predicate of eventualities:

(121)  $[[\text{believe}]]^w = [\lambda e.\text{believe}(e)]$

Now, in order to connect (121) with propositional content in Hintikkan fashion, we can assume that the complement clause that *believe* combines with has a denotation like (122):

(122)  $[[\text{that it is raining}]]^w = [\lambda e.\forall w' \in \text{CON}_{e,w}: \text{rain}(w')]$

Then, (121) and (122) can combine via Predication Modification (appropriately generalized to encompass not just predicates of individuals but also predicates of eventualities). We thereby achieve the result in (123):

(123)  $[[\text{believes that it is raining}]]^w = [\lambda e.\text{believe}(e) \wedge \forall w' \in \text{CON}_{e,w}: \text{rain}(w')]$

The next step is to combine (123) with a thematic functional head that introduces an experiencer argument, as in (124), which combines with (123) via Event Identification (see Kratzer 1996) to yield (125):

(124)  $[[v_{Exp}]]^w = [\lambda x.[\lambda e.\text{Exp}(e,x)]]$

(125)  $[[v_{Exp} \text{ believes that it is raining}]]^w = [\lambda x.[\lambda e.\text{believe}(e) \wedge \text{Exp}(e,x) \wedge \forall w' \in \text{CON}_{e,w}: \text{rain}(w')]]$

When the subject merges in, we get (126):

(126)  $[[\text{Beatrix } v_{Exp} \text{ believes that it is raining}]]^w = [\lambda e.\text{believe}(e) \wedge \text{Exp}(e,b) \wedge \forall w' \in \text{CON}_{e,w}: \text{rain}(w')]$

Finally, we assume default existential closure over the eventuality argument to yield the final product in (127):

(127)  $[[\text{Beatrix } v_{Exp} \text{ believes that it is raining}]]^w = \exists e[\text{believe}(e) \wedge \text{Exp}(e,b) \wedge \forall w' \in \text{CON}_{e,w}: \text{rain}(w')]$

## 2.6 Attitudes, Event Semantics, and Decomposition

How can we ensure that the clause *believe* combines with has the denotation in (122)? We can get this effect by assuming that it contains an appropriately defined left-peripheral modal functional head. For concreteness, let's assume that the complementizer *that* (or its silent counterpart, for embedded clauses that lack an overt *that*) itself carries this function:

(128)   $[[that]]^w = [\lambda p.[\lambda e.\forall w' \in \text{CON}_{e,w}: p(w')]]$

On this view, complementizer *that* combines with a sentence via Intensional Functional Application, returning a predicate of eventualities that is true of an eventuality if and if only all of the worlds compatible with the propositional content of that eventuality in the evaluation world are worlds in which the relevant sentence is true. This is sometimes known as the decompositional approach to attitude reports, since it involves 'decomposing' the attitude verb in such a way that the quantification over possible worlds is attributed to a separate functional head rather than to the attitude verb itself.

How should we decide between the approach in (129) and the approach in (130)? That is, how can we decide whether the quantification over possible worlds in an attitude report is contributed by the attitude verb itself or by a left-peripheral modal functional head in the complement clause?

(129)   $[[believe]]^w = [\lambda p.[\lambda x.[\lambda e.believe(e) \wedge \text{Exp}(e,x) \wedge \forall w' \in \text{CON}_{e,w}: p(w')]]]$

(130)   $[[believe]]^w = [\lambda e.believe(e)]$

While this question should ultimately be linked up with broader theoretical considerations about thematic separation (see Williams 2015 for an overview), it is also possible to weigh the options based on evidence particular to attitude reports. And one of the most interesting lines of evidence in favor of the approach in (130) comes from the existence of verbs whose attitude semantics is closely tied to the syntax of their complement. Here we consider three such cases.

The first is due to Moulton (2009), who observes the contrast in (131): when a perception verb like *see* combines with a bare infinitive (lacking *to*), as in (131-a), the result is a PERCEPTUAL REPORT that leaves it open whether the perceiver believes the content associated with the object of perception. But when a perception verb combines with an infinitive containing an overt subject and the marker *to* (henceforth, following the literature, an 'exceptional case marking' or ECM infinitive), the result is a perceptual report that does entail that the perceiver believes the content associated with the object of perception:

(131) a. Martha saw Fred driving too fast, but she believed he wasn't.
b. Martha saw Fred to be driving too fast, #but she believed he wasn't. (Moulton 2009: 128)

To make sense of this contrast without having to posit ambiguity in the verb *see*, Moulton proposes that there is just one verb *see*, but that ECM infinitives contain a silent modal functional head that contributes belief semantics. Consistent with this analysis is the observation that in general, ECM infinitives correlate with belief semantics; most notably, *believe* can combine with an ECM infinitive:

(132) Martha believes Fred to be happy.

This opens up the possibility that *believe* uniformly just contributes a predicate of eventualities, and it is its complement — whether it takes the form of a finite clause or an ECM infinitive — that contributes the modal quantification.

There is an apparent exception to the generalization that ECM infinitives always correlate with belief semantics, and this exception will lead us directly into our next case study. In particular, the complement to *want* in (133) bears the same superficial shape as an ECM infinitive, but (133) does not ascribe a belief; it ascribes a desire:

(133) Martha wants Fred to be happy.

However, an important difference between (132) and (133) is that in the latter case only, *for* can be inserted before the embedded subject:

(134) a. *Martha believes (very strongly) **for** Fred to be happy.
b. Martha wants (very strongly) **for** Fred to be happy.

Facts like this lead to the conclusion that another class of infinitives in English needs to be recognized, namely *for-to* infinitives, which sometimes but not always bear an overt *for*. In Grano 2016b, building on Bresnan (1972), Pesetsky (1992), Portner (1997), and others, I show that *for-to* infinitives often correlate with priority MODALITY in the sense of Portner 2007, occurring with verbs that have to do with desires, goals, or subjective evaluations:

(135) John hoped/wished **for** Bill to leave.

(136) John planned/intended/decided **for** Bill to leave.

## 2.6 Attitudes, Event Semantics, and Decomposition

(137)  John was happy/sad/angry **for** Bill to leave.

This led me to conclude that just as ECM infinitives contribute belief semantics, *for-to* infinitives may contribute priority semantics. And later, in Grano 2019a, I put this analysis to use to help make sense of the data in (138). When *persuade* combines with an infinitive, it means roughly 'cause to intend', whereas when *persuade* combines with a finite clause, it means roughly 'cause to believe':

(138) a.  Mary persuaded John to leave.
 ≈ Mary caused John to form an intention to leave.
 b.  Mary persuaded John that it was raining.
 ≈ Mary caused John to form a belief that it is raining.

I argue in Grano 2019a that there is just one verb *persuade* and that the different interpretations are contributed by the complement clause: the CONTROL infinitive in (138-a) is a *for-to* infinitive which is analyzed as a priority modal that triggers an intention semantics, whereas the finite clause in (138-b) contributes a different flavor of modality that triggers a belief semantics.

Similar phenomena have also been observed cross-linguistically. In our third case study, Bogal-Allbritten (2016) shows that in Navajo there is a verb, *nisin*, which is used for both belief and desire reports. In some contexts, this leads to ambiguity, as in (139):

(139)  Nahodoołtį́į́ł  nisin
 AREALS.rain.FUT 1s.attitude.IMPF
 'I think it will rain.' OR 'I want it to rain.'
 (Bogal-Allbritten 2016: 63–64)

Bogal-Allbritten (2016) furthermore shows that there are particles that can be used to disambiguate between the two kinds of meaning:

(140) a.  Nahałtin  **sha'shin** nisin.
 AREALS.rain.IMPF probably 1s.attitude.IMPF
 'I think it is probably raining.'
 b.  Nahałtin  **laanaa** nisin.
 AREALS.rain.IMPF wishful 1s.attitude.IMPF
 'I wish that it were raining.'  (Bogal-Allbritten 2016: 67)

As argued by Bogal-Allbritten (2016), these facts support the approach to attitude semantics wherein it is the complement clause that contributes the modal quantification: *nisin* is a general attitude verb, and the complement determines what kinds of worlds are being quantified over.

All that being said, the decompositional approach to attitude reports also faces some important challenges that have yet to be tackled. One has to do with fine-grained variation in attitude semantics. By way of background, consider first the difference between a belief report (141) and a desire report (142):

(141)   John believes that it is raining.

(142)   John wants it to be raining.

As we will discuss in detail in Chapter 6, *want*-sentences differ in non-trivial ways from *believe*-sentences that threaten any analysis that treats them as logically parallel (say, by simply treating (141) as quantifying over belief worlds and (142) the same except quantifying over desire worlds). This much is not a problem for the decompositional approach; to the contrary, it may even be a feature. The reason is that the syntax of the complement varies, so that we can associate finite complements with a Hintikkan semantics and nonfinite complements (more specifically, given the discussion above, *for-to* infinitives) with whatever semantics turns out to be right for desire ascriptions. And the decompositional approach can even be leveraged to explain combinatoric restrictions that hold between attitude verbs and the syntax of their complements:

(143)   *John believes for it to be raining.

(144)   *John wants that it is raining.

We might explain (143)–(144) by appealing to the idea that *believe* and *for it to be raining* are both descriptions of contentful eventualities, but impose mutually incompatible requirements on the described eventuality, leading to incoherence (and likewise for *want* and *that it is raining*).

But the problem is that there are also some attitude verbs that display hybrid behavior and that can combine with finite clauses. In particular, Anand and Hacquard (2013) consider *hope* (and its negative counterpart *fear*), and assign it a semantics that can be informally exemplified by (145):

(145)   John hopes that it is raining.
        a.  Belief component: John believes that it might be raining (but is not sure that it is).
        b.  Desire component: Rain is more desirable to John than no rain.

## 2.7 Discussion Questions

Another attitude verb considered by Anand and Hacquard (2013) is *doubt*, to which they assign a semantics informally sketched in (146):

(146) John doubts that it is raining.
   a. Belief component: John believes that it might be raining (but is not sure that it is).
   b. Likelihood component: No rain is more likely to John than rain.

It is unclear whether these truth conditions can be captured while maintaining a uniform modal semantics for finite clauses and varying only the predicate of eventualities associated with the embedding verb. Instead, capturing these fine-grained semantic differences while maintaining the decompositional approach may require proliferating the inventory of modal functional heads that finite complement clauses can instantiate. This would be familiar from our investigation of infinitives, where we identified a distinction between ECM infinitives and *for-to* infinitives. But when it comes to finite clauses, it is not clear that there is any independently detectable syntactic difference between complements to *believe* and complements to verbs like *hope* or *doubt*. Consequently, the relative contribution of the attitude verb and its complement in contributing to the semantics of an attitude report remains an open question.

## 2.7 DISCUSSION QUESTIONS

(i) Aside from belief reports, there are other, non-attitude sentences standardly analyzed as involving universal quantification over possible worlds, including sentences with necessity modals such as *must*. For example, (147) can be characterized as true if and only if all worlds compatible with the available evidence in the actual world are worlds in which it is raining.

(147) It must be raining.

Do *must*-sentences like (147) obey closure under entailment, conjunction, and logical equivalence, and anti-closure under negation? Or does the universal quantification approach to *must* face some of the same problems as the Hintikkan approach to belief reports?

(ii) Above we entertained the possibility that (148-a) and (148-b) have the same truth conditions and that intuitions to the contrary have a pragmatic source. What might a pragmatic account of this contrast look like? In other words, what conversational implicature might be carried by (148-b) but not (148-a), and why?

(148) a. Beatrix thinks that woodchucks are **woodchucks**.
b. Beatrix thinks that woodchucks are **groundhogs**.

(iii) A recurring theme in this chapter has to do with which of our intuitions about attitude reports are semantically underpinned and which are pragmatically or extra-linguistically underpinned. In her paper 'Belief Sentences and the Limits of Semantics,' Partee says parenthetically:

> There is of course room for widely differing opinions about how much of the burden will fall on semantics proper within a larger theory of language use and reasoning. I sometimes think that all the semantics alone should tell us about sentence [sic] of the form "John believes that ..." is, in effect, "There is something (some proposition?) that John believes". But that would probably predict too many such sentences to come out true.
>
> (Partee 1982: 96)

Do you think this is a reasonable possibility? Or is Partee right that it would be too weak (predict too many belief sentences to be true)?

(iv) Aside from attitude reports, another area of semantics that seems to call for hyperintensionality concerns licensing of cross-sentential anaphora, as brought out by the following minimal pair, attributed by Heim (1982: 21) to Partee:

(149) a. I dropped ten marbles and found **all of them, except for one**. It is probably under the sofa.
b. I dropped ten marbles and found **only nine of them**. It is probably under the sofa.

The first sentence in (149-a) is logically equivalent to the first sentence in (149-b), and yet only the former makes available an appropriate antecedent for *it* in the second sentence. Can one approach to hyperintensionality make the right distinctions for both attitude reports and for cross-sentential anaphora, or might these phenomena point to two separate kinds of hyperintensionality?

## 2.8 FURTHER READING

For general background on the semantic theory assumed in this book, see Heim and Kratzer 1998, and see von Fintel and Heim 2011 for an accessible introduction to possible worlds semantics and intensional phenomena. See also Soames 2010: chapt. 3 for a critique of possible worlds semantics.

Important work on the Hintikkan approach to attitude semantics includes Hintikka 1969; Stalnaker 1984, 1987; Yalcin 2018. Treating objects of attitudes as sets of possible worlds is but one approach among a vast sea of alternatives. Some alternatives have been reviewed above; other approaches include making use of such notions as propositions as model-theoretic primitives (Thomason 1980; see also Pollard 2008, 2015), vague propositions (Moore 1999), attitudinal objects and truthmaker theory (Moltmann 2013b, 2017, forthcoming), measurement theory (Matthews 2007, reviewed by Dresner 2010), and cognitive act types (Hanks 2011, 2015; Soames 2014, 2015, 2019).

There are also many resources for further exploring the various approaches to hyperintensionality surveyed in Section 2.5. On **impossible worlds** (Section 2.5.3), see Jago (2007, 2015); Berto (2017), and see Berto 2013; Nolan 2013 for overviews. On **situation semantics** (Section 2.5.4), see Moltmann (forthcoming) for an approach to attitude reports that uses situations and actions, based in part on Fine's (2017) truthmaker semantics. On **structured propositions** (Section 2.5.5), see Cresswell 1985 (reviewed by Gupta and Savion 1987) and Cresswell 2002, and for an approach that combines possible worlds semantics with structured meanings, see Pagin 2019. Pagin combines a Hintikkan semantics for belief reports with a structured meaning component that acts as a filter to block certain kinds of intuitively invalid substitutions that would otherwise be predicted to go through. On **sententialism** (Section 2.5.6), see the criticism in Church 1950; Cresswell 1980; Schiffer 1987, 2003; Clapp 2002 and the solutions or rebuttals offered in response in Lepore and Loewer 1989; Seymour 1992; Ludwig and Ray 1998; Higginbotham 2006; Felappi 2014; Ludwig 2014. Finally, on **Interpreted Logical Forms** (Section 2.5.7), see Larson and Segal 1995; Dusche 1995; den Dikken et al. 1996; Ludlow 2000; Higginbotham 2009, and for criticism, see Fiengo and May 1996; Clapp 2002.

# 3 Attitude Reports and Proper Names

## 3.1 INTRODUCTION

We use proper names to refer to individuals. Accordingly, a rather simple theory would hold that a proper name denotes nothing more and nothing less than the individual it refers to. This implies that when two proper names refer to the same individual, such as *Superman* and *Clark Kent* in the DC Comics series and later adaptations, they have identical denotations. Along with some basic assumptions about COMPOSITIONALITY, this then implies that one should be able to replace *Superman* with *Clark Kent* in a sentence without altering the truth conditions of that sentence. And at first blush, this seems to hold up: if Superman is Clark Kent, then the truth conditions of (1-a) (which we'll stipulate are met; i.e., suppose (1-a) is true) seem to be identical with the truth conditions of (1-b). There could be no scenario where one is true but the other false.

(1)    a.   **Superman** can fly.      *true*
       b.   **Clark Kent** can fly.      *true*

But this intuition famously breaks down in attitude reports, where, for example, those of us acquainted with the Superman stories readily accept (2-a) as true but would most likely be inclined to reject (2-b) as false. This is known as FREGE'S PUZZLE (after Frege 1892), and it figures centrally in the philosophical literature on propositional attitude reports.[1]

(2)    a.   Lois Lane believes that [**Superman** can fly].      *true*
       b.   Lois Lane believes that [**Clark Kent** can fly].      *false?*

---

[1] As an example of its centrality, it is noteworthy that the *Stanford Encyclopedia of Philosophy*'s entry 'Propositional Attitude Reports' (McKay and Nelson 2014) takes Frege's puzzle as its central theme and means of organizing various approaches to attitude reports.

## 3.1 Introduction

In a nutshell, this chapter is about trying to reconcile the tension between (1) and (2). And we might as well begin by acknowledging that, on some level, it is not hard to see what is going on here. Although *Superman* and *Clark Kent* refer to the same individual, the two names are associated with two different personas: Superman is the cape-wearing superhero capable of flight and other powers, whereas Clark Kent is the mild-mannered bespectacled reporter for the *Daily Planet*. Lois Lane is acquainted with both personas, but does not realize that they belong to the same individual. Thus she would be prepared to assent sincerely to the assertion "Superman can fly" but not to the assertion "Clark Kent can fly," and this is what seems to underpin the intuition that (2-a) is true but (2-b) false. (This is what Berg 1988 calls the "assentialist" intuition.) But as we shall see, it is one thing to have an intuitive grasp of the source of the puzzle and quite another thing to build an adequate theory of the semantics of attitude reports and of proper names that delivers the intuitively correct results for cases like this while at the same time avoiding other pitfalls.

Prominent approaches to Frege's puzzle can be sorted into three categories based on where they locate the solution: in the semantics, in the pragmatics of inference (CONVERSATIONAL IMPLICATURE), or in the pragmatics of what's given (INDEXICALity).[2] The semantic solution proceeds by complicating the semantics of proper names, treating them as being on a par with definite descriptions in not only referring but also encoding a *way* of referring, so that co-referential proper names (just like co-referential definite descriptions) end up being extensionally equivalent but intensionally distinct. Frege's own solution to the puzzle falls into this category, though it faces serious challenges emanating in no small part from the work of Kripke (1979, 1980). Solutions in terms of the pragmatics of inference hold that the perceived non-equivalence of pairs like (2-a–b) is not actually a reflection of their semantics proper but instead a reflection of pragmatic reasoning: using a particular proper name in the complement of an attitude predicate often invites the inference that the attitude holder is acquainted with the referent in question *via that name*, in a way that influences our judgments about truth conditions (see especially Salmon 1986; Soames 1987, 2002). On this view, (2-b) is literally true but instead merely *seems* false. Finally, solutions in terms of the pragmatics of what's

---

[2] The terms 'pragmatics of inference' and 'pragmatics of what's given' – used to refer to conversational implicature and indexicality(/presupposition) phenomena, respectively – are borrowed from Portner (2005).

given hold that attitude reports covertly encode contextually specified information (HIDDEN INDEXICALS) about how the attitude holder thinks of the referents expressed in the complement clause, and one factor that influences how these indexicals are valued is the choice of proper names used in the report (see especially Crimmins and Perry 1989).

In what follows, we will have a more detailed look at each of these three solution strategies (Sections 3.2–3.4, respectively). Then, in Sections 3.5 and 3.6, we expand our empirical reach by considering two additional puzzles that have important implications for how we approach Frege's puzzle, namely Kripke's (1979) puzzle and Saul's (1997, 2007) puzzle involving apparent substitution failures in simple (non-attitude) sentences.

## 3.2 THE NON-RIGID DESIGNATOR APPROACH

The first hypothesis to consider involves giving up on the idea that the sole semantic function of a proper name is to contribute a referent. Frege's own solution to the puzzle worked along these lines: he proposed to associate with each proper name both a reference (*Bedeutung*) and a sense (*Sinn*), where a sense contains the referent's 'mode of presentation', a *way* of making reference to an individual. In terms of the background theory of this book, this means treating proper names as being on a par with definite descriptions: like co-referential definite descriptions, co-referential proper names would be treated as *extensionally* equivalent (picking out the same referent at the evaluation world) but *intensionally* distinct (possibly picking out different referents at one or more other possible world). (Cf. also Russell 1905; Searle 1958; Gluer and Pagin 2006 for variants of this view.)

For definite descriptions, this is uncontroversial. For example, it so happens that in the actual world, the first man on the moon was also, on an earlier space mission, the back-up Command Pilot for Gemini 11. In particular, both of these designations uniquely pick out Neil Armstrong. So (3-a) holds (let $w_0$ be the actual world). But we can easily imagine other possible worlds where things went differently, and so, as indicated in (3-b), the two definite descriptions are not intensionally equivalent.

(3) a. [[the first man on the moon]]$^{w_0}$
    = [[the back-up Command Pilot for Gemini 11]]$^{w_0}$
  b. [$\lambda w$.[[the first man on the moon]]$^{w}$]
    $\neq$ [$\lambda w$.[[the back-up Command Pilot for Gemini 11]]$^{w}$]

## 3.2 The Non-rigid Designator Approach

Because of the extensional equivalence of these definite descriptions, simple sentences like (4-a–b) are correctly predicted to be truth-conditionally equivalent, but because of their intensional non-equivalence, attitude sentences like (5-a–b) are correctly predicted not to be truth-conditionally equivalent.

(4)    a. Armstrong was **the first man on the moon**.
       b. Armstrong was **the back-up Command Pilot for Gemini 11**.

(5)    a. Maggie believes that Armstrong was **the first man on the moon**.
       b. Maggie believes that Armstrong was **the back-up Command Pilot for Gemini 11**.

On a Frege-style approach, we would say the same thing about proper names: it so happens that Clark Kent and Superman refer to the same individual, as in (6-a) (here, let's understand $w_0$ as the world in which the Superman stories are set, rather than as the actual world), but – so the approach would go – the two names do not pick out the same referent at every possible world, and therefore they are intensionally distinct, as in (6-b).

(6)    a. $[[\text{Clark Kent}]]^{w_0} = [[\text{Superman}]]^{w_0}$
       b. $[\lambda w.[[\text{Clark Kent}]]^w] \neq [\lambda w.[[\text{Superman}]]^w]$

If this approach is correct, then Frege's puzzle is solved: in the same way that we don't consider it a puzzle that co-referential *definite descriptions* in attitude contexts resist substitution, the same would go for co-referential proper names. But to avoid the charge of circularity, the Frege-style solution depends crucially on whether we can muster independent support for the idea that co-referential proper names are intensionally distinct. It is easy to find independent evidence that co-referential *definite descriptions* are intensionally distinct. Consider, for instance, that (7) is a logically coherent counterfactual conditional. Now compare that with (8). Here, things are not so clear: if we are being charitable, we might interpret 'might not have been Clark Kent' as 'might not have gone by the name "Clark Kent"' or maybe 'might not have assumed the persona associated with the name "Clark Kent"', both of which certainly are logically coherent properties to attribute to Superman. But does the literal meaning of (8) admit such an interpretation, or is such an interpretation pragmatically driven?

(7)    If things had gone differently, **the back-up Command Pilot for Gemini 11** might not have been **the first man on the moon**.

(8) ?If things had gone differently, **Superman** might not have been Clark Kent.

The Frege-style approach to proper names stands in contrast with an approach traceable to John Stuart Mill, who wrote that "Proper names ... denote the individuals who are called by them; but they do not indicate or imply any attributes as belonging to those individuals" (1843: 40, cited by Abbott 2010: 14). In terms of the background theory of this book, this means that co-referential names have not only the same EXTENSION, as in (9-a), but also the same INTENSION, as in (9-b): Clark Kent and Superman denote the same individual regardless of the choice of evaluation world. And if this approach is correct, then Frege's puzzle persists.[3]

(9) a. $[[\text{Clark Kent}]]^{w_0} = [[\text{Superman}]]^{w_0}$
    b. $[\lambda w.[[\text{Clark Kent}]]^w] = [\lambda w.[[\text{Superman}]]^w]$

That co-referential proper names are intensionally equivalent is the essence of Kripke's (1980) highly influential view in the Millian tradition that proper names are RIGID DESIGNATORS, picking out the same individual at every possible world (see also Donnellan 1970 for an important precursor). We've already had a taste of the rationale behind this view in the oddness of (8). Now let's consider the issues at stake in more detail. Portner (2005) summarizes Kripke's argument as follows. Take the proper name *Confucius*. If this proper name non-rigidly designates, then it must correspond to some definite description that can be used to pick out an individual as we move from one world to the next. For example, maybe it picks out *the most famous Chinese philosopher*. But this cannot be right, or else we would expect (10)–(11) to behave similarly. They don't: (10) invites a coherent exercise in counterfactual reasoning, whereas (11) asks us to entertain a logical contradiction.

(10) Suppose **Confucius** were not **the most famous Chinese philosopher**.

(11) Suppose **the most famous Chinese philosopher** were not **the most famous Chinese philosopher**.

In order to analyze *Confucius* as being shorthand for some definite description, it would have to be an *essential* property of Confucius – something that we could not coherently imagine him lacking.

---

[3] In a theory in which attitude reports trigger hyperintensional semantics, then one would also have to ask whether co-referential names are hyperintensionally equivalent. See Ripley 2012 for a solution to Frege's puzzle in terms of HYPERINTENSIONALITY, and Jago 2015 for criticism.

## 3.3 The Pragmatic Approach

And Kripke even suggests a candidate: maybe it is indeed an essential property of an object that it has whatever origins it had. In the case of Confucius, for example, maybe it is an essential property of his that he was born to whatever parents he was born to. But this is not a viable approach to the meaning of the name *Confucius*, because we can successfully use the name without having any clue who his parents were: in other words, essential properties can be discovered empirically. In Kripke's words: "Some properties of an object may be essential to it, in that it could not have failed to have them. But these properties are not used to identify the object in another possible world, for such an identification is not needed" (1980: 53).

Now, one way of reacting to this reasoning would be to hypothesize that proper names rigidly designate in ordinary modal contexts like counterfactual conditionals but that in attitude contexts they non-rigidly designate. (See Tancredi 2010 for a suggestion along these lines.) Kripke (1979) urges caution about this kind of view as well. If people do associate something like Fregean senses with proper names, are these senses public or private? If public, it remains to be shown, for example, that Cicero and Tully (two names for the same Roman orator) have "any special *conventional, community-wide* 'connotation' in the one lacking in the other" (Kripke 1979: 244). If they are private, that raises its own concerns: as Kripke points out, it is not clear that private senses will always be rich enough to uniquely pick out a referent, thereby duplicating the substitution puzzle. For example, someone might know Cicero as a famous Roman orator and Tully as a famous Roman orator, and not associate any other information with these two names, yet nonetheless believe (mistakenly) that Cicero and Tully are two distinct individuals. So, even if we were to treat attitude contexts as special, Kripke argues, Fregean senses do not do the work that they are supposed to do in solving the puzzle (see Kripke 1980: 80–82, as well as Kripke 1979: 246–247).

Based on considerations like these, the prospects for locating the solution to Frege's puzzle in the semantics of proper names themselves seem bleak, leading many scholars to seek solutions elsewhere.

### 3.3 THE PRAGMATIC APPROACH

A crucial question to ask about Frege's puzzle is whether the intuition that (12-a) is true but (12-b) false is an intuition based solely on the semantically circumscribed truth conditions associated with these sentences.

(12) a. Lois Lane believes that **Superman** can fly.
b. Lois Lane believes that **Clark Kent** can fly.

The pragmatic approach to Frege's puzzle begins with the hypothesis that (12-a) and (12-b) really do have identical truth conditions after all, and our intuition has led us astray. Of course, pursuing this line brings with it the obligation to come up with some plausible explanation for *why* our intuition has led us astray. And the usual suspect would be Gricean pragmatics: sometimes, our intuitions about the truth conditions of a sentence go beyond its semantically circumscribed truth conditions and include as well inferences based on conversational implicature.

This tension between semantics and pragmatics in theorizing about truth judgments is similar to the distinction between grammaticality and acceptability in syntax: in the generative tradition, grammaticality is a theoretical notion having to do with whether a structure can be generated by a grammar. As native speakers of a language, we do not have direct access to intuitions about whether a given string of words can be parsed into a grammatical structure; instead, we only have intuitions about whether a given string of words sounds more or less acceptable as a sentence of the relevant language. Grammaticality is one factor that may influence acceptability, but it is not the only one, and so the question of grammaticality is only partly an empirical one. theory influences the decision as well. Returning to the case at hand, if we have otherwise impeccable reasons for thinking that proper names rigidly designate, pursuing a pragmatic account of our intuitions about proper name substitution does not seem unreasonable.

The idea that substitution pairs like (12-a–b) are after all truth-conditionally equivalent and that our judgment about this is clouded by pragmatic factors is most prominently associated with Nathan Salmon (see especially Salmon 1986) and Scott Soames (see especially Soames 1987, 2002). The basic idea is that, despite what our intuition tells us, (12-b) *is* true. It merely strikes us as false, because there is pragmatic pressure when reporting attitudes to use terms that the attitude holder herself would use to report the attitude. Since Lois Lane would not use the name *Clark Kent* to name the individual she believes can fly, (12-b) is an odd way of reporting a true belief – so odd that it ends up striking us as false.

This approach is attractive insofar as it keeps the semantics as simple as possible: there is no need to complicate the theory of proper names or the theory of attitude reports. But it also comes with the burden to address at least two pressing questions. First, is there empirical

## 3.3 The Pragmatic Approach

support for a pragmatic approach? That is, does the phenomenon in question display the familiar hallmarks of conversational implicature? Second, is there conceptual support for a pragmatic approach? That is, can the relevant implicature be subsumed under some general Gricean conversational principle for which there is independent evidence?

Let's consider first the question of empirical support. One of the chief hallmarks of a conversational implicature is that it is cancellable. For example, (13-a) ordinarily gives rise to the inference that the two reported events happened in the order in which they are reported. But (13-a) can be felicitously followed by (13-b). The fact that (13-b) does not contradict (13-a) shows that the temporal sequencing inference is cancellable and therefore a conversational implicature.

(13) a. They got married and had kids ...
b. ... but not that in that order.

Against that backdrop, consider the sequence in (14-a–b).

(14) a. Lois Lane believes that Clark Kent can fly ...
b. ... but she wouldn't say so using the name 'Clark Kent'.[4]

Consistent with the pragmatic approach, (14-b) does not seem to contradict (14-a). However, this is not decisive evidence in favor of the pragmatic approach, because another possibility is that a belief report like (14-a) is ambiguous between one reading that is sensitive to distinctions between co-referential names and another reading that is not, and what (14-b) does is force the latter reading. And there is independent support for the existence of such an ambiguity: it is a manifestation of the familiar *de dicto/de re* distinction that we take up in Chapter 4. This is a typical kind of conundrum that arises in some cases where a sentence seems to associate with two closely related but distinct readings. Is this distinction built into the semantics, so that the sentence is actually ambiguous in some way? Or does the semantics merely deliver one general reading, and the semblance of ambiguity is a consequence of optional pragmatic enrichment? The cancellation test for implicature, when it goes through, as it seems to here, is of no help, because it is consistent with both possibilities.

Let's now consider the question of conceptual support. Salmon and Soames, in their work on the topic, both appeal to Grice's maxim of Quantity, the relevant portion of which says, "Make your

---

[4] This formulation is borrowed from Saul 2007: 11.

contribution as informative as is required (for the current purposes of the exchange)" (Grice 1967). Saul sums it up this way:

> Since we generally require information about not just what belief is held, but how that belief is held, adherence to the maxim of Quantity would demand that the speaker attempt to convey information about how a belief is held. An audience, then will assume that a speaker is choosing a belief-reporting sentence which is suggestive of the guise under which the belief is held.
>
> (Saul 1998: 371)

Saul attempts to give teeth to this account by grappling with a difficult question: Exactly what is the implicature, in any given case, associated with a belief report? A first stab would be to say that a belief report conversationally implicates that the believer "is disposed to assent to the proposition in the embedded clause, when presented to him (at that time) under the sentence in the embedded clause" (1998: 373). But this will not do, because of examples like (15), where we judge (15-a) as true but (15-b) potentially false, even if we don't think that the ancient astronomer in question would have understood the English sentences used in these embedded clauses. (Hesperus is also known as the Evening Star and Phosphorus as the Morning Star – but as it happens, they are the same celestial body, namely Venus.)

(15)    a.   The ancient astronomer believed that Hesperus is Hesperus.
        b.   The ancient astronomer believed that Hesperus is Phosphorus.

Saul ultimately argues that a belief-reporting sentence of the form *A believes that S* conversationally implicates that "A believes that S under a guise similar to 'S'," where a guise counts as similar to 'S', "for the purposes of a particular belief-reporting utterance, just in case the speaker would take it to be an appropriate guise for the purposes of her utterance (upon being sufficiently informed)" (1998: 383). This appeal to similarity is highly reminiscent of Davidson's (1968) *samesaying*, discussed in Chapter 2 above in connection with SENTENTIALISM.

It should also be mentioned that there is another family of approaches that shares with those approaches considered here the idea that Frege's puzzle is not to be explained in terms of narrow semantics, but that also reject a pragmatic account. See for example Braun 1998 and Saul 2007. Saul (2007), in particular, defends an account that appeals to psychological processing rather than to conversational implicature. A key source of evidence Saul uses is the existence of substitution failures even in simple (non-attitudinal, non-modal) sentences. On this, see Section 3.6 below. Braun (1998) similarly argues that just as someone could fail to recognize that (16-a) and (16-b) express the same proposition, someone could also fail to recognize that (17-a) and (17-b) express the same proposition.

(16) a. Superman is strong.
 b. Clark Kent is strong.

(17) a. Lois Lane believes that Superman is strong.
 b. Lois Lane believes that Clark Kent is strong.

And, Braun argues, in the latter case, this could be so even if the person in question is rational and moreover believes that Superman is identical with Clark Kent. This is sufficient, Braun argues, for explaining the intuition, without appealing to conversational implicature. Braun calls it the Psychological Explanation.

## 3.4 THE HIDDEN INDEXICALS APPROACH

Suppose one is committed to the assumption of rigid designation for proper names as well as the assumption that our anti-substitution intuitions about co-referential proper names are rooted in semantics rather than in conversational implicature or in psychology. Is there any other way out of the puzzle? Or would we be committed to the view that substitution of co-referential names always preserves truth conditions? At first blush, it would seem as though to deny this would be to deny compositionality and hence threaten the whole program of semantic interpretation that we're invested in.[5] But there is an escape hatch: maybe there is more than meets the eye to belief reports like (18-a–b). In particular, maybe they have different truth conditions despite the rigid designation of proper names, because belief reports incorporate hidden indexicals that get contextually resolved in ways that can be influenced by the choice between *Superman* and *Clark Kent*.

(18) a. Lois Lane believes that **Superman** can fly.
 b. Lois Lane believes that **Clark Kent** can fly.

A theme running throughout solutions to Frege's puzzle is the idea that when one believes a proposition, one believes it *in a particular way*. Another way of putting this is that belief is *mediated*: believing

---

[5] For an approach to Frege's puzzle carried out by denying compositionality, see Fine (2003, 2007). For a reply, see Pickel and Rabern 2017.

something is not merely having the appropriate attitude toward some proposition but moreover taking that proposition in a particular way. Fleshing out the nature and locus of this mediation is what holds the promise of solving Frege's puzzle. The Fregean solution, as we saw, was to build the mediation right into the semantics of the proper names themselves: a name like *Superman* is endowed not just with referential capacity but with a particular way of grasping its referent. The pragmatic solution is to delegate that mediation to conversational implicature: all the semantics tells us is that there is *some* way in which an attitude holder accepts a proposition, and enrichments beyond that are merely invited inferences. But there is yet a third approach that aspires to have its cake and eat it too, maintaining the rigid designator theory of proper names while at the same time treating anti-substitution intuitions as semantic rather than pragmatic. This is the so-called hidden indexicals approach.

Approaches in this general vein include Schiffer 1977, 1992; Perry 1979; Crimmins and Perry 1989; Crimmins 1992; Richard 1990; Forbes 2006, among others. One choice point among these theories has to do with whether the indexical content is to be dealt with as a separate argument of *believe*. On this kind of approach, exemplified by Crimmins and Perry (1989), *believe* is semantically a three-place relation between an individual, a proposition, and a mode of presentation. This sits uncomfortably with the fact that, syntactically, *believe* is just a two-place predicate. On the other kind of approach, exemplified by Richard (1990), *believe* is semantically a two-place predicate, albeit with an enriched notion of what the object of the belief predicate is, one that encodes mode of presentation. See Section 3.8 below for pointers to some of the critical reactions that these approaches have inspired.

## 3.5 KRIPKE'S PUZZLE

Frege's puzzle is standardly presented as a substitution puzzle: two proper names are not interchangeable in attitude contexts, even when they are co-referential. What Kripke (1979) argues is that essentially the same puzzle can be replicated even without substitution.

KRIPKE'S PUZZLE rests on two seemingly innocuous assumptions. The first is what Kripke calls the *disquotational principle*: "If a normal English speaker, on reflection, sincerely assents to 'p,' then he believes that p" (1979: 248–249) (where 'p' is "any appropriate standard English sentence"). And a similar principle likewise holds for any other language.

## 3.5 Kripke's Puzzle

The second assumption is what Kripke calls the *principle of translation*: "If a sentence of one language expresses a truth in that language, then any translation of it into any other language also expresses a truth (in that language)" (1979: 250).

Against that backdrop, Kripke invites us to consider a monolingual French speaker, Pierre, who has never been outside France. He has heard about London (through its French name *Londres*), and based on what he has heard about it, sincerely assents to the French sentence *Londres est jolie* ('London is pretty'). So by the French version of the disquotational principle, we can conclude *Pierre croit que Londres est jolie* ('Pierre believes that London is pretty'). And by the principle of translation, we conclude that Pierre believes that London is pretty.

Now comes the plot twist: at some point, Pierre ends up moving to London, albeit without knowing that it is the same city that he learned about under the name *Londres*. He instead knows his new city under its English name *London*. As it happens, the part of London in which he now resides is a rather unattractive one, and so Pierre (having now learned a sufficient amount of English) assents to the English sentence *London is not pretty*. By the English version of the disquotational principle, Pierre believes that London is not pretty.

So now we have a situation wherein it seems that Pierre both believes that London is pretty and believes that London is not pretty. No belief revision has taken place, as Pierre still has the same old opinion of the city he learned of as *Londres*. And yet we would not want to accuse Pierre of a logical contradiction. Of course, on some level, it is very easy to see what is going on here: Pierre has opposite impressions of what he believes to be two distinct cities, and yet in fact they are one and the same. The puzzle – as emphasized by Kripke – is that there seems to be no satisfactory answer to the question: Does Pierre believe, or does he not believe, that London is pretty?

Lest one think that the French/English *Londres/London* distinction play a crucial role in this case, Kripke presents another case where translation plays no role whatsoever. Suppose Peter learns about Paderewski the famous pianist, and thereby forms the belief that Paderewski had musical talent. Peter then learns about Paderewski, the Polish Prime Minister, and concludes that Paderewski the pianist and Paderewski the Prime Minister were probably not the same individual but rather two people who shared the same name. Having the Prime Minister in mind and not thinking highly of the musical skills of politicians, he thereby forms the belief that Paderewski had no musical talent. But little does Peter know, Paderewski the pianist and Paderewski the

Prime Minister are one and the same individual. Now we have the same dilemma. There seems to be no satisfactory answer to the question: Does Peter believe, or does he not believe, that Paderewski had musical talent?

Kripke's puzzle undermines any attempt to solve Frege's puzzle by appealing to the idea that co-referential proper names have distinct senses. In Pierre's case, *London* and *Londres* are translational equivalents, and in Peter's case, there is only one name involved: *Paderewski*. There is no contrastive pair of co-referential proper names on which to hang a difference in sense. So where does that leave us? Focusing on the Paderewski case, an intuitively satisfying response to the question of whether Peter believes that Paderewski has musical talent goes something like the following: 'Yes and no. Peter believes that Paderewski had musical talent insofar as he knows of a pianist named Paderewski whom he believes had musical talent, but at the same time Peter does not believe that Paderewski had musical talent insofar as he knows of the Polish Prime Minister named Paderewski whom he does not believe had musical talent.' This suggests that, in an important way, *beliefs* are more finely grained than the linguistic strategies that we ordinarily deploy for reporting them; i.e., a belief report like 'Peter believes that Paderewski had musical talent' has an indeterminate truth value unless more information is supplied. And this intuition fits quite well with the hidden indexicals approach to Frege's puzzle. For Crimmins and Perry (1989), for example, the sentence 'Peter believes that Paderewski has musical talent' is both true and false, because the truth of the sentence turns on contextually resolved content concerning Peter's notion of Paderewski. In a separate but related vein, Bach (1997) approaches Kripke's puzzle by arguing that the complement clause of a belief report does not *specify* the content of a belief but rather merely *describes* or *characterizes* it in a way that underdetermines the actual content of the belief.

Kripke's puzzle also has an interesting status with respect to approaches to Frege's puzzle that are based on direct sensitivity to form. Larson and Ludlow, for example, in their approach to attitude reports in terms of Interpreted Logical Forms (see Section 2.5.7 above), propose to explain Kripke's puzzle by saying that it involves "a case of homophony between what are in fact two syntactically distinct objects" (1993: 319): *Paderewski$_I$* and *Paderewski$_{II}$*. For a critique of this view, see Fiengo and May 1996. One objection these authors raise is that, given Peter's situation, (19) seems truthful.

(19)   Peter believes that there are two people named 'Paderewski'.

(Fiengo and May 1996: 359)

Yet for Larson and Ludlow, it should come out false, since "what resides within the quotation marks is either *Paderewski*$_I$ or *Paderewski*$_{II}$, and Peter would believe that each of these accrues to only one individual" (Fiengo and May 1996: 359).

## 3.6 SUBSTITUTION IN SIMPLE SENTENCES

Saul (1997) observes that although substitution of co-referential proper names has typically been taken to be a puzzle that arises only in attitude contexts, a similar puzzle can arise in simple sentences as well. For example, suppose (20) is true; in that situation, according to Saul, (21) nonetheless seems false.

(20)   Clark Kent went into the phone booth, and **Superman** came out.

(21)   Clark Kent went into the phone booth, and **Clark Kent** came out.

(Saul 1997: 102)

Saul (1997) entertains two possible solutions to cases like this. First, we might entertain the hypothesis that names are ambiguous between referring to individuals and referring to temporal stages of an individual. So on its temporal stage interpretation, *Clark Kent* refers just to those disjoint temporal stages of the relevant individual at which he is presenting himself not as a superhero but rather as a reporter, and this accounts for the intuition that (21) seems false: when the individual in question comes out of the phone booth, it is a 'Superman' rather than a 'Clark Kent' temporal stage of the relevant individual that emerges.

The second possible solution that Saul (1997) entertains is a pragmatic one, wherein (21) is literally true but pragmatically misleading. If this is right, then we need to ask whether to likewise pursue a pragmatic account of proper names in attitude reports, *à la* Salmon and Soames, and if not, justify why anti-substitution intuitions in attitude reports should be explained one way and anti-substitution intuitions in simple sentences a different way.

In later work, Saul (2007) develops yet another approach in terms of psychological processing: in a nutshell, even if we know that Superman and Clark Kent are the same person, we mentally store information associated with these two names separately, and this clouds our intuitions when faced with substitution pairs like (20)–(21). This approach is designed with simple sentences in mind, but in an appendix, Saul discusses how it might be extended to attitude contexts as well.

## 3.7 DISCUSSION QUESTIONS

(i) Aside from the kinds of cases considered by Saul (1997) (see Section 3.6 above), another kind of sentence that gives rise to anti-substitution intuitions outside attitude contexts is exemplified by the following pair, where, intuitively, (22) is true but (23) is false.

(22) **Superman** was so-called because of his superhuman abilities.

(23) **Clark Kent** was so-called because of his superhuman abilities.

What implications might this have for theories of proper names? Does it challenge the view that names are rigid designators? Or can it be made consistent with that view via an appropriately sophisticated semantics for *so-called*?

(ii) As discussed in Chapter 2, synonymous expressions like *woodchuck* and *groundhog* sometimes give rise to anti-substitution intuitions in attitude contexts, just like co-referential proper names. To what extent might the various proposed solutions to Frege's puzzle extend straightforwardly to these kinds of cases as well?

(iii) Can Frege's puzzle be replicated in intensional contexts other than attitude reports (e.g. sentences with modal auxiliaries and counterfactual conditionals)? How might the answer to this question bear on the choice between the various proposed solutions to Frege's puzzle? To what extent do the different solutions predict that Frege's puzzle should be found only with attitude reports and not with intensional contexts more generally?

(iv) Although Frege's puzzle is, on some level, a puzzle for natural language semantics, the great majority of the work on this topic is found in the philosophy literature rather than in the linguistics literature. Why do you think this might be?

## 3.8 FURTHER READING

The literature on attitude reports and proper names is vast. Overviews that I have found to be particularly helpful in preparing this chapter include: McKay and Nelson 2014; Abbott 2010: Chapt. 5; Saul 2007:

## 3.8 Further Reading

Chapt. 1. Indispensable classic readings include Frege 1892; Kripke 1979. For a representative sampling of solutions, also recommended are Salmon 1986, Soames 1987 (for the pragmatic approach), Crimmins and Perry 1989 (for the hidden indexicals approach), and Saul 2007 (for the psychological processing approach). For criticism of the hidden indexicals approach, see Saul 1993; Sider 1995; Soames 1995. See also Bonardi 2019 for recent work on proper names and coordination in attitude contexts.

# 4 The *de dicto / de re* Ambiguity

## 4.1 INTRODUCTION

The sentence in (1) is verified by two rather different kinds of scenarios.

(1)  Beatrix wants to marry a philosopher.

In one kind of scenario, Beatrix has a desire to marry. She has no particular mate in mind, though she believes that philosophers generally make for excellent marriage partners. Such a scenario primes the so-called *de dicto* reading of (1), rendered unambiguously in (2-a). In the other kind of scenario, suppose, for example, that Beatrix meets someone at a bar. They hit it off, and Beatrix (perhaps hastily) forms the desire to marry this person. Little does Beatrix know, the person in question is a philosopher. Such a scenario verifies the so-called *de re* reading of (1), rendered unambiguously in (2-b).[1]

(2)  a. *Unambiguous* de dicto *paraphrase of (1)*: Beatrix wants her eventual spouse to be a philosopher.
     b. *Unambiguous* de re *paraphrase of (1)*: There is a philosopher that Beatrix wants to marry.

(One can also imagine a variant of the second scenario in which Beatrix is aware that the person in question is a philosopher. Such a scenario is also verified by (1), and can be subsumed under the *de re* reading, which allows for unawareness but does not require it.)

As a very rough first approximation, we might say that the *de dicto* reading of (1) involves construing *philosopher* in such a way that its content constitutes a crucial component in how Beatrix conceptualizes

---

[1] If you're familiar with the distinction between specific and non-specific indefinites, you might be wondering how this is any different from that. Indeed, there is a connection, but also an important distinction. We will coax this out eventually in Section 4.3.3.

## 4.1 Introduction

her desire, whereas the *de re* reading involves construing *philosopher* in such a way that its content serves as a means on the part of the speaker (the reporter of the attitude) to characterize some component of the content of the attitude, irrespective of whether Beatrix is aware of the accuracy of such a characterization.

The *de dicto/de re* ambiguity is not unique to desire ascriptions; it is found with the full gamut of propositional attitude reports. For example, in parallel fashion with (1)–(2), the belief report in (3) is ambiguous between the two readings in (4).

(3)   Beatrix believes that she will marry a philosopher.

(4)   a.   *Unambiguous* de dicto *paraphrase of (3)*: Beatrix believes that her eventual spouse will be a philosopher.
      b.   *Unambiguous* de re *paraphrase of (3)*: There is a philosopher that Beatrix believes she will marry.

The question before us is how to build a syntax-semantics for attitude reports like (1) or (3) that clarifies the source of this ambiguity and assigns appropriate truth conditions to each reading. We will begin, in Section 4.2, by considering what is quite possibly the simplest and oldest approach, which can be traced to Russell (1905). It involves treating the *de dicto/de re* ambiguity as a kind of scope ambiguity. Such an approach has a number of virtues, which we will lay out. Offsetting these virtues, however, one major source of difficulty for the scope theory is its seemingly erroneous prediction that *de re*-interpreted expressions always have wide quantificational scope. Apparent counterexamples to this prediction will be discussed in Section 4.3, followed by a tour of alternative theories that such counterexamples have prompted, in Section 4.4. These alternative theories loosen the relationship between the *de dicto/de re* contrast and quantificational scope, but they share with the scope theory the fundamental idea that the *de dicto/de re* ambiguity is reducible to whatever mechanism determines an expression's world of evaluation. Challenging this fundamental idea is a puzzle first pointed out by Quine (1956), which we discuss in Section 4.5 alongside a very different kind of approach to the *de dicto/de re* ambiguity that owes much to the pioneering work of Kaplan (1968) and his attempt to solve Quine's puzzle. This will leave us with two broadly disparate kinds of approaches to the ambiguity (the scope approach and what we might call the Quine–Kaplan approach), and so we will close in Section 4.6 by stepping back and asking: Should one approach ultimately be subsumed under the other, or are both needed in a comprehensive theory of the *de dicto/de re* ambiguity?

Before we begin, a note of clarification: throughout this chapter I will be using the terms *de dicto* and *de re* as labels for *readings of attitude reports*. In some of the philosophical literature, one also finds the terms *de dicto* and *de re* as labels for kinds of *attitudes* (irrespective of how they are reported). Burge (1977), for example, defines *de dicto* belief as a belief that is "fully conceptualized," i.e., a belief whose correct ascription "identifies it purely by reference to a 'content' all of whose semantically relevant components characterize elements in the believer's conceptual repertoire" (1977: 345–346). In contrast, *de re* belief is defined by Burge as a belief "whose correct ascription places the believer in an appropriate nonconceptual, contextual relation to objects the belief is about" (1977: 346). I will not take a stance on whether there is such a thing as a *de dicto* attitude or a *de re* attitude, nor whether (if there is such a thing) *de dicto* attitudes can only be truthfully reported by *de dicto* attitude reports and *de re* attitudes only by *de re* attitude reports. But these are very interesting questions for the interface between semantics and philosophy of mind.

## 4.2 THE SCOPE THEORY

Consider again the following example:

(5) Beatrix believes that she will marry a philosopher.

(6) a. *Unambiguous* de dicto *paraphrase*: Beatrix believes that her eventual spouse will be a philosopher.
   b. *Unambiguous* de re *paraphrase*: There is a philosopher that Beatrix believes she will marry.

The scope theory of the *de dicto/de re* ambiguity, applied to this example, works as follows. Suppose for now that the indefinite expression *a philosopher* denotes an existential quantifier, as in (7).

(7) $[[\text{a philosopher}]]^w = [\lambda f.\exists x[x \text{ is a philosopher in } w \wedge f(x)]]$

If we parse (5) so that this quantifier remains inside the complement clause, then it will have a logical form (henceforth LF) like (8) (I assume that object-position quantifiers undergo covert quantifier raising – see Heim and Kratzer 1998: Chapt. 7), which will feed the truth conditions in (9).[2]

---

[2] Two notes regarding (8). First, in order to save space, there are several places in this chapter where I will represent LFs using bracketing rather than tree drawings. (8) is the first such case. Second, in (8), '$\lambda_1$' is to be read as the piece of syntax that

## 4.2 The Scope Theory

(8) [ Beatrix believes that [ [ a philosopher ] $\lambda_1$ she will marry $t_1$ ] ]

(9) $\forall w' \in \text{DOX}_{b,w}: \exists x[x$ is a philosopher in $w' \land b$ marries $x$ in $w']$

This seems to captures the *de dicto* reading: at each of Beatrix's DOXASTIC ALTERNATIVES, Beatrix marries a philosopher.[3] The particular individual whom Beatrix marries may vary from one world to the next, but what never varies is that at each world, the person Beatrix marries is a philosopher.

But suppose the covert quantifier movement also has the option of targeting the root node, i.e., combining with the matrix clause and therefore taking scoping over the attitude predicate.[4] This will yield an LF like (10) and corresponding truth conditions in (11).

(10) [ [ a philosopher ] [ $\lambda_1$ Beatrix believes that [ she will marry $t_1$ ] ] ]

(11) $\exists x[x$ is a philosopher in $w \land \forall w' \in \text{DOX}_{b,w}: b$ marries $x$ in $w']$

The truth conditions in (11) seem to accurately capture the *de re* reading: at each of Beatrix's doxastic alternatives, it is the same individual whom she marries. This individual happens to be a philosopher in the actual world, but nothing in the truth conditions requires that Beatrix be aware of this.

In a nutshell, the scope theory of the *de dicto/de re* ambiguity works by capitalizing on the idea that the evaluation world used in interpreting a nominal expression is determined by structural position: if the nominal expression is embedded under an intensional predicate like *believe* that shifts the evaluation world of its complement, the *de dicto* reading arises, whereas if the nominal expression is outside the scope of any intensional predicate, then the evaluation world will be the actual world and the *de re* reading arises. This is a welcome result from the perspective of theoretical parsimony: our syntax-semantics for attitude reports and intensionality interacts correctly with our

---

triggers Predicate Abstraction in the sense of Heim and Kratzer 1998. In Heim and Kratzer's notation, this would be represented simply as the bare index '1'. I depart from them in using the notation '$\lambda_1$', in order to be more transparent about its semantic effect.

[3] We ignore for now the very salient *de se* reading of *she* in this example and instead assume for simplicity's sake that the sentence is evaluated against an assignment function whereby *she* refers to Beatrix. See Chapter 5 for approaches to *de se* attitude reports.

[4] A possible concern here is that there is independent reason to think that quantifier raising is unable to span a clause boundary. We will revisit this concern in Section 4.3.1 below.

syntax-semantics for quantifier movement to derive the ambiguity as a scope ambiguity, with no novel machinery needed.

To be sure, the scope theory faces numerous serious challenges that we will review in detail below. But first, it should be acknowledged that the scope theory also makes a number of accurate predictions that provide a benchmark against which alternative approaches should be evaluated. Here we will consider five accurate predictions of the scope theory.

First, the scope theory accurately predicts that attitude reports are *de dicto/de re*-ambiguous not wholesale but rather only with respect to particular nominal expressions embedded in the complement clause of the attitude predicate. In the above example, the indefinite description *a philosopher* plays a crucial role in the ambiguity, and on the scope theory this is by virtue of its capacity for optional covert movement to the matrix clause. Attitude reports that lack candidates for movement, such as (12), harbor no such ambiguity (assuming that weather *it* is semantically vacuous).[5] And attitude reports that have multiple candidates for movement correspondingly have multiple ambiguities. Consider the sentence in (13). This sentence is four-ways ambiguous, because each of the two indefinite descriptions *a linguist* and *a philosopher* can freely be read *de dicto* or *de re*, yielding the possibilities indicated in (13-a–d). This follows automatically from the scope theory, since each of the two nominals acts independently and each can either remain in the complement clause or move to the matrix level.

(12) Beatrix believes that it is raining.
(No *de dicto/de re* ambiguity)

(13) Beatrix believes that a linguist will marry a philosopher.
  a. Beatrix believes that [a linguist]$_{de\ dicto}$ will marry [a philosopher]$_{de\ dicto}$.
  b. Beatrix believes that [a linguist]$_{de\ dicto}$ will marry [a philosopher]$_{de\ re}$.

---

[5] The prediction changes if we take the view that event descriptions contain an event pronoun that can be read *de re*. See Kratzer (1998b) for a development of such a suggestion. In a related vein, Cable (2011) presents evidence suggesting that some verbs like *juggle* admit *de re* interpretations. Cable argues that this is compatible with the view that only nominal expressions can be read *de re*, provided verbs like *juggle* are semantically decomposed into a complex predicate ('do juggling'). Finally, Sudo (2014) (as well as Fodor 1970; Schwager 2011) argues that under some conditions, predicates can be read *de re* if they are contextually equivalent to a *de dicto*-interpreted predicate, where contextual equivalence is (roughly speaking) extensional equivalence in all the worlds compatible with the common ground.

## 4.2 The Scope Theory

    c. Beatrix believes that [a linguist]$_{de\ re}$ will marry [a philosopher]$_{de\ dicto}$.
    d. Beatrix believes that [a linguist]$_{de\ re}$ will marry [a philosopher]$_{de\ re}$.

A second accurate prediction of the scope theory is that it captures two signature properties that distinguish *de re*-interpreted nominals from *de dicto*-interpreted nominals: co-extensional substitution and existential entailments. To recycle an example from Quine (1951) that we used in Chapter 2, suppose that all creatures that have kidneys also have hearts, and vice versa. Then, (14-a) entails (14-b) only if *a creature with a kidney* is interpreted *de re*. By scoping the nominal out of the intensional context, the normal rules of co-extensional substitution apply. But without such scoping out, the substitution is blocked by virtue of the fact that some of Beatrix's doxastic alternatives may be ones in which there are creatures with hearts but no kidneys, or vice versa. (See, however, Section 4.5.3 below for some possible counterexamples to such substitution.)

(14)    a. Beatrix believes she will marry a **creature with a kidney**.
        b. Beatrix believes she will marry a **creature with a heart**.
        (valid only on the *de re* reading of (14-a))

As for existential entailments, consider (15). Given the non-existence of unicorns, (15) is necessarily false on the *de re* reading, since this reading asserts that there is some unicorn in the actual world. On the *de dicto* reading, on the other hand, it is possibly true, provided that there are unicorns in at least some of Beatrix's doxastic alternatives.

(15)    Beatrix believes she will marry a unicorn.

A third accurate prediction of the scope theory is that not just attitude predicates but any expression that shifts the world of evaluation can in principle trigger a *de dicto*/*de re* ambiguity. On the scope theory, what is crucial is whether the world of evaluation associated with the nominal expression is tied to the actual world or to the worlds quantified over by a world-shifting expression. And attitude predicates are just one class of world-shifting expression. Consider the example in (16), where the world-shifter is the modal *must* and the relevant nominal expression is *a philosopher who speaks French*.

(16)    Beatrix must find a philosopher who speaks French.

On the *de dicto* reading, the sentence says that the deontically best worlds are ones in which there is a philosopher who speaks French that Beatrix finds. The found individual may vary from one world to the next, so long as at each world, he or she is a philosopher who speaks French. On the *de re* reading, by contrast, the sentence says that there is some philosopher who speaks French (in the actual world) such that Beatrix must find him or her.

A fourth accurate prediction of the scope theory is that *de dicto/de re* ambiguities are triggered by and calculated relative to attitude predicates and other modal expressions (by virtue of their world-shifting behavior). The sentence in (17), for example, has no *de dicto/de re* ambiguity, because there is no attitude predicate or modal expression for *a philosopher* to outscope.

(17)   Beatrix married a philosopher.

By the same token, a nominal expression embedded under *two* intensional predicates as in (18) gives rise to three readings.

(18)   Beatrix **believes** [that Polly **wants** [to marry a philosopher]].

If *a philosopher* remains in the most deeply embedded clause, then it is *de dicto* with respect to both *want* and *believe*. If *a philosopher* moves to the intermediate clause, then it is *de re* with respect to *want* but *de dicto* with respect to *believe*. On this reading, Beatrix believes that there is some philosopher that Polly wants to marry, but does not necessarily believe that Polly realizes that the individual she wants to marry is a philosopher. Finally, if *a philosopher* moves to the highest clause, then it is *de re* with respect to both attitude predicates: there is some philosopher such that Beatrix believes that Polly wants to marry that philosopher, and the status of this individual as a philosopher does not constitute part of the content of Beatrix's reported belief. The scope theory predicts exactly this range of attested readings.

Finally, a fifth accurate prediction of the scope theory is that not just indefinite descriptions but any world-dependent expression capable of movement should participate in the ambiguity.[6] (19) illustrates the ambiguity with the definite description *the first person to walk on the Moon*. The *de dicto* reading is the more salient one. On this reading, Beatrix believes that the property of being the first person to walk on the Moon and the property of dying in 2012 are shared by the same

---

[6] We will see below (Section 4.5.1) that proper names also seem to participate in the *de dicto/de re* ambiguity, which is a problem for the scope theory if proper names are treated as RIGID DESIGNATORS.

## 4.3  Scope Mismatches

individual. But there is also a *de re* reading available, wherein there is some individual who Beatrix believes died in 2012, and it so happens that that individual was the first person to walk on the Moon, possibly unbeknownst to Beatrix.

(19)  Beatrix believes that the first person to walk on the Moon died in 2012.

Aside from indefinite and definite descriptions, nominal expressions headed by quantificational determiners such as *most* and *every* participate in the ambiguity as well. In (20), for example, the *de dicto* reading is one wherein Beatrix might report her belief as "everyone in this café is a genius" and the belief report could be true even if Beatrix is so grossly mistaken that there is no one in the café in question. On the *de re* reading, by contrast, there is some set of individuals such that every member is believed by Beatrix to be a genius, and it just so happens that (possibly unbeknownst to Beatrix) all the occupants of the café are in that set.

(20)  Beatrix believes that everyone in this café is a genius.

Suppose we take the view that the definite description in (19) has a denotation like (21) and the universal quantifier in (20) has a denotation like (22). Since these denotations are world-dependent, the choice between an *in situ* interpretation and an interpretation in which the expression in question has moved to the matrix level accurately models the ambiguity.

(21)  [[the first person to walk on the Moon]]$^w$ = the unique $x$ such that $x$ was the first person to walk on the Moon in $w$

(22)  [[everyone in this café]]$^w$ = [$\lambda f.\forall x$ [$x$ is in this café in $w$: $f(x)$]]

## 4.3  SCOPE MISMATCHES

A major source of difficulty for the scope theory of the *de dicto/de re* ambiguity is that it is possible, against the expectations of this account, for *de re*-interpreted nominals to have narrow quantificational scope. There are a number of ways of demonstrating this, which we now turn to: scope islands, scope paradoxes, and third readings. We will see that to some extent, the problems are ameliorated if we avail ourselves of CHOICE FUNCTION technology for indefinite expressions. But even if we do so, there remain residual problems that will call for a revision to the scope theory.

### 4.3.1 Scope Islands

The sentence in (23) is scopally ambiguous.

(23)  Some professor reads every journal.   ∃ > ∀ / ∀ > ∃

On the surface scope reading, the sentence reports that there is at least one professor who reads every journal, whereas on the inverse scope reading, the sentence reports that for every journal, there is at least one professor or another who reads it; i.e., the professor may vary from one journal to the next. And we can derive the reading in which the universal quantifier takes wide scope by proposing that this involves covert movement of *every journal* to a position above *some professor*.

But (24) is not similarly ambiguous; i.e., it cannot report a scenario wherein for every journal, there is at least one professor or another who thinks that Maggie reads that journal.

(24)  Some professor thinks [that Maggie reads every journal].

∃ > ∀ / *∀ > ∃

Facts like these have been taken to suggest that finite clauses are islands for covert quantifier movement, that is, that covert quantifier movement cannot escape a finite clause (May 1977; cf. also Grano and Lasnik 2018 for a slightly revised version of the generalization). But if finite clauses are islands for covert quantifier movement and *de re* readings are derived via covert quantifier movement, then we expect no *de re* readings for nominal expressions embedded in finite complements to attitude predicates, contrary to fact.

Now, for *de re* readings of *indefinite* nominal expressions in finite complement clauses, this is not so serious a problem, because indefinites are well known to give rise to apparently wide scope behavior regardless of the kind of syntactic configuration in which they are embedded. Consider (25).

(25)  Every professor thinks [that Maggie reads some journal].

∀ > ∃ / ∃ > ∀

Unlike (24), (25) quite readily admits an inverse scope interpretation, where there is some particular journal (say, *Linguistic Inquiry*) such that every professor thinks that Maggie reads that journal.

Based in part on contrasts like (24)/(25), some scholars have pursued an approach in which finite clauses are indeed islands (explaining (24)) but indefinites are not quantifiers. Instead, indefinites have a different kind of analysis that gives rise to apparently wide scope behavior without actually involving movement. A popular version

## 4.3 Scope Mismatches

of this approach uses choice functions. (See especially Abusch 1994; Reinhart 1997; Winter 1997; Kratzer 1998b; Matthewson 1999. See also Schwarzschild 2002 for a different approach.)

In basic terms, a choice function is a function that inputs a set and returns some member of that set. Suppose we have the sentence in (26) and we want to capture – without using movement – the reading wherein there is one particular cat that was chased by every dog. Then, we can assign *a cat* the denotation in (27). It denotes that individual that is returned by applying © to the denotation of *cat*, where © is a variable over choice functions. The set of possible choice functions is defined in (28): © is a choice function if and only if, when applied to a type $\langle e, t \rangle$ function like that denoted by *cat*, it returns an individual such that, when [[cat]] applies to it, the result is true.

(26)   Every dog chased a cat.

(27)   $[[\text{a cat}]]^w = ©([[\text{cat}]]^w)$
       (where © is a variable over choice functions)

(28)   $\{© |\ \forall f \in D_{\langle e,t \rangle}: ©(f) \in \{x\ |\ f(x) = 1\}\}$

Then, we allow for matrix-level existential closure over choice function variables so that we end up with a semantics like (29) for the sentence of interest in (26). This yields the reading that we are after: there is some choice function © such that every dog chased the individual returned by applying © to [[cat]].

(29)   $\exists©[\forall x\ [x \text{ is a dog}: x \text{ chased } ©([[\text{cat}]])]]$

Now let's return to an attitude report involving a *de re*-interpreted indefinite description, as in (30).

(30)   Beatrix believes that she will marry a philosopher.

We can interpret *a philosopher* using a choice function that is existentially closed at the matrix level. In order to accurately convey the *de re* reading, it must be the case that in all of Beatrix's belief worlds, the individual she marries is a philosopher *in the actual world*. We can guarantee this by assuming, following Reinhart (1997: 393–394), that choice functions always select from the EXTENSION of the NP in the actual world, even when the function is embedded in an intensional context. Then, (30) will end up with the denotation in (31), and we have successfully captured the *de re* reading without resorting to covert movement.

(31)   $\exists©[\forall w' \in \text{DOX}_{b,w}: b \text{ marries } ©([[\text{philosopher}]]^w) \text{ in } w']$

But as we have already seen, it is not just indefinites that give rise to *de dicto/de re* ambiguities; definite descriptions and quantificational expressions in general do as well. One option we might entertain would be to relax the restrictions on covert movement. Maybe a nominal can move out of a finite clause in order to yield a *de re* reading, but is not allowed to do so for other reasons, such as to outscope an indefinite (see e.g. Keshet 2011: 254, who entertains but ultimately rejects such an approach). The problem for this view is that it still makes the prediction that *de re* interpretations should correlate with wide quantificational scope. And this is a bad prediction, as becomes apparent when we look at negative quantifiers like *no*. Consider for example (32).

(32)   John is certain that no female student passed the exam.
(Charlow and Sharvit 2014: 9)

Charlow and Sharvit (2014) observe that (32) does not have a reading paraphrasable as 'No female student is such that John is certain she passed the exam', which is what we would expect if *no female student* underwent covert movement to the matrix level. And yet despite the absence of this interpretation, *no female student* nonetheless admits a *de re* interpretation. Suppose, following Charlow and Sharvit (2014), that John reported his belief as 'None of these individuals passed the exam' while pointing at the relevant individuals, who happen to be the set of all female students. I can then truthfully characterize John's belief as (32) even if John does not realize that the individuals about whom he has the belief constitute the set of female students.

Percus (2000) points out a parallel non-attitude example involving a counterfactual conditional. In (33), *every semanticist* gives rise to a *de dicto/de re* ambiguity in that it can universally quantify either over those individuals who are semanticists at each relevant counterfactual world (the *de dicto* reading) or over those individuals who are semanticists in the actual world (the *de re* reading).

(33)   If every semanticist owned a villa in Tuscany, what a joy the
       world would be.                              (Percus 2000: 177)

And yet the *de re* reading is not one where we are saying that for all actual semanticists *x*, if *x* owned a villa in Tuscany, the world would be a joy. (And this is as expected, since *if*-clauses, like finite complement clauses, are islands for covert quantifier movement.) Instead, we are saying that in all of the relevant counterfactual worlds in which all of the *actual* semanticists own villas in Tuscany, the world is a joy. In other words, *every semanticist* has narrow quantificational scope with respect to the conditional, even on its *de re* reading.

## 4.3 Scope Mismatches

### 4.3.2 Scope Paradoxes

Another way of demonstrating that *de re*-interpreted nominals can have narrow quantificational scope comes from sentences with readings that, on the scope theory of the *de dicto/de re* ambiguity, lead to scope paradoxes. This was first pointed out by Bäuerle (1983) for German, and similar facts hold for English. Consider (34), which is Keshet's (2010a) loose translational variant of one of Bäuerle's sentences.

(34)   George thinks every Red Sox player is staying in some five-star hotel downtown.           (Keshet 2010a: 692)

Imagine a scenario wherein George observes a group of individuals that, unbeknownst to him, constitute the Red Sox team. George forms the belief that there is some five-star hotel downtown, and that every individual in the group he observes is staying there. I can truthfully report this belief with (34). But on the scope theory of the *de dicto/de re* ambiguity, this reading imposes contradictory requirements on the relative LF positions of the universal quantifier and the indefinite:

(35)   a.  ∀ > think
       b.  think > ∃
       c.  ∃ > ∀

The *de re* interpretation of *every Red Sox player* requires it to scope over the attitude predicate (35-a), and the *de dicto* reading of *a five-star hotel downtown* requires it to scope under the attitude predicate (35-b). But the fact that George thinks there is just one hotel at which all the relevant individuals are staying requires the indefinite to outscope the universal (35-c), leading to a scope paradox whereby the universal has to scope both over and under the indefinite.

Keshet (2010a) argues that these facts can be reconciled with the scope theory of the *de dicto/de re* ambiguity, provided we adopt a choice function analysis of indefinites. In particular, Keshet proposes that on the problematic reading, (34) has an LF like (36).

(36)   ∃©[ [every Red Sox player] λ$_1$ [George thinks that $t_1$ is staying at ©(five-star hotel downtown)] ]

In (36), the universal quantifier outscopes the attitude predicate, ensuring its *de re* status, but the choice function associated with the indefinite is existentially bound from above the universal quantifier, getting the relative scope of the indefinite and the universal correct.[7] In order

---

[7] As we saw above in Section 4.3.1, there are reasons to think that quantifiers cannot escape finite complement clauses. But in separate work, Keshet (2011) proposes a

for this account to be successful, however, it also must be the case that the choice function returns an individual that is a five-star hotel downtown not in the actual world but rather in the local evaluation world (which changes as we move from one of George's belief worlds to the next). As Keshet notes, this is a departure from Reinhart (1997), for whom choice functions always yield an individual that has the relevant property in the actual world, even in intensional contexts. As independent support for this departure from Reinhart, Keshet points out that (37) has a reading in which *two uncles* is interpreted *de dicto* but has wide scope over the attitude predicate ('there are two individuals $x$ such that Mary thinks that $x$ is an uncle of hers and that if $x$ dies, she will be rich').

(37)   Mary thinks that if two uncles of hers die, she will be rich.
(Keshet 2010a: 695)

But as we saw in Section 4.3.1 above, there are other contexts where it is crucial that a choice function pick out an individual from the predicate's extension at the actual world. So, Keshet solves the problem of scope paradoxes, but at the expense of complicating the analysis of choice functions. Since the consequences of this complication have yet to be worked out (though see Grano 2019b for some first steps), it would be premature to remove scope paradoxes from the list of possible concerns for the scope theory of the *de dicto/de re* ambiguity.

### 4.3.3   Third Readings

A final way of demonstrating that *de re*-interpreted nominals can have narrow quantificational scope comes from the existence of the so-called third reading, first pointed out by Fodor (1970) (cf. also Geach 1967). Consider the sentence in (38).

(38)   Charley wants to buy a coat like Bill's.   (Fodor 1970: 226)

On what we have been calling the *de dicto* reading, the coat that satisfies Charley's desire can vary from one desire world to the next so long as at each world, it is a coat like Bill's. On what we have been calling the *de re* reading, there is a particular coat that Charley wants to buy, and Charley may or may not know that it is just like Bill's. But Fodor (1970) observes that this sentence also admits a third interpretation (sometimes called FODOR'S THIRD READING). Suppose that Charley does not have a particular coat in mind. Maybe, for example, he is looking

---

means of solving this problem for the scope theory of the *de dicto/de re* ambiguity as well. See Section 4.4.2 below for details.

## 4.3 Scope Mismatches

for a blue single-breasted trench coat. Unbeknownst to Charley, Bill's coat happens to match this description. This scenario can also be reported by (38), despite the fact that *coat like Bill's* is not part of the content of Charley's desire (unlike in the *de dicto* reading) but nor is the desire about a particular coat (unlike in the *de re* reading).

This shows us that we need to distinguish two independent dimensions of the interpretation of an indefinite: specific vs. non-specific and TRANSPARENT VS. OPAQUE. Specificity has to do with whether the indefinite has wide (specific) or narrow (non-specific) quantificational scope, whereas transparency has to do with whether the descriptive content of the indefinite is part of the content of the attitude (opaque) or not (transparent). Then we can say that the *de dicto* reading is non-specific and opaque, the *de re* reading is specific and transparent, and the third reading pointed out by Fodor is non-specific and transparent.[8]

Fodor's third reading is not confined to desire reports; for example, (39) has a parallel 'third reading' interpretation in which Charley believes he will buy some kind of coat (e.g. a blue single-breasted trench coat) that I know happens to be like Bill's, even though Charley may not.

(39)  Charley believes he will buy a coat like Bill's.

The existence of the third reading is a problem for the scope theory of the *de dicto/de re* ambiguity because neither of the two scope options for sentences like (39), schematized here in (40)–(41) (let *c* be the denotation of *Charley*), captures the third reading.

---

[8] The fourth logical possibility, specific and opaque, is also one Fodor claimed to be possible, but it has been argued that such a reading is not actually possible (see e.g. Ioup 1975; Keshet (2011: 255 note 4)). (i), modeled after Keshet 2011, paraphrases this hypothetical reading, and (ii), also modeled after Keshet 2011, has an odd status, suggesting that such a reading is not actually available.

(i)  There's a coat that Charley wants to buy [specific]. He thinks that it is just like Bill's, but actually, it is nothing like Bill's [opaque].

(ii) Charley wants to buy a coat like Bill's. #But actually, it is nothing like Bill's.

However, Szabó (2010) (see also Szabó 2011) argues that such a reading is possible. One piece of evidence Szabó points to is that if *want* is replaced by *think*, then the judgment changes:

(iii) Charley thinks he bought a coat like Bill's. But actually, it is nothing like Bill's.

Szabó develops an approach to specific opaque readings wherein a quantificational determiner can scope out of an attitude predicate (yielding specificity) and leave its restricting noun phrase *in situ* (yielding opacity).

(40)  $\forall w' \in \text{DOX}_{c,w}: \exists x \, [x \text{ is a coat like Bill's in } w' \wedge c \text{ will buy } x \text{ in } w']$

(41)  $\exists x \, [x \text{ is a coat like Bill's in } w \wedge \forall w' \in \text{DOX}_{c,w}: c \text{ buys } x \text{ in } w']$

(40) is inappropriate because it is formulated so that in all of Charley's belief worlds, the coat he buys is just like Bill's, and yet on the third reading, Charley does not necessarily realize that the coat in question is just like Bill's. But (41) is not appropriate either, because it is formulated so that the coat Charley will buy remains constant across Charley's belief worlds, and yet on the third reading, the belief is not tied to any particular coat.

To harp on a familiar refrain, the choice function analysis of indefinites may provide a way out of the conundrum. Suppose we assign (39) an analysis like (42).

(42)  $\forall w' \in \text{DOX}_{c,w}: \exists \copyright [c \text{ will buy } \copyright(\text{coat just like Bill's}) \text{ in } w']$

Narrow quantificational scope (i.e., non-specificity) is guaranteed by virtue of the choice function being existentially closed below the quantification over belief worlds. If we furthermore assume, following Reinhart (1997), that choice functions always yield a member of the NP's extension at the actual world, then we derive transparency as well: at each of Charley's belief alternatives, Charley buys a hat that is just like Bill's actual hat.[9]

### 4.3.4 Summary

The scope theory of the *de dicto/de re* ambiguity erroneously predicts that *de re*-interpreted nominals cannot have narrow quantificational scope. To some extent, the problem is ameliorated if indefinites are analyzed as choice functions rather than as quantifiers. But even if one makes that move, there are residual difficulties: quantifiers other than indefinites such as those headed by *no* and *every* can have *de re* readings even in configurations where they obligatorily take narrow scope. And even restricting our attention to indefinites, it remains to be seen whether choice functions can do all the needed work, given

---

[9] See, however, Schwager 2011, in which Kaufmann (previously Schwager) presents data suggesting that third readings are possible even in cases where the nominal in question has an empty extension in the actual world. This is a problem not only for the scope theory of the *de dicto/de re* ambiguity but also for the alternatives considered in Section 4.4 below. Kaufmann proposes a solution wherein a property in the content of an attitude report "can be replaced by a different property ... as long as the reported property is a subset of the reporting property at all the relevant worlds" (2011: 409) (see also note 3 above). For other recent work on third readings, see also Baron 2016 and Dawson and Deal 2019.

## 4.4 RESOLVING THE MISMATCHES

### 4.4.1 World Pronouns

One popular alternative to the scope theory of the *de dicto/de re* ambiguity involves introducing world pronouns into the syntax, as proposed by Cresswell (1990) and Percus (2000), among others. That is, rather than treating an expression's world variable as a parameter of interpretation whose value is always determined by the world-shifting operator under which it is immediately embedded (or else valued by the actual world if it is not embedded under a world-shifting operator), the suggestion is that we treat world variables as pronouns in the syntax that can be bound at a distance. Consider the sentence in (43).

(43)   Beatrix believes that every cat is a genius.

In the theory we've been pursuing so far, if *every cat* stays in the embedded clause, then its world variable is inescapably bound by the world abstractor associated with the belief predicate, as in (44); the only way to have it interpreted relative to the actual world is via covert movement, as in (45).

(44)   a.  Beatrix believes that [every cat is a genius]
       b.  $\forall w' \in \text{DOX}_{b,w}: \forall x[x \text{ is a cat in } w': x \text{ is a genius in } w']$

(45)   a.  every cat [$\lambda_1$ Beatrix believes [that $t_1$ is a genius] ]
       b.  $\forall x[x \text{ is a cat in } w: \forall w' \in \text{DOX}_{b,w}: x \text{ is a genius in } w']$

But suppose we modify our system so that instead of treating world variables as parameters of interpretation, as in (46), we treat them as arguments in the object language, as in (47). World-dependent expressions then combine with silent world pronouns in the syntax as their first arguments.

(46)   *worlds as a parameter of interpretation*
       a.  $[[\text{cat}]]^w = [\lambda x.x \text{ is a cat in } w]$
       b.  $[[\text{genius}]]^w = [\lambda x.x \text{ is a genius in } w]$
       c.  $[[\text{leave}]]^w = [\lambda x.x \text{ leaves in } w]$
       d.  $[[\text{believe}]]^w = [\lambda p.[\lambda x. \forall w' \in \text{DOX}_{x,w}: p(w')]]$

(47) worlds as arguments in the object language
   a. [[cat]] = [λw.[λx.x is a cat in w]]
   b. [[genius]]= [λw.[λx.x is a genius in w]]
   c. [[leave]]= [λw.[λx.x leaves in w]]
   d. [[believe]] = [λw.[λp.[λx.∀w′ ∈ DOX$_{x,w}$: p(w′)]]]

A sentence like (48), for example, would have a syntax like (49), where *left* combines with a world pronoun, and we furthermore assume that a sentence always contains a world binder in its left periphery.[10]

(48) Maggie left.

(49)

(49) yields the interpretation in (50), which can be connected to the desired truth conditions via the principle in (51), borrowed from von Fintel and Heim (2011).

(50) [λw.Maggie left in w]

(51) **Principle of utterance truth:** An utterance of a sentence (=LF) ϕ in world w is true iff [[ϕ]](w) = 1. (von Fintel and Heim 2011: 104)

On this approach, we can also do away with Intensional Functional Application, since the world binder in an embedded sentence will yield the appropriate intensional type for an intensional predicate like *believe* to combine with via ordinary Functional Application:

(52)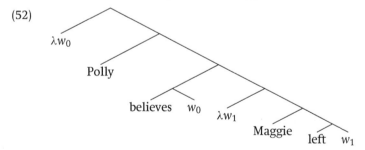

[10] In (49), 'λw$_0$' is to be read as a piece of syntax that triggers Predicate Abstraction, where Predicate Abstraction is now generalized so as to be able to bind not only individual variables but also variables over other types, such as worlds, as needed here. This notation follows von Fintel and Heim 2011: chapt. 8.

## 4.4 Resolving the Mismatches

With these modifications in place, we can derive *de re* readings without movement. Consider for example the LF in (53-a) which will yield the interpretation in (53-b). Here, the world pronoun associated with *genius* is bound by the world binder under *believe* so that this constitutes part of the content of the attitude, but the world pronoun associated with *cat* is bound from the matrix level, thereby giving rise to the *de re* interpretation.

(53) a. $\lambda w_0$ [Beatrix believes-$w_0$ [$\lambda w_1$ that every cat-$w_0$ is a genius-$w_1$]]
 b. [$\lambda w_0. \forall w' \in \text{DOX}_{b,w_0}: \forall x[x$ is a cat in $w_0$: $x$ is a genius in $w'$]]

This approach fully divorces a nominal's *de dicto/de re* status from its quantificational scope, thereby avoiding all of the scope mismatch problems considered in the previous section, and with no need to invoke a choice function analysis of indefinites. Revisiting the problematic examples from the previous section, what we can do in each case is have the matrix-level world binder bind the world pronoun associated with the *de re*-interpreted nominal, while leaving that nominal within the quantificational scope of the relevant attitude verb or modal. This is schematized in (54), with irrelevant details omitted.

(54) a. $\lambda w_0$ [John is certain that no **female student**-$w_0$ passed the exam].
 b. $\lambda w_0$ [If every **semanticist**-$w_0$ owned a villa in Tuscany, what a joy the world would be].
 c. $\lambda w_0$ [George thinks every **Red Sox player**-$w_0$ is staying in some five-star hotel downtown].
 d. $\lambda w_0$ [Charley believes that he will buy a **coat like Bill's**-$w_0$].

The trade-off in adopting the covert world pronoun solution is that we replace an undergeneration problem with an overgeneration problem: unless we place constraints on how a world pronoun can be bound, we predict many more kinds of readings for various sentences than what is actually possible. In particular, the literature has identified several sources of overgeneration for the covert world pronouns approach. Here we consider three.[11] This first one is observed by Percus (2000), who considers the belief report in (55). The constituents *my brother* and *Canadian* both have world-dependent denotations, so if

---

[11] Others not discussed here are the Presuppositional DP Constraint (Musan 1995; Keshet 2008; Romoli and Sudo 2009) and the Nested DP Constraint (Romoli and Sudo 2009).

binding of world pronouns is entirely unconstrained, we predict four possible LFs for this structure, given in (56).

(55)  Mary thinks that my brother is Canadian.  (Percus 2000: 196)

(56) a. $\lambda w_0$ [Mary thinks-$w_0$ [$\lambda w_1$ my brother-$w_1$ is Canadian-$w_1$]]
 b. $\lambda w_0$ [Mary thinks-$w_0$ [$\lambda w_1$ my brother-$w_0$ is Canadian-$w_1$]]
 c. $\lambda w_0$ [Mary thinks-$w_0$ [$\lambda w_1$ my brother-$w_1$ is Canadian-$w_0$]]
 d. $\lambda w_0$ [Mary thinks-$w_0$ [$\lambda w_1$ my brother-$w_0$ is Canadian-$w_0$]]

(56-a) yields the run-of-the-mill *de dicto* reading for *my brother*, and this is indeed an available reading: Percus paraphrases it as 'Mary believes that I have a Canadian brother.' (56-b) yields the *de re* reading of *my brother*, and this is a possible reading as well: 'My brother is such that Mary thinks he is Canadian.' But what about (57-c)? Here, *my brother* is *de dicto* but the predicate *Canadian* is *de re*: 'There is a Canadian such that Mary thinks he is my brother.' This is not a possible reading for the sentence. Finally, in (56-d), both *my brother* and *Canadian* are read *de re*, which is also not a possible reading for the sentence. Percus suggests that the absence of the reading in (56-d) is not a serious problem, in that there are plausibly other principles that rule it out (see 2000: 200 note 18). But the unavailability of the reading associated with (56-c) is a puzzle.

This leaves us with two options. We can either give up on having world pronouns in the syntax and seek some other explanation for the facts that originally led us down this path, or we can keep the world pronouns and explore ways of reining in their binding behavior. Percus explores the latter view, venturing the generalization in (57). On this approach, (57) rules out (56-c). (It does so in part because of Percus's simplifying assumption that *is Canadian* is a verb. But as Percus points out, it would be more accurate to say that *Canadian* is an adjective that combines with a world pronoun, and the resulting structure combines with *is*. So ultimately (57) needs some refinement.)

(57) **Generalization X**: The situation[12] pronoun that a verb selects for must be coindexed with the nearest $\lambda$ above it.

(Percus 2000: 201)

The second overgeneration problem concerns adverbs. Percus (2000) argues that if the adverb *always* in (58) admitted an interpretation in

---

[12] Percus uses situation pronouns rather than world pronouns. The choice between the two is not immediately relevant here.

## 4.4 Resolving the Mismatches

which its associated world pronoun were bound at the matrix level, it would yield an unavailable reading.

(58) Mary thinks that my brother always won the game.
(Percus 2000: 201)

Here's Percus:

> Imagine that Mary wrongly takes Pierre to be my brother, imagine moreover that she is unaware of the fact that Pierre and I played the series of games that I have been talking about, and imagine that Pierre won all of those games.
> (Percus 2000: 204)

The sentence (58) is judged false in this scenario, though if the world or situation pronoun associated with *always* could be bound from the matrix level, it should be judged true. Percus therefore proposes:

(59) **Generalization Y**: The situation pronoun that an adverbial quantifier selects for must be coindexed with the nearest λ above it. (Percus 2000: 204)

Third, Keshet (2008, 2010b) observes (building on similar observations by Musan (1995) regarding temporal interpretation) that sentences like (60) are odd insofar as *married bachelor* leads to a contradiction.

(60) #Mary thinks the married bachelor is confused.
(Keshet 2008: 53)

In a theory with covert world pronouns, however, *married* and *bachelor* each associate with their own world variable. If we were to associate one with the matrix-level world binder and the other with that introduced by the attitude predicate, then we should expect coherent readings of (60), contrary to fact (that is, the belief report could be about a bachelor whom Mary believes is married, or a married person whom Mary believes is a bachelor). Keshet therefore proposes:

(61) **Intersective Predicate Generalization**: Two predicates interpreted intersectively may not be evaluated at different times[13] or worlds from one another. (Keshet 2010b: 388)

---

[13] Here we focus only on world-sensitivity, not time-sensitivity. See Keshet 2010b for more on the relationship between the two.

In short, covert world pronouns give us the flexibility we need to account for *de re*-interpreted nominals with narrow quantificational scope, but they do so at the cost of giving us too much flexibility that must be reined in, and attempts at reining the system in amount to little more than descriptive statements of what the problems are (though see Percus 2000 and Keshet 2010b for efforts at explaining some of the generalizations). This has led some researchers to explore yet other options that give us just the needed flexibility but without too much, in a more principled way. The next two approaches we consider are in this vein.

### 4.4.2 Split Intensionality

Keshet (2008, 2011) proposes a return to view that worlds are a parameter of interpretation rather than pronouns in syntax. In order to account for the scope mismatch facts, Keshet proposes, in an approach he calls SPLIT INTENSIONALITY, that when a predicate needs to combine with an intensional type, this is mediated by an abstractor over the world parameter that projects in the syntax and can be freely inserted as needed to repair type mismatches. That is, rather than interpreting a structure like (62) via Intensional Functional Application, an abstractor over worlds (represented here as '$\wedge$') projects between an attitude verb and its clausal complement as in (63), and composition proceeds via ordinary Functional Application.

(62)  believe$_{\langle st, et \rangle}$ [that it is raining]$_t$       IFA

(63)  believe$_{\langle st, et \rangle}$ [ $\wedge$ [that it is raining]$_t$ ]$_{\langle st \rangle}$       FA

Crucially, this additional piece of syntax creates a landing site for nominal expressions that is below the attitude verb itself (yielding narrow quantificational scope) but above the world abstractor (yielding a *de re* interpretation). For example, (64) on its *de re* reading would have a syntax like (65).

(64)  Mary thinks that everyone in this room is outside.

(Keshet 2011: 268)

(65)  Mary thinks [ [everyone in this room]$_1$ [$\lambda_1$ [$\wedge$ [that $t_1$ is outside]]]

The nominal expression *everyone in this room* moves covertly to the periphery of the complement clause, and it will be read *de re* because it is outside the scope of the world abstractor. But it will nonetheless have narrow quantificational scope, because it sits below *thinks*, which is what effects universal quantification over belief worlds. (Note, though,

## 4.4 Resolving the Mismatches

that this requires some nonstandard assumptions about how generalized quantifiers compose – see Keshet 2011: 266–268 for discussion.)

Keshet (2011) also discusses how Split Intensionality yields an elegant account of Fodor's (1970) third reading (see Section 4.3.3 above). In particular, the sentence in (66) can be parsed in three distinct ways depending on the structural position of the indefinite, yielding the three attested readings. If the indefinite scopes below the abstractor, as in (67-a), it yields the standard *de dicto* reading (opaque, narrow scope). If the indefinite attaches at the matrix level, as in (67-b), it yields the standard *de re* reading (transparent, wide scope). And if the indefinite scopes above the abstractor but below the attitude verb, as in (67-c), it yields Fodor's third reading (transparent, narrow scope).[14]

(66) Charley believes he will buy a coat like Bill's.

(67) a. Charley believes ∧ [ [a coat like Bill's] [ $\lambda_1$ he will buy $t_1$ ] ]
 b. [a coat like Bill's] $\lambda_1$ [ Charley believes ∧ [ he will buy $t_1$ ] ]
 c. Charley believes [a coat like Bill's] $\lambda_1$ [ ∧ [ he will buy $t_1$ ] ]

An important piece of independent support that Keshet appeals to in motivating Split Intensionality has to do with how the *de dicto/de re* ambiguity interacts with syntactic islands. As already discussed above in Section 4.3.1, finite complement clauses are known to be islands for covert quantifier movement, challenging the scope theory of the *de dicto/de re* ambiguity. Split Intensionality is immune to this challenge, because it provides a landing site for nominal expressions that is inside the complement clause (avoiding any island violation) but outside the scope of the world abstractor (triggering *de re* readings). What Keshet shows is that when other kinds of syntactic islands are embedded *inside* a finite complement clause, nominal expressions in the nested island resist *de re* interpretations. Consider the examples in (68).

(68) a. #John believes that [if *any Republican friend of his* were Republican], he wouldn't be friends with him.
 b. #The teacher thinks John should be punished [because Sally wrote *every paper he/John wrote*].
 c. #Mary believes that there's a [nasty rumor going around that *a man in my class* is a man]. (Keshet 2011: 258–259)

---

[14] In contrast to Fodor's third reading, Bäuerle's scope paradox remains a challenge for Split Intensionality. As discussed in Section 4.3.2, Keshet (2010a) suggests a solution to the paradox using choice functions, and that solution is orthogonal to the choice between Split Intensionality and the more traditional scope theory of the *de dicto/de re* ambiguity.

In each case, the bracketed constituent constitutes a standard kind of syntactic island (adjunct islands in (68-a–b) and a complex NP island in (68-c)). If the italicized nominal constituent is read *de dicto*, then the belief report comes across as infelicitous, since it attributes a contradictory belief to the attitude holder. And the crucial observation is that the sentences do indeed come across as infelicitous: the italicized expressions cannot be read *de re*, even to avoid attributing a contradictory belief to the attitude holder. This follows if nominal expressions embedded in islands within complement clauses cannot be read *de re*.

Similarly, consider the coordination example in (69). Coordinate structures are also well known to constitute syntactic islands. And according to Keshet, in a sentence like (69), both conjuncts have to be read either *de re* or *de dicto* together. (69) does not have a reading wherein *a doctor* is read *de re* and *a lawyer* is read *de dicto*, or vice versa. (See, however, Section 4.5.4 below for a possible counterexample to the claim that conjuncts in a coordinate structure must be read uniformly *de re* or uniformly *de dicto*.)

(69)   Mary wants to date a doctor and a lawyer.   (Keshet 2011: 258)

In a system with world pronouns, it is not clear why embedding a nominal expression in an island would prevent its world pronoun from being associated with the matrix world binder. But it is accounted for on Keshet's theory: it falls out from independently known constraints on movement.

In summary, Split Intensionality avoids overgeneration problems associated with world pronouns by returning to the view that a predicate's world of evaluation is inextricably tied to its structural position, while at the same time avoiding undergeneration problems associated with the traditional scope theory by enriching the syntax with a structural position where a nominal can get a *de re* interpretation without escaping the quantificational scope of an attitude verb.

Still, it remains to be seen whether Split Intensionality really does occupy that razor-thin boundary between overgeneration and undergeneration. One potential source of undergeneration for Split Intensionality concerns iterated attitude reports. Just as Split Intensionality predicts that a nominal expression embedded in an island inside a complement clause cannot be read *de re*, it also predicts that a nominal expression embedded under *two* attitude predicates cannot be read *de re* with respect to both attitude verbs: such a reading would require the nominal expression to move above both world abstractors, incurring an island violation. Above in Section 4.2, I claimed that indefinites embedded under two attitude verbs can be read *de re* with respect to

## 4.4 Resolving the Mismatches

both attitude verbs. But given the special status of indefinites, we also need to know whether this extends to other kinds of nominals, and setting up the relevant test cases will require a great deal of care. More research is needed here. See also Keshet and Schwarz 2019 for relevant discussion.

### 4.4.3 Presupposition Projection

A third kind of approach is to try to assimilate the *de dicto/de re* ambiguity into a theory of PRESUPPOSITION PROJECTION (see especially Heim 1992; Geurts 1998; Maier 2006, 2009; Romoli and Sudo 2009). Presupposition projection is the phenomenon whereby a presupposition induced by some lexical item persists even when that lexical item belongs to a sentence embedded under a propositional operator. For example, the definite article *the* in (70) triggers the presupposition that there is a book on the table (existence) and that there is only one book on the table (uniqueness). This existence and uniqueness presupposition persists even when (70) is negated (70-a), questioned (70-b), modalized (70-c), or used in the antecedent of a conditional (70-d).

(70) The book on the table is interesting.

(71) a. The book on the table is **not** interesting.
b. **Is** the book on the table interesting?
c. The book on the table **might/must** be interesting.
d. **If** the book on the table is interesting, I'll want to read it.

But what happens if we embed this presupposition trigger under an attitude verb, as in (72)?

(72) Beatrix **thinks** that the book on the table is interesting.

Conceptually, we can imagine two ways of resolving the presupposition: if it is resolved locally, with respect to Beatrix's belief worlds, then the presupposition ends up being that Beatrix *thinks* there is a unique book on the table. But if it is resolved globally, with respect to the actual utterance context, then the presupposition ends up being that there is in fact a a unique book on the table, and Beatrix may or may not believe this. But – so the idea goes – these two options for resolving the presupposition are precisely the *de dicto* and *de re* readings of *the book on the table*, respectively.

This line of analysis makes a clear prediction: the only kinds of expressions that participate in *de dicto/de re* ambiguities should be presupposition triggers. This prediction avoids some of the overgeneration problems of the world pronouns approach (Section 4.4.1), but it also raises some questions of its own. While the definite article *the* and plausibly some quantificational determiners like *every* trigger existence presuppositions, indefinites clearly do not; consequently, these must be dealt with in some other way, limiting the empirical reach of the account.

If presupposition triggers are not a necessary condition for *de dicto/de re* ambiguities, are they at least a sufficient condition? That is, do *all* presupposition triggers lead to *de dicto/de re* ambiguities? Not if Percus's (2000) Generalizations X and Y hold (Section 4.4.1 above), for it is possible to find main predicates and adverbs that are presuppositional. For example, in (73-a), the main predicate *stopped* triggers the presupposition that I smoked before. Does (73-b) have a reading wherein the presupposition is that I smoked before, irrespective of whether Beatrix believes it? It is not so clear that it does.

(73)    a.  I stopped smoking.
        b.  Beatrix thinks that I stopped smoking.

Similarly, the adverb *anymore* in (74-a) triggers the presupposition that I used to smoke. Does (74-b) have a reading wherein the presupposition is that I used to smoke, irrespective of whether Beatrix believes it?

(74)    a.  I don't smoke anymore.
        b.  Beatrix thinks that I don't smoke anymore.

According to Romoli and Sudo (2009), the answer is negative (though see Heim 1992: 208 for a different take, at least with respect to *stop*), and they suggest that this is because only presuppositional nominals and not presuppositional main predicates and adverbs involve a "direct anaphoric dependency between the presupposition and the assertion" (2009: 434).

In summary, presupposition triggers appear to be neither a necessary nor a sufficient condition for *de dicto/de re* ambiguities. This is not to say that the approach is wrong – it is conceivable that presupposition projection accounts for some manifestations of the ambiguity – but more research will be needed to determine what its limits are.

## 4.5 DOUBLE VISION

Aside from scope mismatches, another major source of difficulty for the scope theory of the *de dicto/de re* ambiguity – and one that will not be so easily solved by the alternative approaches discussed in Section 4.4 – is a puzzle first pointed out by Quine (1956) that has since come to be known (starting with Klein 1978) as DOUBLE VISION. In what follows,

## 4.5 Double Vision

we first lay out the puzzle (Section 4.5.1), then present an influential approach to it based on Kaplan (1968) (Sections 4.5.2 and 4.5.3), and then finally discuss two competing syntactic implementations of that approach (Sections 4.5.4 and 4.5.5).

### 4.5.1 The Puzzle

Quine (1956) invites us to consider the following scenario:

> There is a certain man in a brown hat whom Ralph has glimpsed several times under questionable circumstances on which we need not enter here; suffice it to say that Ralph suspects he is a spy. Also there is gray-haired man, vaguely known to Ralph as rather a pillar of the community, whom Ralph is not aware of having seen except once at the beach. Now Ralph does not know it, but the men are one and the same. Can we say of this *man* (Bernard J. Ortcutt, to give him a name) that Ralph believes him to be a spy?
>
> (Quine 1956: 179)

In this scenario, the sentence in (75) seems true, given that Ralph believes that the man in the brown hat is a spy and the man in the brown hat is in fact Ortcutt. But the sentence in (76) also seems true, given that Ralph believes that the man seen at the beach is not a spy and the man seen at the beach is also in fact Ortcutt.

(75) Ralph believes that Ortcutt is a spy.

(76) Ralph believes that Ortcutt is not a spy.

And yet, we can simultaneously assert (75) and (76) without charging Ralph with being irrational as we ordinarily would if someone believed some proposition and its negation.[15]

At this point we should say something more about proper names. Proper names seem to give rise to the *de dicto*/*de re* ambiguity just as much as other kinds of nominal expressions do, as brought out by thinking about truth judgments associated with sentences like the following. (77) seems true no matter how we read it, because Lois Lane associates the name 'Superman' with the individual who she believes can fly. (78), by contrast, seems true on a *de re* reading of 'Clark Kent'

---

[15] In this respect, there is a striking parallel between Quine's double vision puzzle and Kripke's (1979) puzzle about belief discussed in Chapter 3. The difference is that KRIPKE'S PUZZLE IS a puzzle about *de dicto* belief reports, whereas Quine's puzzle is a puzzle about *de re* belief reports. But given their similarity, it should come as no surprise that Kaplan's (1968) solution to Quine's puzzle (see Section 4.5.2 below) bears a close resemblance to one of the approaches to Kripke's puzzle, namely Crimmins and Perry's (1989) HIDDEN INDEXICALS approach, also discussed in Chapter 3.

but false on a *de dicto* reading, because although there is an individual who Lois believes can fly, she would not recognize that individual by the name 'Clark Kent'.

(77) Lois Lane believes that **Superman** can fly.
(true on both the *de dicto* and *de re* readings)

(78) Lois Lane believes that **Clark Kent** can fly.
(false on the *de dicto* reading; true on the *de re* reading)

As we know from Chapter 3, the interaction between attitude reports and proper names is notoriously vexing. If we take the Mill–Kripke view that proper names are rigid designators (i.e., have world-independent denotations), then not only do we owe an account of FREGE'S PUZZLE, we also have trouble explaining how proper names could give rise to a *de dicto/de re* ambiguity. Neither the scope theory nor any theory based on manipulating a nominal's world of evaluation expects an ambiguity for rigid designators.[16]

But crucially, even if we were to give up on the view that proper names are rigid designators, Quine's puzzle would still be a puzzle. Assume that Ralph does not know that *either* the man in the brown hat *or* the man he saw at the beach is named Ortcutt. But then this means that *both* (75) *and* (76) are *de re* belief reports on their true readings, so we cannot explain away the apparent contradictory beliefs by saying that they are not actually contradictory because one is described by a *de re* report while the other is described by a *de dicto* report. Not only that, Quine's puzzle does not rest on proper names; it can be replicated with other kinds of nominals. For example, replacing *Ortcutt* with *the man in the brown hat* yields the same problem. On its *de re* reading, (79) should be true, but then so should (80). In other words, the problem is that there is an individual who Ralph believes is a spy, and there is an individual who Ralph believes is not a spy, and both of these individuals in question are the man in the brown hat.

(79) Ralph believes that the man in the brown hat is a spy.
(true on both the *de dicto* and *de re* readings)

(80) Ralph believes that the man in the brown hat is not a spy.
(false on the *de dicto* reading; true on the *de re* reading)

---

[16] As Kripke puts it, "[i]t may well be argued that the Millian view implies that proper names are *scopeless* and that for them the *de dicto-de re* ambiguity vanishes" (1979: 272, note 7).

## 4.5 Double Vision

Before looking for a solution, it is worth pointing out that double vision is found with attitude reports only and not with modal expressions more generally. Pearson (2016) illustrates this by continuing Quine's scenario as follows:

> [I]t is Ralph's birthday, and he is considering who might come to his party. He is quite happy to welcome at the party anyone whom he considers a pillar of the community, but not a suspected spy.
>
> (Pearson 2016: 706)

Against this context, Pearson observes that (81-a–b) both have true *de re* readings (showing that *want* patterns like *believe* in triggering the double vision puzzle), whereas (82-a–b) are mutually contradictory. Like *believe* and *want*, the verb *deserve* denotes a relation between propositions and individuals. But unlike *believe* and *want*, it does not ascribe any attitude to the individual. Correspondingly, the intuition is that if Ralph deserves to get what he wants and Ortcutt *is* in fact a pillar of the community, then (82-a) is true and (82-b) is false. But there is no scenario that would make both true.

(81) a. Ralph **wants** to welcome Ortcutt at the party.
b. Ralph **wants** to snub Ortcutt at the party.

(82) a. Ralph **deserves** to welcome Ortcutt at the party.
b. Ralph **deserves** to snub Ortcutt at the party. (Pearson 2016: 706)

The solution we seek for double vision should therefore be tied to some property unique to attitude reports and not shared by modal expressions more generally.

### 4.5.2 Acquaintance Relations

The influential approach to Quine's double vision puzzle that we will review here has two important features. The first is due to Quine (1956) himself, and it is the idea that we need to be able to treat *believe* (and other attitude verbs) not as a two-place relation between an individual and a proposition but rather as a three-place relation between an individual (the attitude holder), another individual (the *res*), and a property.[17] Probably the easiest way to grasp the intuition

---

[17] Actually, for Quine, *believe* denotes an $n + 2$-place relation, where $n$ is the number of nominals in the belief report that are construed *de re*. For the most part in what follows we will be concerned only with attitude reports that have one *de re* interpreted nominal. But it will be worth keeping multiple *de re* reports in mind as we consider various solutions to Quine's puzzle.

underlying this proposal is to observe that sentences like (83) admit paraphrases like (84) that render the status of *believe* as a three-place relation syntactically transparent and that, interestingly, also seem to force the *de re* construal: (84) places the proper name *Ortcutt* outside the complement clause, and we might informally describe (84) as saying that Ralph ascribes spyhood to some individual that the speaker (but not necessarily Ralph) knows as Ortcutt.

(83)  Ralph believes that Ortcutt is a spy.

(84)  Ralph believes of Ortcutt that he is a spy.

The intuition that the syntax in (84) forces a *de re* construal is reinforced by the observation that (85) does not sound contradictory, whereas as (86) does.

(85)  Ralph believes that his horse is graceful. But actually, Ralph doesn't have a horse.

(86)  Ralph believes of his horse that it is graceful. #But actually, Ralph doesn't have a horse.

The second important feature, due to Kaplan (1968) and further developed by Lewis (1979) and Cresswell and von Stechow (1982), is the introduction of acquaintance relations. It begins with the following intuition. In Quine's scenario, there is some individual that Ralph bears a relation to (perhaps we could call it the 'see-wearing-a-brown-hat' relation); this individual (unbeknownst to Ralph) is Ortcutt, and Ralph believes *de dicto* that the man he saw wearing a brown hat is a spy. Meanwhile, there is some individual that Ralph bears some other relation to (call it the 'see-at-the-beach' relation); this individual (also unbeknownst to Ralph) is also Ortcutt, and Ralph believes *de dicto* that the man he saw at the beach is not a spy. Then, (87)–(88) are both true by virtue of the same factors that render (89)–(90) true, respectively.

(87)  Ralph believes that Ortcutt is a spy.

(88)  Ralph believes that Ortcutt is not a spy.

(89)  The individual Ralph saw wearing a brown hat is Ortcutt and Ralph believes *de dicto* that the individual he saw wearing a brown hat is a spy.

(90)  The individual Ralph saw at the beach is Ortcutt and Ralph believes *de dicto* that the individual he saw at the beach is not a spy.

## 4.5 Double Vision

More formally, let $R$ be a three-place predicate that holds between two individuals $x$ and $y$ and a world $w$ if and only if $x$ bears some suitable acquaintance relation to $y$ in $w$ (see Section 4.5.3 immediately below for discussion of what counts as 'suitable'). Then we can analyze (87) and (88) as having the semantic representations in (91) and (92), respectively (where $o$ is Ortcutt and $r$ is Ralph). In prose, (91) states that there is some acquaintance relation $R$ such that Ralph bears $R$ uniquely to Ortcutt in the actual world, and Ralph believes (*de dicto*) that the individual to whom he uniquely bears the $R$ relation is a spy. Similarly, (92) states that there is some acquaintance relation $R$ such that Ralph bears $R$ uniquely to Ortcutt in the actual world, and Ralph believes (*de dicto*) that the individual to whom he uniquely bears the $R$ relation is *not* a spy. (A note on the $\iota$ notation: read $\iota x[f(x)]$ as 'the unique $x$ such that $f(x)$ is true'. So $\iota y[R(r,y,w)]$ is 'the unique $y$ such that $R(r,y,w)$ is true'.)

(91)  $\exists R[\iota y[R(r,y,w)] = o \land \forall w' \in \text{DOX}_{r,w}: \iota y[R(r,y,w')]$ is a spy in $w']$
      (verified by $[\lambda x.[\lambda y.[\lambda w.x$ sees $y$ wearing a brown hat in $w]]])$

(92)  $\exists R[\iota y[R(r,y,w)] = o \land \forall w' \in \text{DOX}_{r,w}: \iota y[R(r,y,w')]$ is not a spy in $w']$
      (verified by $[\lambda x.[\lambda y.[\lambda w.x$ sees $y$ at the beach in $w]]])$

This gets us what we want. Existentially quantifying over $R$ ensures that both (87) and (88) are true in Quine's scenario without portraying Ralph as having contradictory beliefs: (87) is verified by the 'see-wearing-a-brown-hat' relation and (88) is verified by the 'see-at-the-beach' relation.[18] The approach also in effect reduces *de re* belief reports to *de dicto* ones in that both underlyingly involve a two-place relation between an individual and a proposition. The difference is that in the case of a *de re* belief report, some *res* is singled out and related via $R$ to some component in the believed proposition.

---

[18] Here we follow Kaplan in treating $R$ as being existentially bound, but on some other approaches it is treated as being contextually bound (e.g. Heim 1992, 1994; Abusch 1997; Maier 2009). See Anand 2006 for discussion. It should also be noted that the implementation sketched here differs from Kaplan's in several other important respects. For Kaplan, $R$ is a relation between a name, a *res*, and an attitude holder; belief reports involve relations to sentences rather than to propositions; and *de re* belief reports instantiate quantification over names. Here this is recast in a possible worlds framework. The specific formulation in (91)–(92) closely follows that of Percus and Sauerland (2003a) (for more on which see Section 4.5.5 below), although here we make the simplifying assumption that the first argument of $R$ as it appears in the content of the attitude report directly refers to the attitude holder rather than being related to the attitude holder through an an appropriately formulated *de se* semantics.

This approach raises at least two pressing questions. First, what is the nature of the R relation? That is, what counts as a suitable acquaintance relation? Second, how are the representations in (91)–(92) derived compositionally? In other words, what do the LFs that yield them look like? In what follows, we address these questions in turn.[19]

### 4.5.3 The Shortest Spy

What makes an acquaintance relation suitable? Consider the following case based on Kaplan (1968). Suppose Ralph believes there are spies. And suppose he believes, not unreasonably, that no two spies share exactly the same height. Then Ralph must also believe that there is a shortest spy. And if Ralph believes this, then he surely believes that the shortest spy is a spy; i.e., (93-a) is true. But now suppose that Ortcutt is in fact the shortest spy. Significantly, (93-a) together with the fact that *Ortcutt* and *the shortest spy* pick out the same individual in the actual world are not sufficient for verifying (93-b). In other words, (93-b) is false even though (94) is true.

(93)   a.  Ralph believes that the shortest spy is a spy.
      b.  Ralph believes that Ortcutt is a spy.

(94)   The shortest spy is Ortcutt and Ralph believes that the shortest spy is a spy.

So, what blocks us from analyzing (93-b) as (95) and verifying it via the indicated acquaintance relation?

(95)   $\exists R[\iota y[R(r,y,w)] = o \wedge \forall w' \in \text{DOX}_{r,w}: \iota y[R(r,y,w')]$ is a spy in $w']$
      (verified by $[\lambda x.[\lambda y.[\lambda w. y$ is the shortest spy in $w]]]$)

---

[19] Yet another question that has been raised for the acquaintance relation approach to *de re* attitude ascriptions – and one that we will not review here – has to do with counterfactual attitudes (Ninan 2008, 2012; Yanovich 2011). For example, Ralph might see Ortcutt wearing a brown hat and then imagine him *not* wearing a brown hat. I can report that imagining as in (i).

(i)   Ralph imagined that Ortcutt was not wearing a brown hat.

But on the acquaintance relation approach, (i) should come out false, because there are no worlds in which the man Ralph saw wearing a brown hat was not wearing a brown hat. See Ninan (2012) for a development of this criticism and an alternative approach to *de re* attitude ascriptions designed to handle such cases.

## 4.5 Double Vision

Kaplan's solution involves a concept he calls 'vividness':

> Consider typical cases in which we would be likely to say that Ralph knows x or is acquainted with x. Then look only at the conglomeration of images, names, and partial descriptions which Ralph employs to bring x before his mind. Such a conglomeration, when suitably arranged and regimented, is what I call a vivid name.
> (Kaplan 1968: 201)

In this vein, we might say that suitable acquaintance relations are ones that would make us comfortable saying that the attitude holder 'knows' or 'is acquainted' with the *res*. If I see someone wearing a brown hat, or if I see someone at the beach, then there is at least some very weak sense in which it can be said that I 'know' the person, in this case by virtue of having come into visual contact with him or her. But if I merely deduce someone's existence based on general reasoning about height asymmetries, it is quite a stretch to say that I 'know' that person.

Or consider another supportive example due to Kaplan (1968). Holmes observes a murder victim and thereby forms the belief that there is a murderer. Can Holmes be said to 'know' the murderer? The answer seems negative. Correspondingly, (96-a) and (96-b) are not sufficient for verifying (97).

(96) a. Holmes believes that the murderer committed a murder.
     b. Ortcutt is the murderer.

(97) Holmes believes that Ortcutt committed a murder.

In more recent work, Aloni (2005) develops the argument that what counts as a suitable acquaintance relation may vary contextually and that vividness in Kaplan's sense is neither a sufficient nor a necessary condition for a suitable acquaintance relation. One relevant example considered by Aloni is originally due to Bonomi (1995). Simplifying the example somewhat, imagine a scenario where Swann believes that his wife Odette has a lover, and so decides that he wants to kill this lover. Suppose furthermore that Odette does indeed have a lover and, unbeknownst to Swann, his name is Forcheville. Then (98) seems true on a *de re* reading of *Forcheville*.

(98) Swann wants to kill Forcheville.

Given that we accept (98) as a truthful *de re* desire report in this scenario, there must be some suitable acquaintance relation involved, and the only one available would seem to be that given by the definite description *Odette's lover*; i.e., the truth of (98) is grounded in the truth of (99).

(99)   Odette's lover is Forcheville and Swann wants to kill Odette's lover.

But if the definite description *Odette's lover* supplies a suitable acquaintance relation, then the belief report in (100) should have a true *de re* reading by virtue of the truth of (101), contrary to fact.

(100)   Swann believes that Forcheville is Odette's lover.

(101)   Odette's lover is Forcheville and Swann believes that Odette's lover is Odette's lover.

This puts us in a bind: why is it that *Odette's lover* gives us an appropriate acquaintance relation in (98) but not in (100)? Not only that, the example also suggests that vividness ('knowing' or 'being acquainted with' someone) is not a *necessary* condition for a truthful *de re* attitude report, insofar as it would be quite a stretch to say in the context of this story that Swann 'knows' Forcheville.

In response to these and other issues, Aloni develops an account in which acquaintance relations (or, in Aloni's theory, conceptual covers) are invoked via a shift in perspective that is costly and therefore employed only as needed to conform to Gricean pragmatic principles. For Aloni, the crucial difference between (98) and (100) is that in (100), replacing *Forcheville* with *Odette's lover*, as in (102), results in a trivially true sentence, in violation of Grice's maxim of quantity, which enjoins a speaker to be as informative as is required. A similar substitution for (100), on the other hand, as in (103), is not trivially true.

(102)   Swann believes that Odette's lover is Odette's lover.

(103)   Swann wants to kill Odette's lover.

Is it sufficient, then, to say that an acquaintance relation must be non-trivializing? Unfortunately not, as brought out by Aloni's discussion of the following variant on Kaplan's "shortest spy" case. Suppose that Ralph believes that the shortest spy is fat and that, unbeknownst to Ralph, Ortcutt is the shortest spy. This is not sufficient for making (104) true, despite the fact that it would not be trivial to believe that the shortest spy is fat (cf. believing that the shortest spy is a spy).

(104)   Ralph believes that Ortcutt is fat.                    (Aloni 2005: 40)

(105)   Ralph believes that the shortest spy is fat.

## 4.5 Double Vision

For cases like this, Aloni appeals to the idea that it would be uncooperative in the Gricean sense to use (104) in the given scenario when (105) would be a "much more efficient" (2005: 40) alternative since it requires no shift in perspective (i.e., it is a *de dicto* report, and, in our terms, does not invoke any acquaintance relation).

Finally, here is one more example considered by Aloni. It is from the 1999 edition of Bonomi 1983, which Aloni paraphrases as follows:

> Suppose Leo correctly believes that Ugo is the only one in town who has a bush jacket. Leo further believes that Ugo has climbed the Cervino mountain. One night Ugo lends his bush jacket to another friend of Leo, Pio. Wearing it, Pio goes to the theater. Leo sees him and believes he is Ugo and utters: That person has climbed the Cervino.
> (Aloni 2005: 22)

In this context, if vividness were a sufficient condition for a suitable acquaintance, then (106) should be true by virtue of the truth of (107), provided that seeing someone wearing a bush jacket is a suitable acquaintance relation.

(106) Leo believes that Pio has climbed the Cervino. (Aloni 2005: 22)

(107) The man Leo saw wearing a bush jacket is Pio and Leo believes that the man he saw wearing a bush jacket has climbed the Cervino.

But in fact, Aloni suggests, (106) seems acceptable if said immediately after Ugo's utterance, whereas it would be unacceptable if uttered two months later, even if nothing about Leo's belief state has changed in the meantime. This suggests that vividness is not only not a necessary condition for a suitable acquaintance relation but also not a sufficient one, and it further reinforces the idea that what counts as suitable varies by context.

### 4.5.4 *Res* Movement

Implementing the acquaintance relation solution to the double vision problem requires making some modifications to our syntactic assumptions. So far we have been assuming that an attitude predicate denotes a relation between individuals and propositions. But if at least some attitude reports incorporate an acquaintance relation to a *de re* interpreted nominal expression (i.e., to a *res*), then in these cases we need to treat the attitude predicate as a three-way relation between an attitude holder, a *res*, and a property. This then would seem to indicate that we need to isolate the *res* syntactically from the rest of the complement clause so that it can be fed in as an argument of the attitude predicate.

Heim (1994) proposes a syntactic operation of RES MOVEMENT that moves the *de re*-interpreted constituent to a position adjoining the attitude predicate, as in (108).

(108)
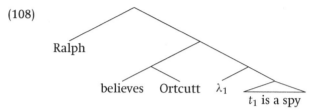

This works in concert with the revised lexical entry for *believe* in (109) which treats the *res* as its first argument, so that we end up with (110) as the representation for (108).

(109) $[[\text{believe}]]^w = [\lambda x.[\lambda f.[\lambda y.\exists R \ [\iota z[R(y,z,w)] = x \land \forall w' \in \text{DOX}_{y,w}: f(w')(\iota z[R(y,z,w')])]]]]$

(110) $\exists R[\iota z[R(r,z,w)] = o \land \forall w' \in \text{DOX}_{r,w}: \iota z[R(r,z,w')] \text{ is a spy in } w' \ ]$

As Heim points out, this approach is not ideal, because it involves a kind of movement that is nonstandard in several ways. For one thing, the moved element targets a position that does not c-command its trace. Also, the λ-binder triggered by the movement does not adjoin to the sister of the moved element, as is usually the case, but rather to the sister of the formed complex [believes Ortcutt]. Not only that, Charlow and Sharvit (2014) point out that proper names embedded in coordinate structures can be read *de re*, as in (111). Thus *res* movement would need to be exempt from the Coordinate Structure Constraint.

(111) John mistakenly believes he has a unicorn, and furthermore, he believes that his unicorn and Mary are fools.
(Charlow and Sharvit 2014: 14)

Aside from having these nonstandard features, there is no independent syntactic motivation for *res* movement; rather, its only motivation is that it enables a compositional implementation of Kaplan's (1968) semantics for *de re* attitude ascriptions. Furthermore, attitude reports with multiple *de re*-interpreted nominals would need structures instantiating multiple instances of *res* movement, and would need revised denotations for *believe* to accommodate the extra arguments (see also note 17 above). Thus there is much to be skeptical about, and many

## 4.5 Double Vision

scholars have voiced this skepticism (e.g. von Stechow and Zimmerman 2005; Anand 2006; Maier 2009; Ninan 2012; Charlow and Sharvit 2014). Based in part on considerations like this, an alternative movement-free implementation has been entertained in the literature, which we now turn to.

### 4.5.5 Concept Generators

Percus and Sauerland (2003a) develop a way of achieving an acquaintance-relation-based semantics for *de re* attitude ascriptions without needing to posit *res* movement. The approach is carried out under the assumption that there are covert world pronouns in syntax (see Section 4.4.1 above), and it relies in part on a rethinking of the syntax of *de re* attitude ascriptions so that (112) on its *de re* reading ends up having a syntax like (113).

(112) Ralph believes Ortcutt is a spy.

(113)

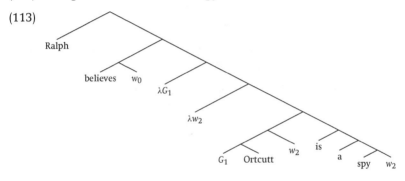

In (113), the *res* combines in the syntax with $G_1$, which denotes a variable over what Percus and Sauerland (2003a) call CONCEPT GENERATORS: functions from individuals to INDIVIDUAL CONCEPTS (type $\langle e, \langle s, e \rangle \rangle$).[20] The left periphery of the complement clause instantiates abstraction over this concept generator variable, so that the complement to the attitude predicate ends up denoting a function from concept generators to propositions (type $\langle \langle e, \langle s, e \rangle \rangle, st \rangle$). The denotation for an attitude verb like *believe* is correspondingly adjusted to accommodate this type as its internal argument; in particular, the proposed denotation, following Percus and Sauerland (2003a), is that in (114).

---

[20] See Baron 2016 for a generalization of concept generators that encompasses *de re* nominals that are not type *e*.

(114) $[[\text{believe}]] = [\lambda \phi_{\langle\langle e,\langle s,e\rangle\rangle,st\rangle}.[\lambda x.[\lambda w.1$ iff there is a concept generator $G$ suitable for $x$ in $w$ such that $\forall w' \in \text{DOX}_{x,w}: \phi(G)(w')]]]$

Now all that remains to be done is to specify what it means for a concept generator to be 'suitable for $x$ in $w$', and in carrying this out, we ensure that this approach achieves the same end as in the Kaplan-based acquaintance relation approach. We do this, basically following Percus and Sauerland (2003a), as in (115).

(115) $G$ is suitable for $x$ in $w$ iff $\text{Dom}(G) \subseteq \{y \mid$ there is a suitable acquaintance relation $R$ such that $\iota z[R(x)(z)(w)] = y$ and $\forall w' \in \text{DOX}_{x,w}: G(y)(w') = \iota z[R(x)(z)(w')]\}$

(115) ensures that in order for a concept generator $G$ to be suitable for $x$ in $w$, every individual in its domain has to be such that there is a suitable acquaintance relation $R$ that $x$ bears uniquely to that individual in $w$ and that, at each of $x$'s doxastic alternatives, $x$ bears $R$ uniquely to the individual returned by applying $G$ to that individual.

The truth conditions that we end up with for (113) are as in (116).

(116) 1 iff there is a concept generator $G$ suitable for Ralph in $w_0$ such that $\forall w' \in \text{DOX}_{r,w}: G(\text{Ortcutt})(w')$ is a spy in $w'$.

If there is indeed a concept generator $G$ that satisfies the conditions in (116), then, given (115), it must be the case that $G([[\text{Ortcutt}]])$ yields some individual concept for which there is a suitable acquaintance relation $R$ such that Ralph bears $R$ uniquely to Ortcutt in the evaluation world and at each of Ralph's doxastic alternatives $w'$, $G([[\text{Ortcutt}]])(w')$ denotes the individual to whom Ralph uniquely bears $R$ at that alternative. In this way, the Kaplanian semantics is carried out without the need for *res* movement, albeit at the cost of the rather baroque assumption that complements to attitude predicates instantiate abstraction over concept generators.

Some work has been done comparing the empirical predictions of *res* movement and concept generators. Charlow and Sharvit (2014), in particular, discuss the phenomenon of bound *de re* pronouns (see also the earlier treatment in Sharvit 2011). Consider the sentence in (117). Focusing just on the *de re* reading of *female student* (i.e., John's belief is about a set of individuals that, possibly unbeknownst to John, constitute the set of female students), and just on the bound reading of *her*, Charlow and Sharvit claim that there is a distinction between what they call the 'simple bound' reading and the 'bound *de re*' reading.

(117) John believes that every female student$_i$ likes her$_i$ mother.
(Charlow and Sharvit 2014: 2)

On the 'simple bound' reading, it is part of the content of John's belief that each target of the liking is the liker's own mother. On the 'bound *de re*' reading, by contrast, John's belief is something along the lines of "This person likes that person's mother; this other person likes that other person's mother," etc., not necessarily being aware of the identity between 'this person' and 'that person' and between 'this other person' and 'that other person'. Charlow and Sharvit argue that this second reading is not easily captured on the *res* movement approach: we would have to allow *believe* to combine with multiple *res* arguments (*her* and *female student*), but then this creates an LF in which *her* is not c-commanded by its binder, erroneously forcing a referential reading and leaving the 'bound *de re*' reading underivable. The concept generator approach, on the other hand, enables the reading: both *res* arguments combine *in situ* with a concept generator variable in the syntax, preserving the c-command relation needed to ensure binding. As long as we allow for an attitude complement to instantiate two concept generator abstractions in its left periphery (i.e., one for each *res*, adjusting the denotation for *believe* accordingly), the 'bound *de re*' reading can be captured.

See also Deal (2018), who argues that in Nez Perce (a highly endangered Sahaptian language native to Idaho) both the *res* movement strategy and the concept generator strategy exist side by side as two distinct ways of achieving *de re* attitude reports.

## 4.6 TAKING STOCK

Over the course of this chapter, we've seen two quite different approaches to *de re*-interpreted material in attitude ascriptions. On one account, *de re*-interpreted material is evaluated with respect to a higher evaluation world than the *de dicto* content of the attitude, achieved either by scoping the material out, or through an analogous mechanism such as treating world variables as pronouns that need not be locally bound or resolving a relevant presupposition globally rather than locally. On the other account, *de re*-interpreted material is related to the attitude holder via an acquaintance relation, achieved syntactically either through movement or through local combination with a concept generator.

It is tempting to view these two approaches as standing in competition with each other, but in an important way, they are not in competition, because their domains of empirical coverage are only partially overlapping. On the one hand, only the former approach is viable for non-attitudinal modals. For example, *deserve* as in (118) is modal but not attitudinal, and yet the sentence still admits both a *de dicto* interpretation (Maggie deserves for her eventual spouse to be a chef) and a *de re* interpretation (there is someone whom Maggie deserves to marry, and that person is a chef). Maggie need not stand in any kind of acquaintance relation with the individual in question on the *de re* reading, so this is a case where scope or an analogous mechanism is called for.

(118)   Maggie deserves to marry a chef.

On the other hand, only the acquaintance relation approach can handle *de dicto/de re* ambiguities with proper names (assuming that proper names are rigid designators) and – regardless of one's assumptions about proper names – it is the only one that can handle double vision puzzles.

But an underexplored question has to do with cases where the two approaches do overlap empirically. For example, does (119) have two *de re* readings, one achieved via scope or some analogous mechanism, and the other achieved via an acquaintance relation?

(119)   Maggie wants to marry a chef.

Perhaps so: since both of these two routes for achieving *de re* semantics seem to be independently needed, it would be stipulative to block one or the other in cases where both will do. On the other hand, it is also conceivable that the two approaches might ultimately be unified in such a way that (119) has only one *de re* reading. Maier (2009), for example, develops an account along these lines; in essence, Maier proposes that acquaintance relations are an automatic by-product of scoping material out of an attitudinal complement. So there may be prospects for a unified account after all.

## 4.7  DISCUSSION QUESTIONS

(i) Above we claimed that the sentence in (120) (repeated from (13)) is four-ways ambiguous because each of the two indefinites can independently be read *de dicto* or *de re*. Can you confirm this claim by coming up with four contrasting contexts that each verify one of the claimed readings?

(120)   Beatrix believes that a famous actor met a musician.

(ii) In Section 4.2, we reviewed five properties of the *de dicto*/*de re* ambiguity that are accurately predicted by the scope theory. To what extent are these properties also accurately predicted by the other approaches considered (world pronouns, Split Intensionality, presupposition projection, and acquaintance relations)?

(iii) The discussion in this chapter of Fodor's third reading focused exclusively on indefinites. Does Fodor's third reading obtain for other kinds of nominal expression as well (e.g. definite descriptions and quantifiers headed by *every* or *most*)? And is this predicted by the approaches to Fodor's third reading that were reviewed?

(iv) On both the *res* movement and the concept generator implementation of the acquaintance relation approach to *de re* attitude reports, the denotation for an attitude predicate gets more and more complicated as the number of *de re*-interpreted nominals in its complement increases. Should this be considered a problem? Is there a way to systematically derive the more complicated denotations from the simpler ones?

## 4.8 FURTHER READING

The literature on *de re* attitude ascriptions can be roughly divided into two groups: one in the tradition of Russell 1905 that seeks an account in terms of scope or analogous mechanisms, and the other in the tradition of Quine 1956 and Kaplan 1968 that seeks an account in terms of acquaintance relations. Important work in the former vein includes Fodor 1970; Cresswell 1990; Percus 2000; Keshet 2008, 2010a, b; Keshet 2011; Romoli and Sudo 2009; Schwager 2011; Dawson and Deal 2019; see also von Fintel and Heim 2011; Keshet and Schwarz 2019; Percus forthcoming for useful overviews. As for the latter vein, see Lewis 1979; Cresswell and von Stechow 1982; Heim 1992, 1994; Abusch 1997; Percus and Sauerland 2003a; Aloni 2005; Anand 2006; Yanovich 2011; Ninan 2012; Charlow and Sharvit 2014; Pearson 2015; Baron 2016; Deal 2018. For approaches couched in Discourse Representation Theory, see also Kamp (1990); Maier (2009); Kamp et al. (2011). Relevant philosophical literature includes Burge 1977; Salmon 2010.

# 5   *De se* Attitude Reports

## 5.1   INTRODUCTION

The starting point for this chapter is that there are three different ways to understand a sentence like (1) that turn on how we interpret the embedded subject *she*.

(1)   Beatrix hopes that she will win.

On one understanding, *she* refers not to Beatrix but instead to some other female individual salient in the context. This is brought out by supplying (1) with the right kind of preceding linguistic context, as in (2), where it is clear that *she* refers not to Beatrix but rather to Maggie.

(2)   Beatrix is going to watch her friend Maggie compete in a tournament. Beatrix hopes that she will win.

This is not the kind of reading that will concern us in this chapter. Instead, we'll be concerned here only with ways of understanding (1) in which Beatrix's hope is *about herself*. And the next observation is that there are two different ways in which Beatrix's hope as reported in (1) could be about herself: one in which she is *aware* that her hope is about herself, and one in which she is *not aware* that her hope is about herself. Absent any context, the former is by a wide margin the most salient reading of (1) – so salient, in fact, that it takes some real work to coax out the latter reading. But it can be done. Imagine, for example, a context in which Beatrix participates in some televised sporting event. Afterwards, she goes home, and becomes somehow incapacitated. Let's say she either gets extremely drunk or else suffers a blow to the head and develops amnesia – drunkenness and amnesia being the two standard devices in the literature for coaxing out the reading that we're after here. Then, she turns on the television, sees herself competing, and – this is crucial – *not recognizing the individual she sees as herself*, forms the hope that the individual she is seeing will win. Now comes the linguistic point: I can use (1) to report this scenario.

## 5.1 Introduction

Summing up so far, we've identified three different ways of understanding the sentence in question, spelled out in (3):

(3) Beatrix hopes that she will win.
   a. Reading a: Beatrix's hope is about someone other than herself.
   b. Reading b: Beatrix's hope is about herself and she is aware that it is about herself.
   c. Reading c: Beatrix's hope is about herself but she is not aware that it is about herself.

The distinction between reading a vs. readings b–c seems pretty straightforward: it is a familiar idea from any introductory syntax course that pronouns like *she* can either be free (referring to someone salient in the context, as in reading a) or bound (linguistically anteceded by something in a higher clause, as in reading b or c). But you might be wondering what the big deal is about the distinction between reading b and reading c. Certainly this distinction has *cognitive* significance for Beatrix: having the thought "I hope I will win" (as in reading b) is after all a very different experience from having the thought "I hope she will win" (ignorant that the individual I hope will win is me, as in reading c). But why think that the distinction has any *linguistic* significance? Indeed, why are we even calling these 'readings' in the first place (implying a genuine ambiguity), as opposed to thinking that there is just one reading that is underspecified in a way that allows us to understand it either as portrayed in (3-b) or as portrayed in (3-c)?

I think that this is a very healthy kind of skeptical reaction, but also that in this case, it so happens that the skepticism can be overcome. In particular, it can be overcome by showing that there are grammatical structures that seem to be sensitive to the distinction. Consider, in particular, (4).

(4) Beatrix hopes to win.

It is no surprise that (4) lacks the reading in (3-a), because (4) differs from (3) in instantiating a well-studied grammatical configuration known as CONTROL, where the unexpressed subject of an infinitive (here, *to win*) cannot be freely interpreted but is instead determined by the embedding clause. What does come as a surprise, though, is that (4) also seems to lack the reading in (3-c); i.e., it intuitively comes across as false in the scenario where Beatrix is drunk or has amnesia and does not realize that her hope is about herself. Instead, (4) seems to have only the reading in (3-b).

Now let me introduce a bit of terminology. When an attitude report is understood in such a way that (i) its content is *about* the attitude holder and (ii) the attitude holder is *aware* that the content of her attitude is about herself (as in (3-b) but not (3-c)), we'll say that it's a DE SE ATTITUDE REPORT.[1] Armed with that terminology, we can say that (3) is *optionally* construed *de se*, whereas (4) is *obligatorily* construed *de se*.[2]

And control turns out not to be a fluke in giving rise to obligatory *de se* readings: as we'll see below, a handful of other cross-linguistically attested grammatical phenomena have been argued to behave likewise, including LOGOPHORS, SHIFTED INDEXICALS, and long-distance reflexives. The question before us, then, is how to enrich our theory of attitude reports to be sensitive to the *de se*/non-*de se* distinction, and how to connect this sensitivity to the grammar in such a way that we can accurately predict where *de se* interpretations are obligatory and where they are merely possible. In what follows, we first offer some clarifying remarks on the relationship between *de se* and semantic binding (Section 5.2). Then, we survey the most popular approach to *de se* attitude reports expressed by control sentences, which involves treating attitude predicates as relations to properties rather than to propositions and having them quantify over CENTERED WORLDS (world-individual pairs) rather than worlds simpliciter (Section 5.3). We then consider a mild variation on this approach whereby the embedded subject in a control sentence is directly keyed to an appropriate intensional parameter (Section 5.4). In Section 5.5, we turn our attention to optionally *de se* attitude reports and review competing approaches to modeling this optionality. Then, in Section 5.6, we evaluate arguments for and against treating *de se* attitude reports as a subspecies of *de re* attitude reports. In Section 5.7, we expand our empirical coverage by surveying three grammatical phenomena other than control that

---

[1] This very useful informal characterization of *de se* attitude reports in terms of the dual features of 'aboutness' and 'awareness' is due to Pearson (2016).

[2] In a way, the foregoing is my attempt to replicate how interest in *de se* attitude reports spread historically from philosophy to linguistics. Here's the actual history, in a nutshell: *de se* attitudes were first discussed in the philosophy literature; important early classics include Castañeda 1966, 1967, 1968; Perry 1979; Lewis 1979 (the last of these is where the terminology *de se* comes from). Meanwhile, the observation in linguistics that attitude reports expressed by control sentences have an obligatory *de se* semantics can be traced back to Morgan 1970 (i.e., before the term *de se* was even coined). It was Chierchia (1989) who finally connected the linguistic facts to the relevant philosophical literature, and developed an influential account based directly on the work of Lewis (1979), as we'll review below.

have also been claimed to trigger *de se* semantics, namely logophors, shifted indexicals, and long-distance reflexives. The central question here is whether the same technology that supports our analysis of *de se* semantics in control sentences works for these other phenomena as well, or whether on the other hand there are multiple routes to *de se*.

## 5.2 DIVORCING DE SE FROM SEMANTIC BINDING

In theorizing about what grammatical mechanism underpins *de se* interpretations, one option that can be dismissed at the outset – although it is initially appealing – is the hypothesis that *de se* semantics is a by-product of binding. That is, one might entertain the idea that control necessarily involves binding and therefore has a necessarily *de se* semantics, whereas ordinary pronouns like *she* are optionally bound and hence optionally *de se*. To be a bit more concrete about this, consider the pattern in (5)–(6). (6) involves some new notation: the use of PRO here embodies the widely held hypothesis in the syntax literature that the subject of the infinitive in a control sentence is syntactically represented by an inaudible pronoun with special distributional and interpretational properties. And the numerical subscripts are intended to show that in (5), *she* can either be bound from the higher clause by *Beatrix* (index 1) or else receive a free interpretation (index 2), whereas in (6), PRO has no choice but to be bound from the higher clause by *Beatrix*.

(5) Beatrix $\lambda_1$ hopes [that she$_{1/2}$ will win].

(6) Beatrix $\lambda_1$ hopes [PRO$_{1/*2}$ to win].

Now here's the initially attractive idea. Maybe matching indices, and the binding relation they represent, always gives rise to *de se*. Maybe, the non-*de se* reading of (5) – where Beatrix's hope is about herself but she doesn't realize it – happens when *she* is not coindexed with *Beatrix* but instead has some other index that just so happens to map onto Beatrix. Since we know independently that this is not an option for (6), obligatory *de se* ensues there.

The problem with this line of reasoning is that *de se* attitude reports are empirically separable from attitude reports that involve binding by the attitude holder into some element in the content of the attitude. Consider the sentence in (7).

(7) [Every boy in this class] $\lambda_1$ thinks [that he$_1$ is a genius].

Even if we restrict ourselves to the bound variable interpretation of the pronoun *he* in the complement clause (every boy *x* is such that *x* thinks that *x* is a genius), the sentence is still ambiguous between a *de se* and a non-*de se* interpretation. As usual, the *de se* reading is the more salient one, but the non-*de se* reading can be brought about by imagining a scenario in which each boy in the class thinks, "that person is a genius," without realizing that the person in question is himself. The conclusion is that we do not want to build a theory in which *de se* interpretations piggyback on binding.

Further reinforcing this conclusion is the observation, due to Hornstein and Pietroski (2010), that sloppy identity under ellipsis does not force a *de se* interpretation. Consider, for example, the sentence in (8), fashioned after Hornstein and Pietroski 2010: 71 ex (7).

(8)  This boy thinks that he is a genius, and so does that one.

In (8), the so-called 'sloppy reading' is one in which the second conjunct is understood to be elliptical for an interpretation in which that boy thinks *himself* a genius (this contrasts with the so-called 'strict reading', where the subject of the elided clause refers back to 'this boy' from the first clause). Crucially, we can construct a non-*de se* scenario under which the sloppy reading would be true. Imagine two boys, each of whom thinks himself a genius without realizing that his thought is about himself. (8) can be read true in such a scenario, showing that sloppy readings do not force *de se* readings. Insofar as sloppy readings are standardly analyzed as being underpinned by a bound variable interpretation, this is another argument against deriving *de se* semantics from binding.

## 5.3 PROPERTIES AND CENTERED WORLDS

The predecessor to the currently predominant approach to *de se* attitude reports is Lewis (1979), and so it will be useful to begin by considering some of the foundational points made in this article. To understand the logic behind Lewis's insights, it is important to note at the outset that on Lewis's understanding of possible worlds, individuals cannot exist in more than one world. An individual may have a close *counterpart* in another world, but strictly speaking the two individuals are distinct. This is a departure from the understanding embodied in the background theory of this book. But I want to adopt it, just for the moment, so that we can better get inside Lewis's head and appreciate his insights from the perspective with which he developed them. In a

## 5.3 Properties and Centered Worlds

moment, we'll see how to translate Lewis's core idea into this book's framework.

Against this backdrop, consider a toy model in which there are just three possible worlds, and each world is inhabited by just three individuals, according to the schema in (9).

(9)    a.   Occupants of $w_1$: $\{a, b, c\}$
       b.   Occupants of $w_2$: $\{d, e, f\}$
       c.   Occupants of $w_3$: $\{g, h, i\}$

Lewis points out that a proposition – modeled as a set of possible worlds – can be modeled equally well as a property, modeled as a set of individuals. Using the toy example in (9), take the proposition $\{w_1, w_2\}$. This can be translated without loss into the property $\{a, b, c, d, e, f\}$, i.e., the set of individuals who inhabit $w_1$ or $w_2$. So rather than modeling belief as a relation to a set of possible worlds, we could equally well model belief as a relation to a set of individuals. The property $\{a, b, c\}$ is the property of inhabiting $w_1$, and likewise the property $\{a, b, c, d, e, f\}$ is the property of inhabiting $w_1$ or $w_2$. So to believe the proposition $\{w_1, w_2\}$ is to identify oneself as being a member of the set $\{a, b, c, d, e, f\}$.

But whereas propositions can always be straightforwardly translated into properties, the reverse is not true: some properties (sets of individuals) *cannot* be translated into propositions (sets of possible worlds). For example, the property $\{a, d, g\}$ in the model sketched above does not correspond to any set of possible worlds. It collects members from all three worlds, but we cannot translate it as $\{w_1, w_2, w_3\}$, because that would correspond to the property that collects up *all* the individuals at each of the worlds, namely $\{a, b, c, d, e, f, g, h, i\}$. Lewis argues that some kinds of attitudes – namely attitudes *de se* – require this extra expressive power afforded by properties but not by propositions. Suppose, for example, that $a$, $d$, and $g$ are all musicians but the other six individuals in the model are not. Then to have $\{a, d, g\}$ as the object of one's belief would be to SELF-ASCRIBE the property of being a musician, i.e., to believe *de se* that one is a musician, to believe that one is a musician while being aware that the individual one believes to be a musician is oneself.

In current theorizing, it is typical to assume an ontology in which individuals can occupy more than one possible world. Once this move is made, sets of mere individuals are no longer fine-grained enough to pick out the kinds of properties that we want to be able to pick out, because an individual's attributes may vary as we move from one world to the next. I may be a musician in the actual world, but since this is a contingent fact about me, there are plenty of other possible worlds in which I am not a musician. But since an individual's attributes *relative to a particular world* are not variable (in any given world, either I'm a musician or I'm not), there is a straightforward fix: model properties as sets of world-individual pairs. After Quine (1969), these are often called centered worlds.

Now let's be more precise about how we can use centered worlds to model a *de se* attitude report, and how this can be achieved compositionally. Consider first that in the Hintikkan tradition, DOXASTIC ALTERNATIVES are modeled as sets of possible words, as in (10).

(10)   $\text{DOX}_{a,w} = \{w' \mid w'$ is compatible with $a$'s beliefs in $w\}$

The intuition behind this view of doxastic alternativeness is described by Cresswell and von Stechow (1982) as follows:

> we imagine $a$ in a world $w$ looking at a screen on which are represented successively all possible worlds. If a world $w'$ appears, either $a$ says, "I don't believe I'm in a world like that", or "for all I believe perhaps I am in a world like that".
>
> (Cresswell and von Stechow 1982: 506)

By contrast, on a centered worlds setup, doxastic alternatives are modeled as sets of world-individual pairs, as in (11).

(11)   $\text{DOX}_{a,w} = \{\langle w',y \rangle \mid$ it is compatible with $a$'s beliefs in $w$ for $a$ to be $y$ in $w'\}$

Sticking with Cresswell and von Stechow's metaphor, we can understand the centered worlds approach to doxastic alternatives by imagining $a$ in a world $w$ looking at a screen on which are represented successively all possible pairings of possible worlds and individuals. If a pair $\langle w',y \rangle$ appears, either $a$ says, "I don't believe I'm an individual like that in a world like that" (either because $a$ does not consider $w'$ a viable candidate for the actual world, or does not consider $y$ a viable candidate for him or herself, or both), or "for all I believe perhaps I am an individual like that in a world like that." In the case of the latter response, that pair is included in the individual's doxastic alternatives.

Now, in English, *believe* does not participate in control configurations.[3] So to carry out this section's goal of analyzing *de se* semantics as expressed by control sentences, let's turn to an attitude verb that

---

[3] This is not true of all languages. Italian *credere* 'believe', for example, admits control complements, with the concomitant obligatory *de se* semantics (Chierchia 1989).

## 5.3 Properties and Centered Worlds

does allow for control, namely *claim*. The control sentence in (12) can only describe a scenario in which Beatrix is aware that her claim is about herself. This can be modeled as in (13), via quantification over Beatrix's "claim" alternatives. The sentence is verified if and only if, at each of those worlds compatible with Beatrix's claims, the individual who Beatrix claims is herself, is a genius.

(12)   Beatrix claims [PRO to be a genius].

(13)   $\forall \langle w', y \rangle \in \text{CLAIM}_{b,w}$: $y$ is a genius in $w'$
where $\text{CLAIM}_{a,w} = \{\langle w', y \rangle \mid$ it is compatible with $a$'s claims in $w$ for $a$ to be $y$ in $w'\}$
'For all those world-individual pairs $\langle w', y \rangle$ such that it is compatible with Beatrix's claims in $w$ for Beatrix to be $y$ in $w'$, $y$ is a genius in $w'$.'

We can achieve this result compositionally via two new assumptions. First, verbs like *claim* denote relations not between individuals and propositions but rather between individuals and properties (characteristic functions of sets of centered worlds), and they carry out quantification over centered worlds, as in (14).

(14)   $[[\text{claim}_{de\ se}]]^w = [\lambda f_{\langle s, et \rangle}.[\lambda x. \forall \langle w', y \rangle \in \text{CLAIM}_{x,w}: f(w')(y)]]$

Second, we need some way of ensuring that the complement to *claim* denotes a type $\langle e, t \rangle$ function, so that it will be able to compose with *claim* via Intensional Functional Application. Chierchia (1989) proposes that PRO is obligatorily bound by a property abstractor directly below the embedding verb, as in (15).[4]

(15)

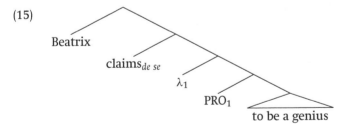

---

[4] On a theory of control in which there is no PRO and control complements are just VPs, nothing special needs to be said: control complements denote properties because the argument associated with the subject position was never saturated in the first place. Such a view is entertained by Chierchia (1984) and Dowty (1985), but has largely fallen out of favor given the syntactic evidence that control complements have subjects. See Landau 2013: Chapt. 3 for a review of the evidence.

A variant of this approach is to assume that PRO is like a relative pronoun in Heim and Kratzer (1998): it is essentially vacuous, but obligatorily moves and thereby triggers abstraction, as in (16). Such an idea was proposed by Percus and Sauerland (2003b) for overt pronouns on their *de se* construal (see Section 5.5 below), and Pearson (2013) extends this line of reasoning to PRO. As long as the semantics ignores PRO (or treats it as the identity function), this approach has the same net result of ensuring a property denotation for control complements.

(16)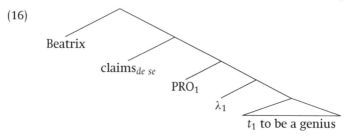

But now, what do we say about sentences wherein *claim* combines with a non-control complement? Do we need to posit a lexical ambiguity for *claim* and all other verbs that combine with both control and non-control complements? Actually, this question is usefully divided into two smaller questions. First, how to analyze *optionally de se* reports like (17)? Does *she* here have the option of behaving like PRO, and that is the reason for the availability of the *de se* interpretation, or is something else going on? This question turns out to be quite a difficult one, and so we'll postpone it to Section 5.5 where it can be properly addressed. But we will address here the second question: how to analyze sentences like (18) where *de se* is not even an option because there are no pronouns that can be connected to the attitude holder.

(17)   Beatrix claims that she is a genius.
       *Relevant reading*: 'Beatrix claims: "I am a genius."'

(18)   Beatrix claims that Maggie is a genius.

Probably the easiest (but also the least interesting) solution is to posit a lexical ambiguity for *claim*, so that in sentences like (18) it denotes a relation between propositions and individuals and it quantifies over worlds, as in (19), whereas for *de se* sentences it denotes a relation between properties and individuals and quantifies over world-individual pairs, as in (20).[5]

---

[5] Of course, this picture must ultimately be further complicated to account for certain kinds of *de re* attitude reports, as discussed in Chapter 4. Here we set this complication aside.

## 5.3 Properties and Centered Worlds

(19) $[[\text{claim}_{de\ dicto}]]^w = [\lambda p_{\langle st \rangle}.[\lambda x.\forall w' \in \text{CLAIM}_{x,w}: p(w')]]$
$\text{CLAIM}_{a,w} = \{w' \mid w' \text{ is compatible with } a\text{'s claims in } w\}$

(20) $[[\text{claim}_{de\ se}]]^w = [\lambda f_{\langle s,et \rangle}.[\lambda x.\forall \langle w',y \rangle \in \text{CLAIM}_{x,w}: f(w')(y)]]$
$\text{CLAIM}_{a,w} = \{\langle w',y \rangle \mid \text{it is compatible with } a\text{'s claims in } w \text{ for } a \text{ to be } y \text{ in } w'\}$

Somewhat more interesting is the possibility of systematically relating denotations like (19)–(20) via a type-shifting rule, as in (21), where *claim*_{de dicto} is defined in terms of *claim*_{de se}. The end result, as in (21-c), is that *claim*_{de dicto} quantifies over world-individual pairs, but the individual component is a vacuous and innocuous 'third wheel', since it does not figure into the scope of the quantifier. Hence we get exactly the same truth conditions as we do with (19). And (21) acts as a template that can be generalized to any attitude verb that accepts both proposition-denoting and property-denoting complements.

(21) $[[\text{claim}_{de\ dicto}]]^w = [\lambda p_{\langle st \rangle}.[\lambda x.[[\text{claim}_{de\ se}]]^w([\lambda w'.[\lambda z.p(w')]])(x)]]$
   a. $= [\lambda p_{\langle st \rangle}.[\lambda x.[\lambda f_{\langle s,et \rangle}.[\lambda a.\forall \langle w'',y \rangle \in \text{CLAIM}_{a,w}: f(w'')(y)]]$
      $([\lambda w'.[\lambda z.p(w')]])(x)]]$
   b. $= [\lambda p_{\langle st \rangle}.[\lambda x.\forall \langle w'',y \rangle \in \text{CLAIM}_{x,w}: [\lambda w'.[\lambda z.p(w')]](w'')(y)]]$
   c. $= [\lambda p_{\langle st \rangle}.[\lambda x.\forall \langle w'',y \rangle \in \text{CLAIM}_{x,w}: p(w'')]]$

Finally, a variation on type-shifting is to assume that there is just one denotation, namely that for *claim*_{de se}, and when it combines with a proposition-denoting expression, a vacuous lambda binder is inserted into the syntax to repair the type mismatch, as in (22). This has the same net result as type-shifting (cf. in this connection Percus and Sauerland's 2003a type-shifting operator PROP). We thereby gain uniformity in what attitude predicates denote, at the cost of semantically extraneous (although innocuous) material in non-*de se* attitude reports. This approach would, however, be rendered more attractive if there were independent reason to believe that all clauses – embedded or not, interpreted *de se* or not – involve left-peripheral lambda abstraction and consequently denote properties. For a defense of such a view, see Pearson 2013.

(22)
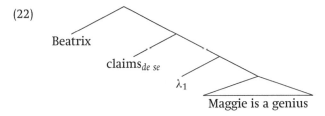

## 5.4 PRO AS AUTHOR-/ADDRESSEE- OR CENTER-DENOTING

On the approach just considered, PRO is either an individual-denoting variable obligatorily bound from immediately above, or a vacuous element whose only semantic effect is to move and thereby induce abstraction. And in order to account for the existence of attitude verbs that can take both control (obligatorily *de se*-interpreted) and non-control (not obligatorily *de se*-interpreted) complements, we had to introduce vacuous abstraction for the latter, achieved either in the syntax or via a type-shifting mechanism for attitude verbs.

There is, however, another kind of approach that exploits the same centered worlds technology for *de se* attitude reports while at the same time giving PRO more substantive content and avoiding vacuous abstraction for non-*de se* reports. The key move enabling such an approach is to enrich the intensional parameters against which linguistic expressions are interpreted in such a way that PRO is directly keyed to one of these parameters. Here we consider two versions of this kind of approach: Anand and Nevins 2004 and Stephenson 2010.

Anand and Nevins (2004) propose that denotations are relativized to a context parameter $c$ (which INDEXICALS are sensitive to) as well as an index parameter $i$ that keeps track of relevant intensional coordinates against which linguistic expressions are evaluated, including at least world and time but also crucially author and addressee. Then, subject-control PRO is a device for picking out the author associated with the relevant index, as in (23), and object-control PRO is a device for picking out the corresponding addressee, as in (24):[6]

(23)  $[[\text{PRO}_{subj}]]^{c,i} = \text{AUTH}(i)$

(24)  $[[\text{PRO}_{obj}]]^{c,i} = \text{ADDR}(i)$    (based on Anand and Nevins 2004: 33)

Correspondingly, denotations for attitude predicates are written so that they take propositions as their first argument (functions from

---

[6] Note that this is *not* an approach in which PRO is a shifted indexical (*contra* what Stephenson 2010: 425 and Landau 2015: 33 claim), because it is the index parameter rather than the context parameter that is responsible for PRO's interpretation. The context parameter plays no important role here. PRO does, however, play a role in Anand and Nevin's argumentation with respect to their approach to shifted indexicals: they use the *de se* nature of PRO to support the idea that the index parameter and the context parameter are type-theoretically identical, both able to pick out, among other things, authors and addressees. See Section 5.7.2 below on shifted indexicals.

## 5.4 PRO as Author-/Addressee- or Center-Denoting

contexts and indices to truth values) and quantify over indices rather than worlds or world-individual pairs (here, $f$ and $g$ are to be read as variables over indices):

(25)  $[[\text{claim}]]^{c,i} = [\lambda p.[\lambda x. \forall f \in \text{CLAIM}_{x,i}: p(c)(f)]]$
 $\text{CLAIM}_{a,f} = \{g \mid g \text{ is compatible with what } a \text{ claims at } f\}$

This gives rise to outcomes like (26) for *de se* attitude reports, the crucial idea being that AUTH($f$) picks out the individual with whom Beatrix self-identifies at each index.

(26)  [[Beatrix claims PRO$_{subj}$ to be a genius]]$^{c,i}$ =
 $\forall f \in \text{CLAIM}_{beatrix,i}$: AUTH($f$) is a genius in $f$
 'All those indices $f$ compatible with what Beatrix claims in $i$ are indices at which AUTH($f$) is a genius.'

In parallel fashion, the ADDR function used for object control would pick out the individual whom the attitude holder identifies as addressee, triggering a *de te* semantics. Whereas *de se* attitude reports are ones in which the attitude holder identifies *herself* as part of the content of the attitude, a DE TE ATTITUDE REPORT is one in which the attitude holder identifies her *addressee* as part of the content of the attitude. As discussed by Landau (2015: 31–32) and Pearson (2016: note 18), this is found with object-control verbs of communication, which are used in INDIRECT SPEECH REPORTS. For example, (27) would be false if Beatrix mistook her addressee Polly for someone else and told Polly, "Polly should leave." Instead, it can only report a situation wherein Beatrix is *aware* that the person she is addressing is the person she is directing to leave.

(27)  Beatrix told Polly [PRO to leave].

A non-*de se*/non-*de te* report, by contrast, differs only in that it lacks any reference to the author or addressee of the index being quantified over, as in (28). In this way, we avoid the vacuous abstraction necessitated by the approach considered in the previous section.

(28)  [[Beatrix claims Maggie is a genius]]$^{c,i}$ =
 $\forall f \in \text{CLAIM}_{beatrix,i}$: Maggie is a genius in $f$
 'All those indices $f$ compatible with what Beatrix claims at $i$ are indices at which Maggie is a genius.'

Anand and Nevins's approach does, however, face at least a few potential shortcomings. Stephenson (2010: 424–430) discusses two. The first is that we have to posit two denotations for PRO, one for subject control and the other for object control. Of course this is not a fatal shortcoming, but all else equal, we would prefer an account that avoids this.

Second, Stephenson points out examples of object-control sentences like (29), where, on Anand and Nevins's account, Sue would have to be analyzed as the addressee in some speech or attitude event. But the weather is clearly not speaking to Sue or bearing any attitude in any literal sense, and consequently it is difficult to see how Sue could be an addressee here.

(29)    The rainy weather discouraged Sue from going for a bike ride.
(Stephenson 2010: 428)

Similarly, consider (30). Unlike object-control verbs of *communication* like *tell*, *persuade* entails the formation of a *de se* intention on the part of the matrix object: (30) entails that Polly formed the *de se* intention: "I will leave." It does not entail anything about Beatrix's mental state and has no *de te* component. (See Chierchia 1989: 18; Landau 2015: 31–32.)

(30)    Beatrix persuaded Polly [PRO to leave].

Examples like (29) and (30) demonstrate that subject vs. object control does not correlate perfectly with *de se* vs. *de te* semantics, against the expectations of Anand and Nevins's proposal.

A third potential shortcoming of Anand and Nevins's account concerns control sentences that do not ascribe any attitude at all, of which we find both subject-control examples, like (31), and object-control examples, like (32).

(31)    Beatrix deserved [PRO to win].

(32)    Beatrix forced Polly [PRO to leave].

Insofar as *deserve* and *force* both have modal semantics, they both quantify over possible worlds, or in Anand and Nevins's system, indices. But given that *deserve* and *force* are not used for reporting mental states or discourse, do the indices they quantify over have authors or addressees? It is not so clear that they do, in which case PRO would, on Anand and Nevins's approach, be undefined, erroneously predicting that (31)–(32) should be semantically defective. To overcome this shortcoming, it seems we would have to posit yet a third variant of PRO that is neither author- nor addressee-denoting (as previously noted by Landau 2015: 36; Pearson 2018: 37).

Stephenson (2010) develops a somewhat different approach that avoids these shortcomings, by treating PRO as center-denoting rather

## 5.4 PRO as Author-/Addressee- or Center-Denoting

than author- or addressee-denoting. To motivate this approach, Stephenson draws on Lasersohn (2005), as well as her own previous work (Stephenson 2007b) and examines some facts regarding so-called predicates of personal taste. Consider the hypothetical exchange in (33). This exchange has a salient reading wherein what Sam asserts is that the cake is tasty to *him* whereas what Sue denies is that the cake is tasty to *her*.

(33) Mary: How's the cake?
Sam: It's tasty.
Sue: No it isn't! (Stephenson 2010: 415)

Stephenson proposes to model this by treating predicates of personal taste like *tasty*, *fun*, and *interesting* as introducing an experiencer argument that can be saturated by a silent nominal $PRO_J$ that is valued by what Stephenson calls, following Lasersohn, the judge parameter, as in (34). This gives rise to truth conditions like (35).[7]

(34) $[[PRO_J]]^{w,j} = j$ (Stephenson 2010: 418)

(35) $[[\text{The cake is tasty } PRO_J]]^{w,j} = 1$ iff the cake is tasty to $j$ in $w$

This approach to intensional parameters is quite similar to that of Anand and Nevins in that on both approaches, denotations become sensitive to individuals. But Stephenson's version is less fine-grained: instead of an author and an addressee, there is just one relevant individual, the so-called center (or, in Lasersohn's terminology, the judge). As Stephenson observes, attitude predicates shift the center to the attitude holder, as borne out by data like (36).

(36) Sam thinks that roller coasters are fun, and Sue does too.
(Stephenson 2010: 409)
*Relevant reading*: Sam thinks that roller coasters are fun *to him*, and Sue thinks that roller coasters are fun *to her*.

On this setup, clauses uniformly have extensions of type $t$ and INTENSIONS of type $\langle s, et \rangle$ (which on this approach is the type of propositions: characteristic functions of sets of centered worlds). Correspondingly, attitude predicates uniformly denote relations between propositions

---

[7] Of course, taste predicates can also be used in a such a way that the implicit experiencer argument refers to an individual salient in the context, as in *The new cat food is tasty*, said by someone watching a cat enjoy a meal. For these cases, Stephenson proposes another kind of silent pronominal, pro, which is not sensitive to the judge parameter.

and individuals (type $\langle\langle s, et\rangle, et\rangle$). For example, *claim* has the denotation in (37).

(37)  $[[\text{claim}]]^{w,j} = [\lambda p_{\langle s, et\rangle}.[\lambda x.\forall \langle w', y\rangle \in \text{CLAIM}_{x,w}: p(w')(y)]]$
  $\text{CLAIM}_{a,w} = \{\langle w', y\rangle \mid \text{it is compatible with } a\text{'s claims in } w \text{ for } a \text{ to be } y \text{ in } w'\}$

Given the proposal that PRO refers to the center, a control complement will have a denotation like (38).

(38)  $[[\text{PRO}_J \text{ to be a genius}]]^{w,j} = 1$ iff $j$ is a genius in $w$

In order to enable *claim* (type $\langle\langle s, et\rangle, et\rangle$) to combine with a clausal complement (type $t$), Intensional Functional Application needs to be rewritten as in (39):

(39)  Intensional Functional Application (centered worlds version): If $\alpha$ is a complex expression formed by combining two expressions $\beta$ and $\gamma$, and $[\lambda w'.[\lambda j'.[[\gamma]]^{w',j'}]]$ is in the domain of $[[\beta]]^{w,j}$, then $[[\alpha]]^{w,j} = [[\beta]]^{w,j}([\lambda w'.[\lambda j'.[[\gamma]]^{w',j'}]])$.

(Stephenson 2010: 419)

Whereas before, Intensional Functional Application repaired the type mismatch that occurred when a function needs to combine with an argument of type $\langle s, \alpha\rangle$ but instead had as its sister an expression of type $\alpha$ (where $\alpha$ is an arbitrary type), now Intensional Functional Application repairs type mismatches that occur when a function needs to combine with an expression of type $\langle s, \langle e, \alpha\rangle\rangle$ but instead has a sister of type $\alpha$. In this way, non-*de se* non-control complements do not involve any kind of vacuous abstraction in the syntax or in the denotations for attitude predicates; instead the burden is shifted onto Intensional Functional Application to induce such abstraction regardless of whether or not the *j* parameter binds anything.

Unlike Anand and Nevins's approach, we avoid having to posit an ambiguity for PRO, since it is always center-denoting regardless of whether subject- or object-control is involved. And we can also handle sentences like (40) repeated from above: for Anand and Nevins's approach, this sentence was problematic because Sue does not constitute an addressee in any ordinary sense; but on Stephenson's approach, all that matters is that Sue constitutes the center associated with the embedded clause, and this seems plausible given that the embedded clause describes the content of an attitude (discouragement) of Sue's.

(40)  The rainy weather discouraged Sue from going for a bike ride.

(Stephenson 2010: 428)

## 5.5 The de re Blocking Effect

How does Stephenson's approach fare concerning control sentences that do not ascribe attitudes, like (41) repeated from above?

(41) Beatrix deserved [PRO to win].

Since PRO in (41) obligatorily refers to Beatrix, the prediction of Stephenson's approach is that Beatrix denotes the center of the embedded clause. And, insofar as predicates of personal taste are also center-sensitive, we can test this prediction by incorporating a predicate of personal taste into the embedded clause:

(42) Beatrix deserved [PRO to eat a tasty cake].

On my judgment, the most natural interpretation of (42) is one in which Beatrix deserved a cake that is tasty *to her*, thereby supporting the prediction of Stephenson's approach, and suggesting that centers need not be attitude holders.

## 5.5 THE DE RE BLOCKING EFFECT

Suppose for concreteness that we adopt some variant of the approaches laid out in Section 5.3 above for *de se* attitude reports expressed by control sentences, and analyze sentences like (43) as having truth conditions like (44).

(43) Beatrix claims to be a genius.

(44) $\forall \langle w', y \rangle \in \text{CLAIM}_{b,w}: y$ is a genius in $w'$

Now, a question arises regarding how we want to analyze sentences like (45) which are *compatible* with a *de se* interpretation but do not force one.

(45) Beatrix claims that she is a genius.
*Relevant reading*: Beatrix claims: 'I am a genius.'

Basically two kinds of answers to this question have been proposed, both of which try to assimilate the *de se* interpretation of (45) to something found elsewhere in the grammar. The first kind of approach is to say that ordinary pronouns like *she* have the option of behaving in relevant respects like a *de se* pronoun (i.e., like PRO), so that (45) has a logical form (henceforth LF) in which *she* is bound from immediately below the attitude verb (or moves to a clause-peripheral position to achieve predicate abstraction), and this LF feeds truth conditions just like (44). On this view, optionally *de se* reports *do* have dedicated *de se* LFs. This view has been advocated by Chierchia (1989); Percus and Sauerland (2003a,b); Anand (2006); Pearson (2018).

The other kind of answer that has been proposed involves assimilating optionally *de se* reports to *de re* reports that are verified by a particular kind of acquaintance relation, namely one of self-identification. The basic idea is this. Recall from Chapter 4 that *de re* attitude reports are amenable to treatments like (46) wherein their truth hangs on the attitude holder standing in some acquaintance relation with a *res*. In (46), the relevant acquaintance relation is something like [λx.[λy.x sees y wearing a brown hat]]. But another kind of acquaintance relation could be [λx.[λy.x identifies him/herself as y]]. Then *de se* readings of optionally *de se* reports can be cashed out as something like (47). Versions of this view have been advocated by Lewis (1979); Reinhart (1990); Maier (2011).

(46)  Ralph believes that Ortcutt is a spy.
 ≈ Ralph believes that the man he saw in the brown hat is a spy (and the man Ralph saw in the brown hat is Ortcutt).

(47)  Beatrix believes that she is a genius.
 ≈ Beatrix believes that the individual with whom she self-identifies is a genius (and the individual with whom she self-identifies is some salient female individual).

Since both approaches recycle technology used elsewhere in the grammar (either from obligatory *de se* reports or from *de re* reports), neither approach seems to have an obvious conceptual advantage over the other. In what follows, we review one potential argument in favor of the dedicated *de se* LF approach, due to Percus and Sauerland (2003b).[8] A second potential argument in favor of the dedicated *de se* LF approach, due to Pearson (2018), will be presented in Section 5.6.2.[9]

Percus and Sauerland (2003b) observe that a pronoun in a dream report like (48) admits two kinds of readings that are distinguishable when John dreams that he is someone other than himself: on one reading, John dreams that he is (for example) Fred and it is Fred (i.e., John's *dream-self*) who gets promoted. On the other reading, John dreams that he is Fred, but it is John (i.e., John's *dream-counterpart*, who exists third-personally in John's dream) who gets promoted. (Of course, there is yet another reading where *he* simply refers to someone salient in the context – this irrelevant reading will be set aside in what follows.)

---

[8] In separate work around the same time, Percus and Sauerland (2003a) present another argument in favor of dedicated *de se* LFs. But Anand (2006) shows that there are some problems for the argument (see in particular Anand 2006: Sect. 1.3 'The Argument from Only'), so I do not review it here.

[9] For yet another argument in favor of dedicated *de se* LFs, see Patel-Grosz (2020).

## 5.5 The de re Blocking Effect

(48) John dreamed that he got promoted.

(Percus and Sauerland 2003b)

Percus and Sauerland (2003b) furthermore generalize based on data like (49) that when a dream report contains *two* embedded pronouns, a dream-self pronoun cannot be c-commanded by a dream-counterpart pronoun. (See also Pearson and Dery 2014 for relevant experimental evidence.)

(49) I dreamed that I was marrying my granddaughter.
   a. In my dream, the dream-self marries the dream-self's granddaughter.
   b. In my dream, the dream-self marries my granddaughter.
   c. #In my dream, I marry the dream-self's granddaughter.
   d. In my dream, I marry my granddaughter.

(Percus and Sauerland 2003b)

In the reading paraphrased by (49-a), both pronouns have the dream-self reading: I dream that I am someone else, who marries his own granddaughter. In the reading paraphrased by (49-d), both pronouns refer to the dream-counterpart: I dream that I am someone else, and observe my dream-counterpart third-personally, who marries his own granddaughter. In (49-b), we have a mixed case: the embedded subject pronoun *I* has the dream-self reading, whereas the possessive pronoun *my* refers to the dream-counterpart. Crucially, however, (49-c) is not an available reading for the sentence in question: the sentence is false in a scenario where I dream I am someone else and observe my dream-counterpart marrying my dream-self's granddaughter. The absence of this reading follows if a dream-self pronoun cannot be c-commanded by a dream-counterpart pronoun, because in this sentence, *my* is c-commanded by *I*.[10]

Percus and Sauerland (2003b) propose to explain this constraint via two proposals. The first proposal is that dream-self pronouns have the interpretation they do because they move to the left periphery of the embedded clause to create a property abstraction (as in Heim and Kratzer's 1998 treatment of relative pronouns, mentioned in Section 5.3 above as one possible approach to ensuring that PRO triggers abstraction). That is, dream-self pronouns are *de se* pronouns like PRO, a proposal consistent with the centered worlds approach to attitude

---

[10] Although the constraint holds for second- and third-person pronouns as well, Percus and Sauerland (2003b) observe that intuitions are sharper when the data are presented with first-person pronouns, so I follow them in focusing on first-person examples here.

alternatives in that the dream-self is the individual who the dreamer dreams is himself at each dream alternative. Dream-counterpart pronouns, on the other hand, are directly bound by the subject of the dream report. The second proposal is that pronoun movement is subject to a superiority constraint, whereby if two pronouns have the same features and one asymmetrically c-commands the other, then the lower one cannot be moved. As long as dream-self and dream-counterpart pronouns share the same features, the fact that (48) lacks the reading in (49-c) is accounted for. But if this is right, it is evidence that optionally *de se* reports do have dedicated *de se* LFs: pronoun movement leads to a dedicated *de se* interpretation, and that movement is indirectly detectable in that it is subject to a superiority effect.

In follow-up work, Anand (2006) – who uses the term '*de re* blocking effect' for the pattern of data in (49) – points out some empirical problems for Percus and Sauerland's analysis, and proposes an alternative account. While a full investigation of his alternative account would take us too far afield, suffice it to say that this alternative account, like Percus and Sauerland's, argues in favor of dedicated *de se* LFs for optionally *de se* reports. There are a number of nuances to the *de re* blocking effect and the analytical details remain controversial, but the key point is that it seems to support the view that optionally *de se* reports do have dedicated *de se* LFs, insofar as the explanation for the effect has to do with some sort of locality restriction that we would expect to constrain dedicated *de se* LFs but not LFs in which *de se* falls out as a special type of *de re*.

## 5.6 DE SE AS A SPECIAL CASE OF DE RE?

In the previous section, we asked whether optionally *de se* reports have dedicated *de se* LFs, a question made viable by the possibility that optionally *de se* reports are just *de re* reports whose acquaintance relation is keyed to the self-identity relation. In this section we ask a more radical question: Can *obligatorily de se* reports be subsumed under *de re* reports? This means asking: Can *de se* pronouns (including PRO and other candidates to be considered in Section 5.7 below) be analyzed as special kinds of *de re* pronouns that are "hard-coded" for the acquaintance relation of self-identity, thereby achieving a theoretical unification of *de re* and *de se*? Here I will not be concerned with the formal details of such an approach; see Schlenker 2003; Anand 2006; Maier 2011; Landau 2015 for some options. Instead, I will review one argument for such a reduction (Landau 2015, 2018) and one argument

## 5.6.1 The Argument from Agreement

Landau (2015, 2018) develops an argument against the centered worlds approach to obligatorily *de se* attitude reports. Consider the minimal pair in (50-a–b) instantiating subject control and object control, respectively. (50-a) is necessarily interpreted *de se* in that Beatrix must realize that her promise concerns herself, and (50-b) is also necessarily interpreted *de se* in that Maggie must realize that her newly formed intention concerns herself. On the centered worlds approach to *de se*, PRO in both examples is bound from immediately below the attitude predicate, as schematized in (51).

(50) a. Beatrix promised Maggie [PRO to leave].
 b. Beatrix persuaded Maggie [PRO to leave].

(51) a. Beatrix promised Maggie [$\lambda_1$ [PRO$_1$ to leave] ]
 b. Beatrix persuaded Maggie [$\lambda_1$ [PRO$_1$ to leave] ]

The problem is that there is evidence that PRO has agreement features that match that of its controller. For example, consider the pattern of licit reflexives in (52). In (52-a), the reflexive must have feminine gender, reflecting PRO's feminine gender, which in turn reflects PRO being subject-controlled by the feminine pronoun *she*, whereas in (52-b), the reflexive must have masculine gender, reflecting PRO's masculine gender, which in turns reflects PRO being object-controlled by *him*.

(52) a. She promised him [PRO to comb herself/*himself].
 b. She persuaded him [PRO to comb *herself/himself].

But in (51), there is no binding relation between the controller and PRO, rather only between the attitude verb and PRO. Conceivably, one could divorce semantic binding from the syntactic procedure that assigns agreements features to pronouns, but what would be suspicious about such an arrangement is the way they work in lockstep: in subject control, PRO bears the subject's phi-features, whereas in object control, PRO bears the object's phi-features. This would end up looking like an accident, when surely it is not.

In response to this, Landau follows Schlenker 2003 and Maier 2011 in taking the position that PRO is a *de re* pronoun keyed to the acquaintance relation of self-identity. Unlike the centered worlds approach, this approach involves binding of PRO by its matrix antecedent rather than from immediately below the attitude predicate, thereby explaining PRO's agreement features. As far as I know, Landau's 'argument from agreement' has yet to be defused by proponents of the centered worlds approach to *de se*.

### 5.6.2 The *de se* Generalization

Pearson (2018) develops a novel argument that unambiguously *de se* expressions like PRO must be analyzed using a dedicated *de se* binding mechanism rather than as a case of *de re* that is fixed to the acquaintance relation of identity. The argument also turns out to extend to some cases of optional *de se* reports, hence bearing on the issues raised in the previous section. The argument is based on the idea that while the *de se* binding approach and the *de se*-as-*de re* approach make identical truth-conditional predictions for some attitude reports, including belief reports, the predictions pull apart for counterfactual attitude reports such as with *dream* and *imagine*.

Pearson uses the minimal pair in (53-a–b) to draw out two distinct readings of pronouns in counterfactual attitude reports. Focusing just on the interpretation of the bolded pronoun, (53-a) makes salient the reading in which *she* refers to Melania (i.e., the individual that Ivanka *imagines* herself to be); this is what Pearson calls, following Ninan (2008), the 'counterfactual-self' construal (generalizing from the label 'dream-self' used in discussing dream reports in particular; see Section 5.5 above). (53-b), by contrast, makes salient the reading in which *she* refers to Melania (i.e., the individual that Melania *believes* herself to be); this is what Pearson calls, also following Ninan (2008), the 'belief-self' construal.

(53) a. Ivanka imagined that she was Melania and **she** was giving an interview as First Lady.
 b. Ivanka imagined that she was Melania and **she** was giving an interview as First Daughter. (Pearson 2018: 13)

Against this backdrop, Pearson defends the generalization in (54):

(54) The *de se* Generalization (Pearson 2018: 14)
 a. If a pronoun or anaphor is unambiguously read *de se*, then it cannot receive a belief-self reading in counterfactual reports with counter-identity.
 b. If a pronoun or anaphor is ambiguous between a *de se* reading and a *de re* reading, then it can receive either a counterfactual-self or a belief-self reading in counterfactual reports with counter-identity.

(54-a) is evidenced by data like (55) while (54-b) is evidenced by data like (53).

(55) a. Ivanka imagined PRO being Melania and PRO giving an interview as First Lady.
b. ?Ivanka imagined that PRO being Melania and PRO giving an interview as First Daughter.  (Pearson 2018: 24)

Ninan (2008) proposes that in counterfactual attitude reports, counterfactual-self readings arise via dedicated *de se* binding, whereas belief-self readings arise as a special case of *de re* readings. Pearson argues that this automatically explains the *de se* generalization: PRO undergoes obligatory *de se* binding and hence only has the counterfactual-self reading, while ordinary pronouns undergo optional *de se* binding and hence optionally have the counterfactual-self reading. And if this is right, then *de se* cannot be fully subsumed under *de re*.

Not only that, in order to be able to account for the second half of the *de se* generalization, then it must also be the case that optionally *de se* pronouns like *he* and *she* can be parsed using either the *de re* approach (yielding the belief-self reading) or the dedicated *de se* binding approach (yielding the counterfactual-self reading).

If it weren't for dedicated *de se* binding, Pearson argues, the *de se* generalization would be difficult to account for. That being said, Pearson explicitly leaves open the question of how to reconcile dedicated *de se* binding with Landau's argument from agreement discussed above. More research will be needed to reconcile the tension between the argument from agreement and the *de se* generalization.

## 5.7 EXPANDING THE EMPIRICAL COVERAGE

Aside from control, there are three other grammatical phenomena that have been claimed to have a special affinity for *de se* semantics. These are: logophors, shifted indexicals, and long-distance reflexives.[11] In what follows, we briefly review each in turn.

---

[11] Yet another claimed means of achieving obligatory *de se* is with emphatic pronominal expressions like *he himself* or *she herself*, as in (i).

(i) Beatrix claims that she herself is a genius.

See, however, Pearson 2017 for evidence against this position.

### 5.7.1 Logophors

Logophors constitute a special class of pronouns that have been identified in some languages, including especially Niger-Congo languages such as Ewe (Clements 1975; Pearson 2015) and Yoruba (Anand 2006). According to Pearson (2015), building on Clements (1975) as well as her own fieldwork on Ewe, logophors have the following special properties.[12] First, they must occur in the scope of a speech or mental attitude predicate. Thus (56-a–b) – wherein the Ewe logophor *yè* is embedded under *be* 'say' and *bòu* 'think', respectively – are both grammatical, whereas (57-a–b) – wherein *yè* appears unembedded (57-a) or embedded under a non-attitude verb like *wɔ* 'do (cause)' – are both ungrammatical.

(56) a. Kofi be yè dzo.
    Kofi say LOG leave
    'Kofi said that he left.'     (Ewe, Pearson 2015: 78)
  b. John bòu be yè nyi honvi.
    John think COMPL LOG COP stupid
    'John thinks that he is stupid.'     (Ewe, Pearson 2015: 94)

(57) a. *Yè dzo.
    LOG leave
    Intended: 'S/he left.'     (Ewe, Pearson 2015: 78)
  b. *Kofi wɔ be yè dzo.
    Kofi do COMPL LOG leave
    Intended: 'Kofi caused himself to leave.'
         (Ewe, Pearson 2015: 96)

Second, logophors obligatorily pick out an attitude holder. Thus in (56-a–b), the logophor obligatorily picks out Kofi and John respectively and does not have the option of being interpreted deictically, and in a sentence like (58) wherein there is more than one potential antecedent but only one is an attitude holder, the logophor can only pick out the attitude holder.

(58) Kofi gblon na Marie be yè dzo.
   Kofi say to Marie COMPL LOG leave
   'Kofi told Marie that he/*she left.'     (Ewe, Pearson 2015: 96)

Third, in iterated attitude reports wherein there is more than one potential antecedent and all are attitude holders, ambiguity ensues. This is illustrated in (59).

---

[12] Here I sketch the basics only. For more thorough coverage, see Pearson 2015.

## 5.7 Expanding the Empirical Coverage

(59) Mari be Kofi xɔse be yè na yè cadeau.
Marie say Kofi believe COMPL LOG give LOG gift
(i) 'Marie said that Kofi believed that she gave him a gift.'
(ii) 'Marie said that Kofi believed that he gave her a gift.'
(Ewe, Pearson 2015: 96)

A theoretically attractive way of accounting for these distributional and interpretive properties is to propose that logophors are endowed with a grammatical feature that must be checked via binding by an attitude predicate; such an approach is pursued by Heim (2002) and von Stechow (2002, 2003). Thus a configuration like (60) is grammatical and correctly predicts that the logophor must pick out Kofi, whereas a configuration like (61) is ungrammatical.

(60) Kofi say [$\lambda_1$ [LOG$_1$ leave]]

(61) [LOG leave]

On this view, logophors are much like controlled PRO, except that (i) logophors must be embedded under attitude predicates, whereas PRO can be embedded under a non-attitude predicate, and (ii) logophors admit long-distance binding in iterated attitude reports, whereas PRO must be bound from the immediately embedding predicate.

Because this approach makes use of the same technology designed to derive the obligatorily *de se* interpretation of controlled PRO, the approach would seem to make the prediction that logophors are likewise obligatorily construed *de se*. And while such a prediction has been claimed to be successfully borne out in Bafut (Niger-Congo, Kusumoto 1998), Yoruba (Anand 2006), and Tangale (Afro-Asiatic, Haida 2009), Pearson (2015) shows that it does not in fact hold for Ewe. For example, four out of five Ewe speakers consulted by Pearson accept as true the sentence in (62-b) in the anti-*de se* scenario depicted in (62-a).

(62) a. *context*: Following a spate of burglaries, a policeman was alerted by CCTV operators that someone was acting suspiciously, and chased after that individual, unaware that it was himself.
b. Sodza xɔse be yè nyi fianfitɔ.
policeman believe COMPL LOG COP thief
'The policeman believed that he was a thief.'
(Ewe, Pearson 2015: 99)

See Pearson 2015 for an attempt to reconcile all of these facts in a way that weaves together recent approaches to *de se* attitude reports with recent approaches to *de re* attitude reports. More cross-linguistic research will be needed to determine whether Pearson's proposal holds up against a wider range of data and languages.

### 5.7.2 Shifted Indexicals

Another class of linguistic expressions that have been claimed to give rise to obligatory *de se* interpretations are so-called shifted indexicals. Observe first that in English, indexical expressions like *I*, *here*, and *now* are fixed by the actual context of utterance, even when embedded under an attitude predicate. This is illustrated in (63) for the first-person pronoun *I*.

(63)   Beatrix believes/says that I was a genius.
       ≠ Beatrix believes/says: "I am a genius."

Facts like this led Kaplan (1989) to the thesis that indexicals are directly referential: their content is indelibly fixed by the context of utterance and consequently unaffected by embedding. In the background theory of this book, we can cash this out by relativizing denotations not only to a world parameter but also to a context parameter $c$ that values indexicals, and stipulating that natural languages lack operators that can manipulate this context parameter. For example, the denotation for the first-person pronoun can be captured as follows, where AUTH is a function from a context to the speaker/author in that context:

(64)   $[[I]]^{w,c} = \text{AUTH}(c)$

Then, in an attitude report like (65), embedding the first-person pronoun under *believe* has no effect on its interpretation, because *believe* manipulates the world parameter but not the context parameter in its complement.

(65)   Beatrix believes that I am a genius.

(66)   $\forall \langle w',y \rangle \in \text{DOX}_{b,w}$: AUTH($c$) is a a genius in $w'$
       'For all those pairs world-individual pairs $\langle w',y \rangle$ such that it is compatible with Beatrix's beliefs in $w$ for Beatrix to be $y$ in $w'$, AUTH($c$) is a genius in $w'$.'

In principle, nothing in the theory presented so far would prevent us from defining an operator that manipulates the context parameter. And this turns out to be a good thing, because it has come to light that in some languages, indexical shift is found (see e.g. Schlenker 2003). One such language is Zazaki (Indo-Iranian), investigated by Anand and Nevins (2004) and Anand (2006). Anand and Nevins (2004) observe

## 5.7 Expanding the Empirical Coverage

that in Zazaki, indexicals do indeed (optionally) shift when they are embedded under the verb *vano* 'say', as illustrated in (67) for the first-person pronoun.[13]

(67) Hɛseni mɨ-ra va kɛ ɛz dɛwletia.
 Hesen.OBL I.OBL-to said that I rich.be.PRES
 'Hesen said that {I am, Hesen is} rich.'
 (Anand and Nevins 2004: 21)

They furthermore rule out the possibility that (67) on its shifted reading instantiates direct quotation. They do so by showing that indexicals in Zazaki can shift even when grammatical dependencies exist between matrix and embedded clause. These include licensing of negative polarity items (68-a) and relativization (68-b); cf. the deviant English examples in (69) that attempt these same grammatical dependencies into quoted material.

(68) a. Rojda ne va kɛ mɨ kes paci kɛrd.
  Rojda not said that I anyone kiss did
  'Rojda didn't say that she kissed anyone.'
  (Anand and Nevins 2004: 22)
 b. čɛnɛkɛ [kɛ Hɛseni va mɨ t paci kɛrda] rindɛka
  girl that Hesen said I kiss did pretty.be-PRES
  'The girl that Hesen said {Hesen, I} kissed is pretty.'
  (Anand and Nevins 2004: 22)

(69) a. *Rojda didn't say, "I kissed anyone."
 b. *The girl that Hesen said, "I kissed" is pretty.

As documented by Anand (2006), Zazaki shifted indexicals give rise to an obligatory *de se* semantics:[14]

(70) a. *context 1:* Hesen says, "I am sick today."
 b. *context 2:* Hesen, at the hospital for a checkup, happens to glance at the chart of a patient's blood work. Hesen, a doctor himself, sees that the patient is clearly sick, but the name is

---

[13] According to Anand and Nevins (2004), all indexicals in Zazaki have the option of shifting under *vano* 'say'. Aside from the first-person pronoun ɛz, other examples of shifting indexicals that the authors document include tɨ 'you', ita 'here', and vɨzeri 'yesterday'.

[14] See also Wechsler 2010 for a development of the proposal that even ordinary unshifted uses of both first- and second-person pronouns, in any language, have a semantics that relies crucially on self-ascription.

hard to read. He says to the nurse when she comes in, "This guy is really sick."

c. Heseni va kɛ ɛz newɛsha.
Hesen.OBL said that I be.sick.PRES
'Hesen said that he was sick.' (acceptable in context 1, unacceptable in context 2)

(Anand 2006: 79)

Anand and Nevins (2004) and Anand (2006) furthermore identify two constraints on Zazaki shifted indexicals. First, the Shift-Together Constraint: if a complement clause contains more than one indexical, they must either shift together or not shift at all; mixed interpretations wherein one indexical shifts and the other does not are ruled out. This is illustrated in (71), where the embedded indexicals ɛz 'I' and to 'you' can (on the shifted reading) refer to Rojda and Bill respectively, or (on the non-shifted reading) refer to the speaker and addressee of the speech report. But they cannot refer to the speaker of the speech report and Bill or Rojda and the addressee of the speech report.

(71) Vizeri Rojda Bill-ra va kɛ ɛz to-ra miradiša.
yesterday Rojda Bill-to said that I you-to angry.be.PRES
'Yesterday Rojda said to Bill, "I am angry at you."'
'Yesterday Rojda said to Bill, "AUTH(c*) is angry at ADDR(c*)."'
*'Yesterday Rojda said to Bill, "AUTH(c*) is angry at you."'
*'Yesterday Rojda said to Bill, "I am angry at ADDR(c*)."'

(Anand and Nevins 2004: 23)

Anand and Nevins (2004) furthermore demonstrate that in sentences with multiple embedding, if an indexical is shifted in the intermediate clause, then an indexical in the lowest clause cannot be anchored to the utterance context. (This is what Anand (2006) calls 'No Intervening Binder'.) This is illustrated in (72). If to 'you' in the intermediate clause undergoes shift and therefore refers to Andrew, then ɛz 'I' in the lowest clause can be interpreted as Hesen (local shifting) or Ali (shifting relative the intermediate clause), but it cannot be interpreted as Andrew (the speaker of the matrix utterance).

(72) (Andrew): Ali mɨ-ra va kɛ Hɛseni to-ra va ɛz braye Rojda-o.
Ali me-to said that Hesen you-to said I brother Rojda-GEN
'Ali said to Andrew that Hesen said to Andrew that {Hesen, Ali, *Andrew} is Rojda's brother.'

(Anand and Nevins 2004: 29)

## 5.7 Expanding the Empirical Coverage

Anand and Nevins (2004) propose to explain this pattern of data with two key ideas. The first idea is that denotations are relativized both to an index $i$ and a context $c$. The index parameter is like the world parameter but extended to encode all the same information that the context parameter encodes, namely world, time, author, addressee, and location. In this way, the index and context parameters are of the same type. This enables the second key idea, which is that indexical shift happens when *vano* 'say' embeds a context-shifting operator OP whose effect is to overwrite the context parameter with the index parameter:

(73)  $[[OP[\alpha]]]^{c,i} = [[\alpha]]^{i,i}$

When such an operator is employed, all subsequent indexicals will shift to the derived context associated with the embedding verb *vano* 'say', neatly deriving the Shift-Together Constraint, the No Intervening Binder Constraint, and the obligatory *de se* semantics.[15]

Among languages for which indexical shift has been documented, interesting points of variation have been discovered in terms of which indexicals shift, which embedding verbs trigger indexical shift, and whether indexical shift is obligatory or optional, which can depend on the embedding verb and the indexical involved. For example, as already mentioned, in Zazaki, all indexicals shift optionally, but only under *vano* 'say'; all other embedding verbs give rise to English-like non-shifting behavior. But in Slave (Athapaskan), the picture is somewhat different (Anand and Nevins 2004; Anand 2006): the first-person pronoun shifts obligatorily under 'say', and optionally under 'tell', 'think', and 'want'. And the second-person pronoun shifts optionally under 'tell'. Aside from that, no other indexicals shift in Slave. Such points of variation can be captured, as Anand and Nevins (2004) and Anand (2006) do, by defining variants of the operator in (73) that target only selected aspects of the context and by imposing distributional restrictions on which embedding verbs can, must, or cannot embed these operators.

Another point of variation among languages that exhibit indexical shift – and one that poses a prima facie problem for the approach developed by Anand and Nevins (2004) and Anand (2006) – concerns the

---

[15] In a different vein, Maier (2009, 2011) proposes to derive the *de se* character of shifted indexicals from a *de dicto* semantics.

Shift-Together Constraint illustrated above for Zazaki. In particular, first-person forms in Amharic appear to violate this constraint, so that in a configuration like (74), 'mixed' interpretations are available:

(74) John lɨj-e ay-ɨttaazzəzə-ññ alə.
 John son-my NEG.3S-obey-1sO say.PERF.3SM
 'John said, "my son will not obey AUTH(c*).'''
 'John said, "AUTH(c)'s son will not obey me."'
  (Anand 2006: 101, Schlenker 2011, glossing simplified)

Anand (2006) proposes to explain this away by positing that the first-person in Amharic is actually ambiguous between a non-shifting indexical and a logophor, and thereby subject to different, looser constraints. But the other way of interpreting this piece of data is to pursue a less constrained approach to indexical shift, as undertaken by Schlenker (2003, 2011). Recall from Chapter 4 that there are two approaches to the way possible worlds are integrated into semantic interpretations: either as a parameter of interpretation, or as pronouns in syntax that can be quantified over and bound at a distance like any other pronoun. Broadly speaking, the former approach is more constrained and hence 'undergenerates', necessitating more sophisticated LFs (as in Keshet 2011), whereas the latter approach 'overgenerates', predicting more readings than are attested and hence necessitating additional constraints (as in Percus 2000). Exactly the same debate plays out for the notion of context: Is it a parameter of interpretation, as in Anand and Nevins (2004) and Anand (2006)? Or should we instead liberalize the system by positing context variables that can in principle be quantified over and bound at a distance? Schlenker (2003, 2011) pursues the latter approach. On that view, indexicals enter the derivation with context variables. Attitude verbs quantify over contexts, and each indexical in its scope can be bound by such a quantifier, or by the matrix context represented in (75) as $c^*$, enabling the kinds of mixed interpretations witnessed in (74) for Amharic.

(75) a. $\lambda c^*$ [John said $\lambda c'$ [my$_c$ son will not obey me$_{c*}$]]
 b. $\lambda c^*$ [John said $\lambda c'$ [my$_{c*}$ son will not obey me$_c$]]

On this approach, unshiftable indexicals (which include e.g. all indexicals in English) are those whose context variable is lexically fixed to $c^*$. Of course, the approach raises important questions about why the Shift-Together Constraint is seemingly operative for many shifting indexicals in many languages. See Schlenker (2011) for a relevant suggestion about how to capture such facts.

Aside from Zazaki and Slave, other languages for which indexical shift has been documented include Amharic, Engenni (Niger-Congo),

## 5.7 Expanding the Empirical Coverage

Aghem (Niger-Congo), Navajo, Ancient Greek, Ancient Egyptian American Sign Language, Catalan Sign Language, and Italian Sign Language (see Schlenker 2011 for references). It is an open question whether shifted indexicals have an obligatory *de se* interpretation in all languages that have shifted indexicals. For example, Schlenker claims in his dissertation (1999: 97) that Amharic shifted indexicals are obligatorily *de se*, though later in the revised 2000 version says that his informant finds the relevant test sentences "almost impossible to assess" (2000: 126). More recently, Malamud says that "Amharic informants showed no hesitation in accepting the *de re* [i.e., non-*de se*] uses of *I* [shifted first-person indexical]" (2006: 106). More research will be needed to get a fuller picture of which options are attested and which are not.

### 5.7.3 Long-Distance Reflexives

Finally, we very briefly consider so-called long-distance reflexives as found in languages like Mandarin Chinese and Japanese. Whereas reflexive (*-self*) forms in English must be bound from within their local clause, as demonstrated in (76), Mandarin reflexive *ziji* can be bound from higher embedding clauses, as seen in (77). (See Huang et al. 2009 for an overview.)

(76)   Beatrix$_i$ says [Maggie$_j$ thinks [Polly$_k$ criticized **herself**$_{*i/*j/k}$]].

(77)   Zhangsan$_i$ shuo [Lisi$_j$ renwei [Wangwu$_k$ piping-le   **ziji**$_{i/j/k}$]].
       Zhangsan say   Lisi  believe Wangwu   criticize-PFV self
       'Zhangsan$_i$ says Lisi$_j$ thinks Wangwu$_k$ criticized himself$_k$/him$_{i/j}$.'

It has been reported in the literature as early as Pan 1995 that when *ziji* is found in an attitude report, it gives rise to obligatory *de se* semantics. For example, according to Huang and Liu (2001), (78) is truthful only if what Zhangsan said was, 'A pickpocket stole *my* purse.' If instead Zhangsan was reporting the theft of a purse without realizing that it was his own purse, then reflexive *ziji* in (78) would need to be replaced with the ordinary third-person pronoun *ta*.

(78)   Zhangsan shuo pashou     tou-le     **ziji**-de  pibao.
       Zhangsan say   pickpocket steal-PFV self-POSS purse
       'Zhangsan said that the pickpocket stole his purse.'
                                                (Huang and Liu 2001)

Wang and Pan (2014), however, dispute the generalization that long-distance *ziji* is obligatorily *de se*. According to these authors, if the speaker of the utterance *empathizes* with the referent in the sense of Kuno and Kaburaki (1977) – i.e., in the case of (78), puts him or herself 'in Zhangsan's shoes', so to speak, then a non-*de se* interpretation (what Wang and Pan call 'indirect' *de se*) becomes available. More research will be needed to determine how exactly long-distance reflexives fit into a comprehensive picture of the syntax and semantics of *de se* attitude ascriptions.

## 5.8 DISCUSSION QUESTIONS

(i) As independent support for the proposal that control complements denote properties rather than propositions, Chierchia (1989) cites the following example of valid reasoning first pointed out by Fodor 1977:

(79) a. *Premise 1:* The cat wanted to eat the cheese.
b. *Premise 2:* The mouse got what the cat wanted.
c. *Conclusion:* The mouse got to eat the cheese.

How does the validity of (79) support the property analysis of control complements? If the control complement in (79-a) instead denoted the proposition that the cat eats the cheese, what would (79-b) mean, and what would we be predicted to be able to validly conclude from (79-a) and (79-b)?

(ii) As discussed in this chapter, in a *de se* belief report, a *de se* pronoun refers to the individual that the attitude holder *believes* herself to be, whereas in a *de se* dream or imagination report, a *de se* pronouns refers to the individual that the attitude holder *dreams* or *imagines* herself to be, respectively. With that in mind, consider a *de se* desire report like (80):

(80) Beatrix wants to win the election.

Does this report that Beatrix wants the individual she *believes* herself to be to win the election, or does it report that Beatrix wants the individual she *wants* to be to win the election? To tease these options apart, consider scenarios in which the individual that Beatrix believes herself to be is distinct from the individual she wants to be. A consideration to keep in mind while reading the next chapter is whether your answer to this question is consistent with the various approaches to *want*-sentences that we will be reviewing.

(iii) Consider the following minimal pair from Hornstein and Pietroski 2010, based on a similar example by Higginbotham (2003):

(81) a. I expected [that I would win].
b. I expected [PRO to win].

As pointed out by Hornstein and Pietroski (2010), these two sentences are truth-conditionally distinct, in that (81-a) would be true but (81-b) false in a scenario in which at some past point in time I had the expectation: "That person will win," not realizing then, but realizing now, that the person in question is me. This leads Hornstein and Pietroski (2010) to join Higginbotham (2009) in suggesting that "PRO is ... even more first-personal than the first-person pronoun itself" (Higginbotham 2003: 512). How might such data be accommodated by the various theories considered in this chapter? *Hint:* Answering this question will likely require us to enrich our theory of attitude reports to take into account time-sensitivity, a topic that we will return to in Section 7.2 below.

## *5.9* **FURTHER READING**

For relevant foundational work in philosophy, see especially Castañeda 1966, 1967, 1968; Perry 1979; Lewis 1979, as well as the recent edited volume García-Carpintero and Torre 2016, which contains works on *de se* thought and communication. See also Ball (2019) for recent work on the status of centered worlds in Lewis's vs. in Stalnaker's approach to attitude ascriptions. Work on *de se* attitude reports in the linguistics literature begins, in some sense, with Chierchia 1989, and crucial subsequent pieces in this research tradition include Schlenker 2003; Percus and Sauerland 2003a; Anand 2006; Stephenson 2007b, 2010; Maier 2009, 2011; Pearson 2013, 2015, 2018; Landau 2018; Patel-Grosz 2020. For somewhat different approaches within the linguistics tradition, see also Higginbotham 2003; Hornstein and Pietroski 2010. Finally, Ninan 2010; Schlenker 2011 serve as useful overviews of the literature.

# 6 Desire Reports and Beyond

## 6.1 INTRODUCTION

If we treat *believe*-sentences as instantiating universal quantification over the attitude holder's DOXASTIC ALTERNATIVES, as in (1), then a reasonable null hypothesis would be that *want*-sentences are just the same except that the quantification is over the attitude holder's BOULETIC ALTERNATIVES (i.e., all those worlds in which the attitude holder's desires are satisfied), as in (2).

(1) $[[\text{Beatrix believes it's raining}]]^w = \forall w' \in \text{DOX}_{b,w}: \text{rain}(w')$
where $\text{DOX}_{x,w} = \{w' \mid w' \text{ is compatible with } x\text{'s beliefs in } w\}$

(2) $[[\text{Beatrix wants it to be raining}]]^w = \forall w' \in \text{BOUL}_{b,w}: \text{rain}(w')$
where $\text{BOUL}_{x,w} = \{w' \mid w' \text{ is compatible with } x\text{'s desires in } w\}$

As it turns out, a wealth of evidence points toward the conclusion that (2) is wrong: there are simply too many differences between *believe*-sentences and *want*-sentences, and too many empirical difficulties for the approach in (2), to lend any credence to such a treatment. What exactly should replace (2) is still a matter of some debate, though we do know quite a bit about the various issues that any adequate proposal must be able to answer to. In what follows, we review some of the more salient issues and the proposals that they have prompted (Sections 6.2 through 6.7). We then scale up to take a broader look at semantic variation among attitude predicates (Section 6.8).

## 6.2 BELIEF-RELATIVITY

We begin with an observation due to Heim (1992) that exposes a problem for treating *want*-sentences as instantiating universal quantification over bouletic alternatives. Heim asks us to consider the sentence in (3).

## 6.2 Belief-Relativity

(3)  I want to teach Tuesdays and Thursdays next semester.

(Heim 1992: 195)

About this sentence, Heim says:

> Suppose this sentence is intuitively true as spoken by me today. Is it therefore the case ... that I teach Tuesdays and Thursdays next semester in all the worlds that are compatible with everything I desire? No. In worlds that are compatible with everything I desire I actually don't teach at all.
>
> (Heim 1992: 195)

In other words, universal quantification over bouletic alternatives seems to endow *want*-sentences with a semantics that is too strong: such an analysis predicts that we should be able to use *want*-sentences truthfully only when they describe a state of affairs that would hold in those worlds where all of the attitude holder's desires (no matter how wild or far-fetched) are fulfilled. And this is simply not the case, as Heim's example attests to. So then the question is: What is the right way of weakening the semantics of *want*-sentences?

Predominant approaches in the formal semantics literature take as their starting point the intuition that the semantics of *want*-sentences is intimately bound up with the attitude holder's beliefs. In Heim's (3), for example, what is intuitively needed is for the semantics to allow us to ignore those worlds incompatible with the attitude holder's beliefs: just considering alternatives that are realistic from the point of view of the attitude holder – where the attitude holder does indeed teach next semester – a Tuesday-Thursday teaching schedule is preferable to any other realistically possible teaching schedule.

There are a number of proposals in the literature for cashing out this basic idea; here I will introduce two that have been quite influential, and we will consider refinements and alternatives as we proceed. The first is what I will call the *better-worlds* approach and it is the one that Heim (1992) proposes. The second is what I will call the *best-worlds* approach and it has one of its clearest articulations in von Fintel (1999) (but prior to this can also be found in some form or another in Giorgi and Pianesi 1997 and Portner 1997). In what follows, I introduce each in turn.

### 6.2.1 The Better-Worlds Approach

Heim's (1992) better-worlds approach to the semantics of *want*-sentences takes inspiration from Stalnaker (1984), who wrote, in a now frequently quoted passage, "wanting something is preferring it to certain relevant alternatives, the relevant alternatives being those possibilities that the agent believes will be realized if he does not get what he want" (1984: 89). Taking seriously the *if*-clause in Stalnaker's characterization of what wanting is, Heim proposes that *want*-sentences have a conditional semantics, whereby (4-a) has truth conditions that are roughly paraphrasable as (4-b).[1]

(4)    a.   Beatrix wants it to be raining.
       b.   Beatrix prefers how she believes things will be if it is raining to how she believes things will be if it is not raining.

In order to cash out (4-b) in formal terms, we need a semantics for belief, a semantics for conditionals, and a semantics for preference (comparative desirability).

For belief semantics, Heim adopts the standard Hintikkan approach of universal quantification over doxastic alternatives. Since this has already been extensively reviewed in Chapter 2, we will not dwell on it any more here.

For conditional semantics, Heim follows an approach combining components from Stalnaker 1968 and Lewis 1973 that works in such a way that a conditional sentence like (5) has the semantics in (6). According to (6), an *if*-clause $p$ is mapped onto a function $\text{Sim}_w$ that returns that subset of $p$-worlds maximally similar to the evaluation world $w$. If all of these worlds are worlds in which the consequent of the conditional is true, then the conditional sentence is true.

(5)    If it is raining, Beatrix will leave.

(6)    $\text{Sim}_w([\lambda w'.[[\text{it is raining}]]^{w'}]) \subseteq [\lambda w'.[[\text{Beatrix will leave}]]^{w'}]$
       where $\text{Sim}_w(p) = \{w': w' \in p$ and $w'$ resembles $w$ no less than any other world in $p\}$        (Heim 1992: 195)
       'Those worlds in which it is raining that are maximally similar to $w$ are all worlds in which Beatrix will leave.'

Finally, for comparative desirability, Heim defines a relation $>_{a,w}$ that compares desirability of worlds relative to an attitude holder $a$ and an evaluation world $w$, as in (7-a). Heim also extends its definition, as in (7-b), so as to be able to compare desirability of propositions (sets of possible worlds).[2]

---

[1] I am grateful to Milo Phillips-Brown (pers. comm.) for suggesting (4-b) as an informal paraphrase of Heim's proposed semantics.
[2] Heim (1992) uses the 'less-than' symbol (<) for comparative desirability. Here I follow Villalta (2008) in replacing it with the greater-than symbol (>), because I find it more intuitive to think of 'more desirable' as being 'greater than' rather than 'less than'.

## 6.2 Belief-Relativity

(7) For any $w$, $w'$, $w''$:
   a. $w' >_{a,w} w''$ iff $w'$ is more desirable to $a$ in $w$ than $w''$
   b. $X >_{a,w} Y$ iff $w' >_{a,w} w''$ for all $w' \in X$, $w'' \in Y$ (Heim 1992: 197)

Putting together the assumed semantics for belief, conditionals, and comparative desirability, (8) exemplifies a first approximation of Heim's semantics for *want*-sentences. In procedural terms, it says: consider all those worlds compatible with Beatrix's beliefs. At each one of those worlds, check to see whether maximally similar worlds in which it is raining are all more desirable to Beatrix than maximally similar worlds in which it is not raining. If this is the case for each of Beatrix's belief worlds, then the sentence is true; otherwise, the sentence is false.

(8) $[[\text{Beatrix wants it to be raining}]]^w =$
   $\forall w' \in \text{DOX}_{b,w}: \text{Sim}_{w'}(\text{raining}) >_{b,w} \text{Sim}_{w'}(\neg\text{raining})$

As it happens, (8) is still not quite Heim's final semantics for *want*-sentences. The reason is that in (8), nothing prevents the Sim function from picking out worlds incompatible with Beatrix's beliefs, because it could be that at least some rain worlds maximally similar to at least some of Beatrix's belief worlds are not themselves among Beatrix's belief worlds (and likewise for non-rain worlds). A potential reason for wanting to disallow this comes from the minimal trio in (9).

(9) a. Beatrix wants it to be raining.
   b. Beatrix wishes that it were raining.
   c. Beatrix is glad that it is raining.

What is the difference between *want*, *wish*, and *be glad*? One salient difference is that *wish*-sentences are used to say something about the relative desirability of worlds that are not among the attitude holder's doxastic alternatives, whereas *be glad*-sentences are used to say something about the relative desirability of worlds that are among the attitude holder's doxastic alternatives. Heim proposes that *want*-sentences are somewhere in between, used to report the relative desirability of worlds that partially overlap with the attitude holder's doxastic alternatives; i.e., propositions that the attitude holder considers to be possible (unlike *wish*) but not guaranteed (unlike *be glad*). Strengthening the analytical connection between desire reports and conditional sentences, Heim notes a striking parallel between the varieties of desire reports exemplified by (9) and the varieties of conditionals exemplified by (10): the indicative conditional in (10-a) is 'want'-like in that rain is taken to be possible but not guaranteed, the counterfactual conditional in (10-b) is 'wish'-like in that rain is presupposed to be counterfactual, and the *because*-sentence in (10-c) is 'be glad'-like in that rain is taken for granted.

(10) a. If it is raining, Beatrix is staying inside.
b. If it were raining, Beatrix would be staying inside.
c. Because it is raining, Beatrix is staying inside.

To implement this idea, Heim modifies the semantics so that before the proposition named by the complement to *want* and its negative counterpart are run through the Sim function, they are each intersected with the attitude holder's doxastic alternatives, as in (11). Since the Sim function can only return subsets of the propositions it applies to, this intersection ensures that the output of the Sim function will only contain worlds compatible with the attitude holder's beliefs.[3]

(11) $[[$Beatrix wants it to be raining$]]^w =$
$\forall w' \in \text{DOX}_{b,w}$: $\text{Sim}_{w'}(\text{DOX}_{b,w} \cap \text{raining}) >_{b,w} \text{Sim}_{w'}(\text{DOX}_{b,w} \cap \neg\text{raining})$

Does Heim's semantics account for the Tuesday-Thursday example repeated in (12)? It does: on Heim's approach, (12) would be used to assert that at each of the attitude holder's belief worlds, maximally similar worlds in which she teaches Tuesdays and Thursdays are all more desirable than maximally similar worlds in which she does not teach Tuesdays and Thursdays.

(12) I want to teach Tuesdays and Thursdays next semester.

In Heim's scenario where the attitude holder believes that she will teach no matter what, maximally similar worlds in which she does not teach Tuesdays and Thursdays are worlds in which she teaches on some other schedule, not worlds in which she does not teach at all. So the sentence ends up not saying anything about the absolute desirability of teaching Tuesdays and Thursdays, but rather only about the relative desirability of teaching Tuesdays and Thursdays as opposed to teaching on some other possible schedule. And this is exactly what we want.

---

[3] Heim's semantics actually still looks somewhat different from (11), because Heim employs a dynamic semantic framework rather than a static one. One of the reasons Heim uses a dynamic semantics is to help carry out an overarching aim of her paper, which is to account for some facts about how presupposition triggers behave when embedded in attitude reports (see Section 6.7 below). Since the static/dynamic distinction is orthogonal to our immediate concerns here, I follow Villalta's (2008) translation of Heim's approach into a static framework.

## 6.2 Belief-Relativity

### 6.2.2 The Best-World Approach

Having sketched Heim's better-world semantics for *want*-sentences, let's now consider von Fintel's (1999) version of the best-worlds approach. Whereas Heim's approach borrows technology from the semantics of conditionals, von Fintel's approach borrows technology from Kratzer's (1981) highly influential doubly relative semantics for modals. By way of background, consider the deontic modal sentence in (13) (adapted from von Fintel and Heim 2011: Chapt. 5, to which the reader is referred for more thorough discussion of Kratzer's semantics for modals).

(13)   Maggie has to pay a fine.

A naive first approximation of a possible worlds analysis of (13) would amount to something like, 'All those worlds in which the rules are obeyed are worlds in which Maggie pays a fine.' The problem with this is that typically one pays a fine because one has broken a rule. So in all of those worlds in which the rules are obeyed, it is not in fact the case that Maggie pays a fine, because in those worlds, Maggie's fine-prompting infraction never occurred. Kratzer's (1981) solution to this problem was for modals to be interpreted relative to two parameters: a MODAL BASE and an ORDERING SOURCE. Then, in calculating the truth conditions of (13), we proceed something like this: consider all of those worlds in which the circumstances of this world up until now (including Maggie's fine-prompting infraction) have occurred. This is the modal base. Then, order those worlds according to how closely they approximate the deontically 'ideal' worlds in which all rules are obeyed. This is the ordering source. Those worlds that most closely approximate this ideal set are all worlds in which Maggie pays a fine.

Technically, this is achieved by defining an ordering relation as in (14). Read $<_P$ as 'better than, relative to the set of ideals named by $P$'. Then, according to (14), a world $w$ is better than a world $w'$ relative to $P$ iff the ideals that are realized in $w'$ is a proper subset of the ideals that are realized in $w$. Then we define a function $\max_P$ that takes a set of worlds and returns that subset of those worlds that come closest to satisfying the ideals named by $P$, as in (15).

(14)   Given a set of worlds $X$ and a set of propositions $P$: $\forall w, w' \in X$:
$w <_P w'$ iff $\{p \in P: p(w') = 1\} \subset \{p \in P: p(w) = 1\}$
(von Fintel 1999: 115)

(15)   Given a set of worlds $X$ and a strict partial order $<_P$: $\forall X \subseteq W$:
$\max_P(X) = \{w \in X: \neg \exists w' \in X: w' <_P w\}$   (von Fintel 1999: 116)

Applying this technology to *want*-sentences, the proposal is that the modal base is the set of worlds compatible with the attitude holder's beliefs (doxastic alternatives), and the ordering source is given by the attitude holder's desires (bouletic alternatives). This is illustrated in (16). In procedural terms, it tells us: look at all those worlds compatible with Beatrix's beliefs. Then, pick out just that subset of her belief worlds that best satisfy her desires. If, in all of those best worlds, it is raining, then the sentence is true; if not, the sentence is false.

(16)  [[Beatrix wants it to be raining]]$^w$ = $\forall w'$ $\max_{BOUL_{b,w}}(DOX_{b,w})$: raining($w'$)

Like Heim's better-worlds approach, the best-worlds approach also accounts for the Tuesday-Thursday example: we look at all of the worlds compatible with the attitude holder's beliefs, and then consider that subset that best satisfies the attitude holder's desires. If the attitude holder teaches Tuesdays and Thursdays in all of those worlds, then the sentence is true, and this is fully consistent with a scenario where there are even better worlds – but crucially not among the attitude holder's belief worlds – in which the attitude holder does not teach at all.

Having now sketched both the better-worlds and the best-worlds approach to *want*-sentences, we turn next to some further empirical considerations that will prompt some refinements.

### 6.2.3 A Doxastic Presupposition

An immediate problem for both the better-worlds approach and the best-worlds approach to *want*-sentences as sketched above is the prediction that *a believes p* entails *a wants p* (for arbitrary values of *a* and *p*). This is a bad result: for example, if I *believe* that I will die in ten days, this does not by any stretch of the imagination entail that I *want* to die in ten days.

Consider first the better-worlds approach. Suppose that Beatrix believes that it is raining. This fact alone is sufficient to verify (17), because $DOX_{b,w}$ ∩ ¬rain and therefore $Sim_{w'}(DOX_{b,w}$ ∩ ¬rain) denotes the empty set, and it is trivially the case that every world in $Sim_{w'}(DOX_{b,w}$ ∩ rain) is more desirable to Beatrix than any world in the empty set, because there are no worlds in the empty set.

(17)  [[Beatrix wants it to be raining]]$^w$ =
$\forall w' \in DOX_{b,w}$: $Sim_{w'}(DOX_{b,w}$ ∩ rain) $>_{b,w}$ $Sim_{w'}(DOX_{b,w}$ ∩ ¬rain)

In fact, by parity of reasoning, the better-worlds approach also erroneously predicts that *a believes ¬p* entails *a wants p*: suppose Beatrix

## 6.2 Belief-Relativity

believes that it is not raining. Then, $\text{Sim}_{w'}(\text{DOX}_{b,w} \cap \text{rain})$ denotes the empty set, and it is trivially the case that all of the worlds in the empty set are more desirable to Beatrix than any of the worlds in $\text{Sim}_{w'}(\text{DOX}_{b,w} \cap \neg\text{rain})$.

Heim (1992) recognizes this problem and proposes to solve it via a rather gentle modification to her semantics: we tack a condition onto the $\text{Sim}_w$ function, so that when it applies to a set of possible worlds $p$, the output is defined only if $p$ is not the empty set:

(18) $p$ is in the domain of $\text{Sim}_w$ only if $p \neq \emptyset$; where defined, $\text{Sim}_w(p) = \{w': w' \in p \text{ and } w' \text{ resembles } w \text{ no less than any other world in } p\}$
(Heim 1992: 198)

This ends up having as a consequence that if Beatrix believes that it is raining, or if Beatrix believes that it is not raining, then the sentence *Beatrix wants it to be raining* is neither true nor false but simply undefined. More generally, the consequence is that *a wants p* presupposes that $p$ is consistent with but not entailed by $a$'s beliefs. So the erroneous prediction about entailment relations is blocked by treating the entailed *want*-sentences as presupposition failures.

Consider now the best-worlds approach. Suppose again that Beatrix believes that it is raining. Just like on the better-worlds approach, this belief alone is sufficient to verify (19): (19) tells us that the *want*-sentence is true iff some subset of Beatrix's belief worlds (namely those that best satisfy her desires) are worlds in which it is raining. But if Beatrix believes that it is raining (i.e., if *all* of her belief worlds are ones in which it is raining), then it is trivially the case that any subset of those belief worlds are also all ones in which it is raining.[4]

(19) $[[\text{Beatrix wants it to be raining}]]^w = \forall w' \max_{\text{BOUL}_{b,w}}(\text{DOX}_{b,w}): \text{rain}(w')$

Von Fintel's (1999) solution is essentially to translate Heim's solution into the best-worlds framework: we do this by tacking a condition onto *want* itself, such that after all its arguments are fed into it, its output is defined only if $\text{DOX}_{a,w} \cap p \neq \emptyset$ (*a* considers $p$ possible) and $\text{DOX}_{a,w} \cap \neg p \neq \emptyset$ (*a* does not consider $p$ certain):

(20) $[[\text{Beatrix wants it to be raining}]]^w$ is defined only if $\text{DOX}_{b,w} \cap \text{rain} \neq \emptyset$ and $\text{DOX}_{b,w} \cap \neg\text{rain} \neq \emptyset$.

---

[4] This is the same logic responsible for the fact that the restriction of a universal quantifier is a downward-entailing environment: for example, if all dogs are friendly, it follows that all big dogs are friendly.

If defined, $[[\text{Beatrix wants it to be raining}]]^w =$
$\forall w' \max_{BOUL_{b,w}}(\text{DOX}_{b,w}): \text{rain}(w')$

This correction has the same consequence as it does on the better-worlds approach: the erroneously predicted entailments are, in some sense, blocked, by virtue of coming out as presupposition failures.

### 6.2.4 Refining the Presupposition

Let's take stock. We started out with some considerations pointing to the conclusion that *want*-sentences incorporate belief semantics in an intimate way, and we looked at two implementations of this idea. These implementations made the belief/desire connection a little *too* intimate, erroneously predicting that belief reports trivially entail corresponding desire reports. To remedy this, we appealed to presupposition: *want*-sentences presuppose that the attitude holder considers the desired proposition possible but not guaranteed. This presupposition offsets the belief/desire intimacy, imposing a healthy distance between the two, in a way that seems to get the balance just right. Or does it?

Heim (1992) notes that both the 'possible' and the 'not guaranteed' components of the proposed presupposition seem to face counterexamples. In particular, she considers the sentences in (21)–(22). (21) is problematic insofar as it could be used felicitously in a situation where John believes he will go to the movies tonight, in apparent violation of the 'not guaranteed' presupposition. And (22) is problematic insofar as it is felicitous even in the presence of an explicit denial of possibility, in apparent violation of the 'possible' presupposition: it is a counterfactual attitude report.

(21)  (John hired a babysitter because) he wants to go to the movies tonight.

(Heim 1992: 199)

(22)  I want this weekend to last forever. (But I know, of course, that it will be over in a few hours.)    (Heim 1992: 199)

In response to the problem raised by (21), Heim proposes a core revision to her semantics: rather than having *want*-sentences incorporate DOX, as in (23), Heim suggests that we should instead analyze *want*-sentences as incorporating a superset of DOX (what von Fintel, in later adopting the revision, dubs DOX*), defined as those worlds that the attitude holder believes are possible irrespective of how the attitude holder may choose to act, as in (24).

(23)  $\text{DOX}_{x,w} = \{w' \mid w'$ is compatible with $x$'s beliefs in $w\}$

## 6.2 Belief-Relativity

(24)  DOX*$_{x,w}$ = {$w'$ | $w'$ is compatible with everything $x$ believes to be the case in $w$ no matter how he chooses to act}

Heim observes that we routinely use *want*-sentences to report on intentions to act, and intended outcomes are typically not just believed to be possible but rather believed to be certain, a certainty grounded by the intention itself: if I intend to go out tonight, then (barring bizarre circumstances), of course I believe I will, because the intention is a commitment to see to it that I do. (This is well studied in the philosophy literature: see especially Bratman 1987, though see also Ludwig 1992, who argues that under some conditions, it is possible for someone to intend to do something even if they believe it is impossible.)

This solution thus pries apart the belief/desire connection ever so slightly more. In (21), John going to the movies tonight is presumably entailed by DOX$_{j,w}$, but crucially not by DOX*$_{j,w}$, given that John could choose to act otherwise. The presupposition failure is thereby defused.

And what about the problem of outcomes not believed to be possible? Here Heim is noncommittal: she suggests that either they too involve some superset of DOX$_{x,w}$ too weak to entail impossibility, or that on some level the attitude holder really does consider the outcome possible. As she puts it, "The reasonable part of me knows and is resigned to the fact that time passes, but the primitive creature of passion has lots sight of it" (1992: 200). In a somewhat different vein, Rubinstein (2012) suggests that "possibilities that are relevant for a desire statement may be possibilities that are circumstantially accessible, yet doxastically inaccessible" (2012: 116). Rubinstein (2017) similarly suggests that the relevant alternatives may be "a superset of the doxastic alternatives, arrived at by potentially suspending some of the subject's beliefs" (2017: 118). But it remains be to seen exactly what the rules are for calculating the right supersets.

It has also been observed in the literature that *hope* really does seem to carry the presupposition of possibility that Heim (1992) initially proposed for *want*, as evidenced by examples such as (25), and *hope* is indeed odd in the never-ending weekend sentence, as seen in (26) (see also Section 6.8 below).[5]

(25)  I want/??hope to build a perpetual motion machine.
(Portner and Rubinstein 2012: 472)

---

[5] See Jerzak 2019 for discussion of another potential issue for belief-based approaches to desire ascriptions. Jerzak argues that in some cases, desire reports have truth conditions that are sensitive to information not available to the attitude holder.

(26) ??I hope this weekend will last forever. (But I know, of course, that it will be over in a few hours.)

## 6.3 MONOTONICITY

One important way in which the better-worlds and the best-worlds approaches to *want*-sentences pull apart from each other empirically is in their predictions about monotonicity. As stressed by von Fintel (1999), the best-worlds approach makes *want*-sentences monotonic; more specifically, it predicts that if *a wants p* is true, then for any proposition $q$ such that $p$ entails $q$, *a wants q* is also true (i.e., *a wants p* is upward-entailing on $p$). The reason for this is that on the best-worlds approach, $p$ is mapped onto the scope of a universal quantifier (the restriction being the attitude holder's most desirable doxastic alternatives). So upward-entailingness is guaranteed for the same reason that *All dogs are mammals* and *All mammals are animals* together entail *All dogs are animals*: the subset relation involved in universal quantification is a transitive one. The better-worlds approach, on the other hand, does not predict upward-entailingness: just because, at each doxastic alternative, all the most similar $p$-worlds are better than all the most similar $\neg p$-worlds, there is no guarantee that any given superset of $p$-worlds (call them $q$-worlds) are such that, at each doxastic alternative, the most similar $q$-worlds are all better than all the most similar $\neg q$-worlds. To venture an analogy from the domain of individuals (since individuals are generally far easier to reason about than possible worlds), suppose (counterfactually) that all semanticists are smarter than all non-semanticists, and (perhaps truthfully) that all semanticists are linguists. It does not then follow that all linguists are smarter than all non-linguists. So the predictions of the two approaches are clear. Which is right? As it turns out, deciding whether *want*-sentences are in fact upward-entailing or not is a rather delicate matter.

Let's start with an easy set of cases that both approaches are able to handle. In a passage quoted by both Heim (1992) and von Fintel (1999), Stalnaker writes as follows:

> Suppose I am sick. I want to get well. But getting well entails having been sick, and I do not want to have been sick. Suppose there was a murder. I want to know who committed the murder. But my knowing who committed the murder entails that the murder was committed, and I never wanted the murder to have been committed.
>
> (Stalnaker 1984: 89)

## 6.3 Monotonicity

These cases look like failures of upward-entailingness and hence would seem to support the better-worlds approach over the best-worlds approach. But note a crucial feature of both examples: in the first, the attitude holder *believes* that he is sick, and in the second, the attitude holder *believes* a murder was committed. Hence a proponent of the best-worlds approach would be justified in saying that what's wrong with the inferences is not that they are false but rather that they incur a presupposition failure: as seen in Section 6.2.3, we have independent reasons for thinking that *want*-sentences presuppose that the attitude holder is not convinced that the desired outcome is guaranteed.[6] So examples like Stalnaker's are not helpful in deciding between the best-worlds and the better-worlds approaches.

Now let's turn to another kind of example, discussed by Heim (1992), building on a similar example by Asher (1987). Consider the following pair of sentences:

(27) a. Nicholas wants a free trip on the Concorde.
 b. Nicholas wants a trip on the Concorde.
 (Heim 1992: 194, based on Asher 1987: 171)

Heim writes of these sentences:

> [I]magine that Nicholas is not willing to pay the $3,000 that he believes it would cost him if he flew to Paris on the Concorde, but he would love to fly on the Concorde if he could get the trip for free. Under these circumstances [(27-a)] is true, yet [(27-b)] is false, despite the fact that taking a free trip on the Concorde, of course, implies taking a trip on the Concorde.
> 
> (Heim 1992: 194)

Is this a knockdown argument against the best-worlds approach? It turns out not to be, because a best-worlds proponent could reply

---

[6] Stalnaker's examples bear a striking resemblance to Prior's (1958) "Paradox of the Good Samaritan" involving deontic reasoning. The paradox is that we do not want (i) to entail (ii), and yet Jones helping Smith who has been robbed entails Smith having been robbed.

(i) It ought to be the case that Jones helps Smith who has been robbed.

(ii) It ought to be the case that Smith has been robbed.

This puzzle can be approached in the same way we approach its *want* variant, by endowing *ought* (and perhaps modals more generally) with the condition that the proposition they combine with (here, worlds where Smith has been robbed) not be true in all the modal base worlds (here, worlds compatible with the circumstances) (see e.g. von Fintel and Heim 2011: 63). In the modal semantics literature, this is sometimes known as the Diversity Condition (see e.g. Condoravdi 2002).

(as von Fintel does) that in testing for upward-entailingness one must control for changes to the context. If Nicholas believes that flying the Concorde costs $3,000, then in reasoning about what he wants, we consider only those worlds where this belief is true, and because of this none of the most desirable worlds are ones where he takes a trip on the Concorde. But if the context then changes so that Nicholas forms the belief that a free trip on the Concorde is possible, this affects the set of worlds compatible with Nicholas's beliefs and therefore affects the computation of what he wants: in this revised set of belief worlds, the most desirable worlds are indeed ones where he takes a trip on the Concorde (and does so for free).

In fact, von Fintel argues not only that the Concorde example is consistent with the best-worlds approach but even more strongly that only the best-worlds approach and not the better-worlds approach accurately predicts that paired desire reports like (28) or (29) in fact sound contradictory. In other words, if we do not introduce any contextual factors that affect the set of worlds being quantified over from one desire report to the next, then *want*-sentences seem to be upward-entailing after all.

(28) #Nicholas does not want a trip on the Concorde but he does want a free trip on the Concorde.

(29) #Nicholas wants a free trip on the Concorde but he does not want a trip on the Concorde.

Other authors have expressed similar intuitions pointing toward the correctness of an upward-entailing analysis of *want*-sentences. Crnič (2011: 172), for example, cites (30-a–b) as valid inferences, and Condoravdi and Lauer (2016: 32) contend that (31) "seems to be a valid piece of reasoning" (though they ultimately propose a non-monotonic semantics for *want* and suggest that (31) involves allowing indefinites to take wide scope and quantify over properties; see also Section 6.4 below).[7]

---

[7] Crnič (2011) also discusses one systematic source of apparent counterexamples to upward entailingness, namely disjunction introduction. For example, (i-a) seems not to entail (i-b), against the expectations of an upward-entailing analysis. This observation has a long history in the deontic logic literature, where it is known as Ross's Paradox, after Ross 1941. Crnič suggests a way of reconciling this with an upward-entailing analysis, but assessing it here would take us too far afield into the semantics of free choice and exhaustification, so I encourage interested readers to consult Crnič 2011.

(i) a. John wants to send this letter.
 b. John wants to send this letter or burn it.

## 6.3 Monotonicity

(30) a. I want to read five books → I want to read one book
b. I want to meet Mary and Sue → I want to meet Mary

(31) John wants to get a poodle, so he wants to get a dog.

In a similar vein, Fara (2013), reacting to a view popular in philosophy that the content of a desire report specifies exactly what it would take for the desire to be satisfied, discusses examples like (32)–(33).

(32) Fiona wants to catch a fish. (Fara 2013: 250)

(33) Charlotte wants to have some champagne. (Fara 2013: 250)

As Fara points out, (32) could intuitively be truthful in a situation where "Fiona wants to catch a fish that's big enough to make a meal; a minnow will not do" (2013: 250); similarly, (33) could intuitively be truthful in a situation where "Charlotte wants enough champagne to feel it go to her head; a thimbleful will not do" (2013: 250). (See also earlier work published by Fara as Graff 2003, as well as Lycan 2012 and Condoravdi and Lauer 2016.)

Although Fara does not explicitly connect these observations to the debate over upward-entailingness, they are directly relevant to it: if *want*-sentences are upward-entailing as the best-worlds approach would have it, then their content merely specifies *necessary conditions* for what it would take to satisfy the desire, rather than necessary and sufficient conditions. So Fara's observations seem to support an upward-entailing analysis.

That being said, Fara's reasoning has not gone unchallenged: in a reply paper, Braun (2015) suggests that what could be going on in examples like (32) is that Fiona wants to catch a meal-sized fish, and then reflects on this desire and realizes that in order to catch a meal-sized fish, she has to catch a fish, and thereby forms another desire, namely the one stated in (32). If she were to then catch a minnow, the desire named in (32) would in fact be satisfied, but her desire to catch a meal-sized fish would not be. In other words, we need to be careful not to make entailments out of what could instead be assumptions about how rational agents (should) reason. And this caution should of course look familiar from studying belief reports.[8]

---

[8] See also Moltmann (forthcoming), who interprets Fara's observations as calling for an analysis in which complement clauses in desire- and need-related attitude reports specify necessary satisfaction conditions only, whereas complement clauses in belief- and claim-related attitude reports specify necessary and sufficient satisfaction conditions.

## 6.4 CONJUNCTION INTRODUCTION AND CONFLICTING DESIRES

Recall from Chapter 2 two basic logical properties of *believe*-sentences on the Hintikkan approach: first, *believe*-sentences are closed under conjunction, in that, for an arbitrary attitude holder $a$ and arbitrary propositions $p$ and $q$, *a believes p* and *a believes q* together imply *a believes $[p \wedge q]$*. And second, paired *believe*-sentences whose contents contradict each other are themselves contradictory. As we discussed there, these are arguably desirable features of a semantics for belief reports, at least insofar as we want the semantics to be normative on how we think rational agents ought to behave.

But the situation is different for *want*-sentences. Levinson (2003) asks us to imagine an individual John who is planning his summer vacation. He considers Paris and Rome both desirable travel destinations, but does not want to expend the time or money needed to visit both cities, even though he believes that visiting both cities is in principle possible. In such a scenario, (34) seems truthful and felicitous, apparently showing us that *want*-sentences are not closed under conjunction, or, to use Levinson's terminology, do not obey conjunction introduction. And crucially, (34) does not even portray John as irrational. Thus, even if we wanted our attitude semantics to be normative on rationality, we would still not want *want*-sentences to obey conjunction introduction.

(34) John wants to visit Paris and John wants to visit Rome, but John does not want to visit Paris and Rome.

Consider now, as Levinson (2003) does, a slight variant on the previous scenario. As before, John considers Paris and Rome both desirable travel destinations, but this time he outright lacks the monetary resources to visit both cities and consequently believes that visiting both cities would be impossible. In this scenario as well, it is possible to say, without contradiction, that John wants to visit Paris and John wants to visit Rome. In other words, the semantics of *want*-sentences needs to allow for conflicting desires without resulting in contradiction. Other examples of conflicting desires culled from the literature are illustrated in (35)–(40). We see here examples where the two desires in question logically (35)–(37) or circumstantially (38) preclude each other, or else preclude each other given what the attitude holder believes (39)–(40). (The latter sort are what Rubinstein 2017 calls the "Doxastic Problem" for desire reports.)

(35) I want to play tennis (because I enjoy it), but at the same time I don't want to play tennis (because I have to teach).
(adapted from Davis 1984; Levinson 2003)

## 6.4 Conjunction Introduction and Conflicting Desires

(36) John wants to move in with his girlfriend, but he also wants to keep living alone. He can't make up his mind.
(Condoravdi and Lauer 2016: 24)

(37) I want it to rain tomorrow so the picnic gets canceled, but I (also) want it to not rain tomorrow so I can go hiking.
(adapted from Condoravdi and Lauer 2016: 24)

(38) Robert wants to marry Jane, but Robert also wants to marry Sue (and bigamy is not possible). (adapted from Portner 2005: 164)

(39) [I believe that I will teach Tuesdays and Thursdays next semester if and only if I work hard now:]
I want to teach Tuesdays and Thursdays next semester but I do not want to work hard now. (adapted from Villalta 2008: 478)

(40) [Al knows that he'll see the concert only if he takes the long drive:]
Al wants to see the concert, but Al doesn't want to take the long drive. (adapted from Phillips-Brown 2018)

The best-worlds approach to *want*-sentences erroneously predicts both that *want*-sentences should obey conjunction introduction and that paired *want*-sentences with contradictory contents should themselves be contradictory. On the best-worlds approach, if John wants to visit Paris, this means that all of his best doxastic alternatives are ones where he visits Paris. And if John wants to visit Rome, all of his best doxastic alternatives are ones where he visits Rome. The only way for this to be the case is if all of his best doxastic alternatives are ones in which he visits both Paris and Rome. This follows from the same reasoning that guarantees that if all dogs are animals and all dogs are quadrupeds, then all dogs are quadruped animals. And by the same token, if there are no doxastic alternatives where John visits both Paris and Rome, then we end up with a logical contradiction.[9]

A number of solutions have been proposed for solving the problem of conjunction introduction and conflicting desires. As recently reviewed by Phillips-Brown (2018), most of these solutions fall into one of two major categories. One category entertains the idea that *want*-sentences do not have a fixed ordering source: preferences can be ranked in

---

[9] Assessing whether Heim's better-world semantics for *want*-sentences also makes the same erroneous predictions regarding conjunction introduction and conflicting desire is less straightforward. For relevant discussion, see Levinson (2003: 229–230); Crnič (2011: 171); and Phillips-Brown 2018.

different ways. Levinson (2003) and Crnič (2011) both propose versions of this idea. Suppose, for example, that John's desire to visit Paris is validated relative to an ordering source that places high value on studying French, whereas John's desire to visit Rome is validated relative to an ordering source that places high value on studying Italian. Then, there is no contradiction. (And although the terminology 'ordering source' suggests the best-worlds approach, this solution can also be implemented in the better-worlds approach, by countenancing multiple flavors of comparative desirability.) As Phillips-Brown (2018) discusses, the major challenge facing this solution is that it needs to be reined in with principles telling us what ordering sources are available in any given context. Consider again the example in (41). There are scenarios compatible with (41) in which there is no way of reading (42) as being true. But if we are allowed to use an ordering source that places high value on seeing the concert, then we erroneously predict that (42) has a true reading relative to that ordering source. Of course this is not fatal for the multiple ordering sources approach, but it remains to be seen whether it can be reined in in a principled way.

(41) [Al knows that he'll see the concert only if he takes the long drive:]
Al wants to see the concert, but Al doesn't want to take the long drive.  (adapted from Phillips-Brown 2018)

(42) Al wants to take the long drive.

The other category of solutions entertains the idea that *want*-sentences do not have a fixed modal base. In particular, Villalta (2008) proposes that the modal base can include worlds outside the attitude holder's doxastic alternatives (cf. also Rubinstein 2012, 2017 and Section 6.6 below). The primary challenge facing this approach is similar to the one facing the multiple ordering sources approach: we are owed a principled account of which worlds outside the attitude holder's doxastic alternatives are allowed into the modal base. Phillips-Brown (2018) entertains a couple of possibilities but points out problems for both and ends up proposing an alternative account of conflicting desires whereby *want*-sentences have just one fixed ordering source, together with a modal base that employs what Phillips Brown calls *coarse worlds*: worlds that do not decide the truth of every proposition. (This builds on Yalcin's 2018 question-sensitive semantics for belief reports, reviewed in Section 2.4.2 above.) The modal base can vary in terms of which propositions it assigns truth values to, but it is fixed in the sense that it never contradicts the

## 6.4 Conjunction Introduction and Conflicting Desires

attitude holder's beliefs. Phillips-Brown argues that this gives us the kind of flexibility we need to handle conflicting desires in an appropriately constrained way.

Another recent approach to conflicting desires that deserves mention is that proposed by Condoravdi and Lauer (2016). These authors propose that an agent at a world has a set of preference structures, each structure encoding some preference source such as desire, inclination, personal moral code, or obligation. Each one of these preference structures is modeled as a set of propositions plus an importance ranking. On their view, *want*-sentences are underspecified for preference structure, and in that sense this view is similar to the one mentioned above wherein we allow multiple ordering sources. But these authors also allow for conflicting desires even with a fixed preference structure by proposing that the truth of a sentence *a wants p* simply depends on $p$ being a member of the set of highest-importance-ranked propositions in the relevant preference structure associated with $a$. There are no inherent constraints on the logical relationship among these propositions, so the set can freely contain contradictory propositions. (This is similar to the Montague–Scott approach to belief reports: see Section 2.4.3 above.) That being said, the lack of logical relationships also means that *want*-sentences end up not being monotonic. Condoravdi and Lauer suggest that apparently monotonic behavior can be analyzed by scoping the offending material outside the *want*-predicate. But it is unlikely that all apparent cases of monotonicity can be handled in this fashion: see especially Fara 2013 and Section 6.3 above.

Finally, yet another style of approach is found in the work of Levinson 2003 and Lassiter 2011. As already mentioned above, Levinson's approach involves multiple ordering sources. But in addition to multiple ordering sources, Levinson's (2003) account of *want*-sentences also has a probabilistic component that borrows concepts from expected utility theory. Levinson argues that we need such a component to account for sentences involving risk assessment like *John wants to buy home insurance*, which intuitively may be true even if John's absolutely ideal outcome would be to not buy insurance and never need it (cf. also van Rooij 1999). See also Lassiter 2011 for an approach similar to Levinson's but without multiple ordering sources. For Lassiter, *want*-sentences are true iff the expected value of the desired outcome is significantly greater than the average expected value of contextually supplied alternatives. According to Lassiter, this approach enables a scenario where visiting Paris and visiting Rome can both be wanted even if they conflict with each other, provided there are enough alternatives entering the calculation to bring down the average expected value of the standard of comparison. For reactions to this style of analysis, see also Büring 2003, as well as von Fintel 2012 (whose focus is on a similar problem associated with deontic modals).

Ultimately the verdict is still out on the proper way of handling conflicting desires. Whatever the correct solution ends up being, it seems likely that it will also help make sense of two other intuitively related and noteworthy properties of *want*-sentences, namely GRADABILITY and FOCUS-sensitivity, to which we now turn.

## 6.5 GRADABILITY

It has occasionally been noted in the literature that, unlike *believe*, *want* behaves like a gradable predicate (Levinson 2003; Villalta 2008; Lassiter 2011; Anand and Hacquard 2013; Grano 2017b). For example, the following data taken from Grano 2017b: 593 show that, unlike *believe*, *want* participates in comparative constructions (43-a)/(44-a) and superlatives (43-b)/(44-b), and admits degree modifiers like *very much* (43-c)/(44-c).

(43) a. John wants to go to Paris **more than** he wants to go to London.
 b. What John wants the **most** is to be happy.
 c. John wants **very much** to leave.

(44) a. ?John believes he'll go to Paris **more than** he believes he'll go to London.
 b. ?What John believes the **most** is that he'll be happy.
 c. ?John believes **very much** that he'll leave.

(Grano 2017b: 593)

Neither the best-worlds approach nor the better-worlds approach to *want*-sentences are equipped to handle such data without adjustments to the proposals. In the best-worlds approach, the ordering source built into the meaning of *want* singles out the most desirable worlds, sealing off any access to less desirable worlds that would be needed to handle a comparison of relative desirability like (43-a). The better-worlds approach, while based on a notion of comparative desirability of worlds, also falls short, since the standard of comparison is hardwired in and therefore cannot be manipulated in the way that something like (43-a) would require.

In order to handle cases like (43-a), then, what seems to be needed is to strip out from the meaning of *want* the superlativity (on the

## 6.5 Gradability

best-worlds approach) or the fixed standard of comparison (on the better-worlds approach). Villalta (2008) makes a proposal exactly along these lines.

By way of background, an influential approach to modeling gradability that has been explored extensively for gradable adjectives like *tall* or *happy* is to enrich the semantic ontology to include degrees, and to analyze such adjectives as relations between degrees and individuals, as sketched in (45) for *tall*. (See e.g. Kennedy 1999, and see Morzycki 2016 for a useful overview.)

(45)  $[[tall]] = [\lambda d.[\lambda x.x \text{ is tall to degree } d]]$

The degree argument in (45) is very useful for analyzing the semantics of sentences like (46-a–e), where the bolded material can be understood as in some way or another saturating, quantifying over, or otherwise manipulating that degree argument.

(46)  a. John is **six feet** tall.
b. John is **very/extremely** tall.
c. John is tall **enough to reach the ceiling**.
d. John is **as** tall **as Bill**.
e. John is tall**er than Bill**.

Somewhat trickier are sentences like (47), where those committed to a degree-based semantics have to say something special about how the degree argument is dealt with in the absence of any other material that takes care of it.

(47)  John is tall.

The usual strategy is to posit a silent morpheme or type-shifting operator POS (short for 'positive') that manipulates the degree argument in such a way that (48) ends up having truth conditions along the lines of 'John's height meets or exceeds some contextually determined threshold' (see especially Kennedy 2007).

Villalta proposes a similar treatment of *want*, as a relation between degrees, propositions, and individuals, as in (48). This degree argument can then be manipulated in the same way that it is for a gradable adjective like *tall*, enabling the kinds of structures seen in (43) above.

(48)  $[[want]] = [\lambda d.[\lambda p.[\lambda x.x \text{ wants } p \text{ to degree } d]]]$

What about *want*-sentences that do not involve an overt degree morpheme? Villalta (2008) suggests that unmodified *want*-sentences involve a silent degree morpheme, but rather than assigning it a positive semantics as is needed for gradable adjectives, she assigns it a superlative semantics so as to result in (her version of) Heim's better-worlds semantics for *want*-sentences: the desired proposition is asserted to be more desirable than *any* relevant alternative. (Recall that for Heim, the relevant alternatives are calculated by taking the negation of the desired proposition. Though Villalta has a different take on this – see Section 6.6 below.)

Is it right to assign a superlative semantics to unmodified *want*-sentences? One potential reason for thinking otherwise has to do with the coherence of formulations like (49). If bare *want*-sentences like *John wants to go to Paris* build in a superlative semantics, then (49) should be contradictory in the same way as *John is the tallest of all but Bill is even taller than John*. Compare also (50), where we get an incoherent result by bringing in explicit superlative morphosyntax.

(49)    John wants to go to Paris, but he wants to go to Rome **even more**.

(50)    #John wants **most of all** to go to Paris, but he wants to go to Rome **even more**.

It should also be pointed out that building gradability into the semantics of *want*-sentences will not automatically solve the problem of conflicting desires discussed in the previous section: even if we use an equative structure (*as ... as*) to explicitly equate two degrees of desire, it is still possible for their contents to conflict without contradiction, as seen in (51).

(51)    John wants to move in with his girlfriend {**just as much as**/**to exactly the same degree that**} he wants to keep living alone.

For a recent take on gradability in attitude reports, see Pasternak 2019.

## 6.6 FOCUS-SENSITIVITY

Building on earlier observations by Dretske (1972, 1975) (cf. also von Fintel 1999), Villalta (2008) argues that, unlike *believe*, *want* is focus-sensitive; i.e., the truth conditions of *want*-sentences can be affected by what in the complement of *want* is focused.

Villalta has us consider a scenario wherein teaching schedules and teaching assignments are being discussed at a department faculty meeting. Lisa would prefer Lara to teach syntax rather than John, but given that John is the only option for teaching syntax, she would prefer that he teach syntax on a Tuesday-Thursday schedule rather on a Monday-Wednesday-Friday schedule. Then the crucial observation

## 6.6 Focus-Sensitivity

is that in this scenario, (52-a) is truthful because it has a meaning along the lines of (52-b), whereas (53-a) is false because it has a meaning along the lines of (53-b). (I follow Villalta here in using all caps to signal the focused constituent.)

(52) a. Lisa wants John to teach syntax ON TUESDAYS AND THURSDAYS.
(Villalta 2008: 496)
b. ≈ John teaching syntax on Tuesdays and Thursdays is more desirable to Lisa than John teaching syntax on other kinds of weekly schedules.

(53) a. Lisa wants JOHN to teach syntax on Tuesdays and Thursdays.
(Villalta 2008: 496)
b. ≈ John teaching syntax on Tuesdays and Thursdays is more desirable to Lisa than someone else teaching syntax on Tuesdays and Thursdays.

Villalta uses these and other facts to argue for a modified version of Heim's better-worlds semantics for *want*-sentences, given in (54), which incorporates a new relation of comparative desirability $>_{DES_{a,w}}$ that can be defined in terms of Heim's relation $>_{a,w}$.[10] Whereas Heim's semantics involves universal quantification over the attitude holder's doxastic alternatives, Villalta's revised approach involves universal quantification over a set of contextually supplied propositional alternatives (the connection to belief still operative in that the propositional alternatives are presupposed to be consistent with the attitude holder's doxastic alternatives). And whereas Heim's semantics involves the relative desirability of *p*-worlds over maximally similar ¬*p*-worlds, Villalta's semantics involves the relative desirability of *p*-worlds over the contextually supplied alternatives. Building on Rooth's (1982, 1992) theory of focus interpretation, the computation of the alternatives is affected by focus, thereby leading to an account of the data in (52)–(53) above.

---

[10] Aside from focus-sensitivity, Villalta argues that her revision to Heim's semantics is also supported by facts about *want*-sentences in scenarios where more than two alternatives are present. But see Rubinstein 2012: 111–117 for a reply to this argument, showing that the data are in fact consistent with Heim's (1992) negation-based version of the better-worlds analysis. It should also be pointed out that (54) is not Villalta's final semantics for *want*-sentences; she ends up proposing a revised degree-based variant on p. 515, discussed in Section 6.5 above.

(54) $[\![\text{want}_C]\!]^g(p)(a)(w)$ is defined iff $\forall q \in g(C)$: $\text{DOX}_{a,w} \cap q \neq \emptyset$
if defined, $[\![\text{want}_C]\!]^g(p)(a)(w) = 1$ iff ...
$\forall q: q \neq p \wedge q \in g(C): p >_{DES_{a,w}} q$
where for any $p, q \subseteq W$, $p >_{DES_{a,w}} q$ iff $\forall w'' \in q \, \exists w' \in p$ such that $w' >_{a,w} w''$, and it is not the case that $\forall w' \in p \, \exists w'' \in q$ such that $w'' >_{a,w} w'$  (Villalta 2008: 480)

It seems highly plausible that there is a deep analytical connection between the facts from the last three sections concerning conflicting desires, gradability, and focus-sensitivity: all point toward the conclusion that *want*-sentences are more relative and more context-sensitive than *believe*-sentences.

## 6.7 PRESUPPOSITION PROJECTION

One might be struck by the fact that so much of the discussion in this chapter has been framed as a reaction to the initial hypothesis that *want*-sentences express universal quantification over bouletic alternatives. Suppose we had instead started with the hypothesis that *want*-sentences express some relation between individuals and propositions while remaining neutral about the nature of that relation, similar to the Montague–Scott approach to belief reports offered as a possible reaction to the PROBLEM OF LOGICAL OMNISCIENCE in Section 2.4.3 above. Then, we would have not made any faulty predictions about entailment relations between *believe*-sentences and *want*-sentences (Section 6.2.3), the felicity of desire ascriptions with contents believed to be inevitable or impossible (Section 6.2.4), monotonicity (Section 6.3), or conjunction introduction and conflicting desires (Section 6.4). Meanwhile, gradability (Section 6.5) and focus-sensitivity (Section 6.6) would have both still required some treatment, but not necessarily one that necessitates reference to the attitude holder's doxastic alternatives.

So is there any good reason to think that *want*-sentences involve the attitude holder's doxastic alternatives if one is not pre-committed to an underlyingly Hintikka-like architecture for attitude reports? No doubt there are important connections between desire and belief, but why think that this is the business of grammar? To address this question we will come back full circle to Heim (1992) and consider her paper's framing motivation, which is to make sense of some puzzling facts about PRESUPPOSITION PROJECTION.

In particular, Heim begins with an observation due to Karttunen (1974) that, "if the complement of an attitude sentences presupposes *p*, then that sentence as a whole presupposes that the attitude-holder believes *p*" (Heim 1992: 183). For example, (55) presupposes that Patricks owns a cello. Heim observes that whereas at first glance (55) seems to carry the same presupposition, (56) reveals that the presupposition can actually merely be that Patrick *believes* that he owns a cello.

(55) Patrick wants to sell his cello. (Heim 1992: 183)

(56) Patrick is under the misconception that he owns a cello, and he wants to sell his cello. (Heim 1992: 183)

Why should desire reports cause ordinary presuppositions to turn into presuppositions about the attitude holder's beliefs? Heim's proposal is that this is because at some level of representation, computing the meaning of (55) involves adding the proposition named by *Patrick sells his cello* to the set of worlds constituting Patrick's beliefs, thereby inducing a presupposition about belief, exactly parallel to the way an unembedded use of *Patrick sells his cello* would be added to the set of worlds constituting the Common Ground, thereby inducing a presupposition about the Common Ground.

Much subsequent work on *want*-sentences, although largely building on Heim's approach, has been motivated by concerns other than presupposition projection; von Fintel (1999), for example, is interested in the distribution of negative polarity items, and Villalta (2008) is interested in the relative distribution of indicative and subjunctive MOOD in Spanish. Geurts (1998) and Maier (2015) both deal with presupposition projection in *want*-sentences, and both follow Heim in making important use of the idea that *want*-sentences have a doxastic component. Maier, in particular, proposes that "desires and other non-doxastic attitudes are asymmetrically dependent on beliefs" (2015: 205).

To be sure, the behavior of *want*-sentences with respect to presupposition projection does not *prove* that *want*-sentences have a doxastic component. But it does constitute grammatical evidence in favor of such a connection, and one that does not depend on any special starting assumptions about how attitude reports are supposed to work. Any fully adequate semantics for *want*-sentences ultimately owes us an account of the observed presupposition projection facts.

## 6.8 THE TYPOLOGY OF ATTITUDE PREDICATES

In (57) we take stock of the empirical differences between *want* and *believe* that have been the focus of this chapter.

(57) a. *want* incorporates belief semantics; *believe* does not incorporate desire semantics.
b. *want* gives rise to (apparently) non-monotonic behavior; *believe* does not.
c. *want* (apparently) does not obey conjunction introduction; *believe* does.
d. Paired *want*-sentences can have conflicting contents without portraying the attitude holder as irrational; paired *believe*-sentences generally cannot.
e. *want* is gradable; *believe* is not.
f. *want* is focus-sensitive; *believe* is not.

Should we pursue a theory in which all of these differences are deeply connected? Or should we pursue a more modular approach whereby some or all of these differences are independent from one another? The answer to that question will depend in no small part on the extent to which the observed clustering of properties is accidental or principled. And to investigate this question, we need to scale our investigation up to other attitude predicates both in English and in other languages. Indeed, one of the major interests in probing the fine-grained semantic differences between *believe* and *want* lies not just in better understanding the semantics of these two verbs *per se* but also in using them as a starting point for investigating semantic uniformity and variation across the full range of attitude predicates that are attested in natural language.

In this connection, Stalnaker (1984) adopts the term *acceptance* as a "broader concept than belief; it is a generic propositional attitude concept with such notions as presupposing, presuming, postulating, positing, assuming and supposing as well as believing falling under it". Stalnaker goes on to say that, "To accept a proposition is to treat it as a true proposition in one way or another – to ignore, for the moment at least, the possibility that it is false." As a diagnostic, he suggests that "one may say that a propositional attitude concept is an acceptance concept if the attitude is said to be *correct* whenever the proposition is true" (1984: 79–80). On the linguistic end, we might correspondingly follow Stalnaker's lead in hypothesizing that the verbs *believe, presuppose, presume, postulate, posit, assume*, and *suppose* all name attitudes of acceptance. And if they all pattern as *believe* does with respect to the properties enumerated in (57), that would constitute support for the view that this clustering of properties is not accidental.

Two natural follow-up questions are: Is *want* also a member of a broader family of attitude predicates that share the same basic

## 6.8 The Typology of Attitude Predicates

properties? And are there yet other attitude predicates that cannot be neatly categorized as *believe*-like or *want*-like? In the remainder of this section we'll take up these two questions in turn.

Turning first to the question of *want*'s kinship, I first want to lay bare an obvious syntactic fact that we have been ignoring up to this point: in English, *believe* can combine with finite clauses whereas *want* cannot:

(58)    a.   Beatrix believes that it will rain tomorrow.
        b.   *Beatrix wants that it will rain tomorrow.

Could this syntactic difference be a correlate of one or more of the semantic differences we have uncovered? Consider also Stalnaker's proposal that belief is an attitude of acceptance – what could be more acceptance-like than an unembedded finite clause, whose canonical function is to present a proposition as being true? This parallelism between the form of unembedded assertions and the form of complements to *believe* was not lost on Stalnaker, who quoted Fodor's position that "it could hardly be an accident that declarative sentences of English constitute the (syntactic) objects of verbs like 'believe'" (Fodor 1978: 503, quoted by Stalnaker 1984: 59).

What this suggests is that we might sort attitude predicates into two classes depending on whether they can combine with a finite clause, and then investigate the semantic concomitants of the two classes. As it turns out, the relative distribution of finite and nonfinite clauses in English ends up being somewhat messy. Much of the mess is cleaned up by recognizing that there are several kinds of nonfinite clauses: one must distinguish (at least) raising infinitives, CONTROL infinitives, *for-to* infinitives, and exceptional case-marking (ECM) or raising-to-object infinitives. With these finer-grained categories, interesting semantic correlates are discoverable; see e.g. Moulton 2009, who argues that ECM infinitives occur only in doxastic contexts, as well as Grano 2016a (cf. also Portner 1997), where I argue that *for-to* infinitives are essentially the opposite, occurring only in non-doxastic contexts.

And if we turn to the Romance languages, we find a similar phenomenon with a somewhat cleaner distribution and whose semantic correlates have been investigated much more extensively: mood choice. In Romance languages, finite complement clauses occur with either indicative or subjunctive mood morphology, and the choice is determined in part by the embedding verb. With some important exceptions, translation equivalents of 'believe' tend to combine with indicative complements, whereas translation equivalents of 'want' combine with subjunctive complements. And the facts that emerge when we scale up from 'believe' and 'want' render plausible the hypothesis that mood choice is not idiosyncratic but rather reflects some semantic properties of the embedding verb. Based in part on mood choice facts, Bolinger (1968) proposes a distinction between embedding predicates that are *representational* (similar to Stalnaker's concept *acceptance*), which take the indicative, and embedding predicates that are *volitional*, which take the subjunctive.

Much subsequent work has been concerned with refining these two categories in light of more recent developments in attitude semantics. Giorgi and Pianesi (1997), for example, working with a best-worlds semantics for *want*-sentences, propose that the predicates that select for the subjunctive are those that have a non-null ordering source. In a different vein, Villalta (2008), working with her own variant of the better-worlds semantics for *want*-sentences, proposes that in Spanish, the predicates that select for the subjunctive are those that are gradable. These include translation equivalents of *want, prefer, fear, regret, be glad, be surprised, doubt, order, advise, suggest, make,* and *achieve*. Another influential approach, exemplified by Giannakidou (1998, 1999), proposes that the indicative mood is selected by veridical attitude predicates; veridicality is a concept bearing close similarity to acceptance in Stalnaker's sense and representationality in Bolinger's sense. See also Giannakidou and Mari (forthcoming) for an updated version of this approach based on the notion of subjective veridicality. It has also been argued that the finite/nonfinite distinction, the indicative/subjunctive distinction, and their cross-linguistic analogues play an important role in how children learn the meanings of attitude verbs like *think* and *want*; see e.g. Hacquard 2014 and Hacquard and Lidz 2019.

Aside from mood choice, another phenomenon that has been found to be relevant in identifying categories of attitude predicates has to do with the availability of epistemic interpretations for embedded modals. Anand and Hacquard (2013), in particular, show that the modal verb *have* (which is in principle compatible with both deontic and epistemic interpretations) can have an epistemic interpretation when embedded under *believe*, as in (59), but not when it is embedded under *want*, as in (60). Generalizing out from here, the authors propose that epistemic modals are available only under attitudes of acceptance in Stalnaker's sense, and they propose an account whereby attitudes of acceptance are those attitudes that quantify over an information state, to which epistemic modals bear an anaphoric dependency.

(59) John believes that Paul has to be innocent.

(60) John wants Paul to have to be innocent.
(adapted from Anand and Hacquard 2013)

## 6.8 The Typology of Attitude Predicates

We turn now to the second question raised above: Are there attitude predicates that cannot be neatly categorized as *believe*-like or *want*-like? In a word, yes. One salient example is *hope* (and its negative counterpart *fear*). As discussed by Anand and Hacquard (2013), *hope* is *believe*-like in that it asserts something about the attitude holder's doxastic state: *a hopes p* entails that *a* believes *p* to be possible. Compare (61), repeated from above, which illustrates that *want* tolerates attitude holder-relative counterfactuality, with (62).

(61)   I **want** this weekend to last forever. (But I know, of course, that it will be over in a few hours.)           (Heim 1992: 199)

(62)   #I **hope** this weekend will last forever. (But I know, of course, that it will be over in a few hours.)

At the same time, *hope* is *want*-like in that *a hopes p* also asserts that *a* has a preference for *p*. Given these mixed semantic properties, it is surely no accident that it also displays mixed mood selection behavior: in Spanish, for example, *esperar* 'hope' selects the subjunctive, whereas in French, *espérer* 'hope' selects the indicative (and see Portner and Rubinstein 2012 for a relevant account of mood choice in French). In fact, Anand and Hacquard (2013) show that *hope* is even mixed with respect to the embedded epistemic modal diagnostic: it allows embedded epistemic possibility modals but not embedded epistemic necessity modals.

Another class of attitude predicates that warrant discussion are those that involve commitment to action. In Grano 2017b, for example, drawing in part on Sag and Pollard (1991), I identify predicates that involve an internal mental commitment to take action such as *decide*, *intend*, *plan*, and *try*; predicates that involve a public commitment to take action such as *agree*, *offer*, *promise*, and *swear*; and predicates that involve a cause or attempted cause to create a commitment to take action such as *beg*, *order*, *persuade*, and *urge*. (See also White and Rawlins 2018 on *decide* and Condoravdi and Lauer 2011 on *promise*.)[11]

Focusing on *intend*, I show in Grano 2017b that *intend* patterns in some ways like *believe*, in other ways like *want*, and in yet other ways unlike both. I argue that the *believe*-like properties of *intend* follow from the fact that *intend* involves commitment to action, which endows

---

[11] Similarly to the way assertions are the speech act counterpart of belief, there is also a close connection between directives, on the one hand, and intentions, promises, and persuasions, on the other hand, in that all have to do with commitment to take action. See also Grano 2015 for an exploration of this connection. Rounding out the picture, see Uegaki 2016, 2019 and Mayr 2019 on question-embedding attitude reports.

it with Hintikka-esque rational properties not found with *want*. The *want*-like properties, I argue, follow from the fact that *want* and *intend* are both based on a preference semantics (this builds on Condoravdi and Lauer 2016). And the properties unique to *intend* stem from the fact that *intend*, unlike both *believe* and *want*, establishes a relation of responsibility between the attitude holder and the outcome named by its complement (this builds on Farkas 1988).

The predicate *try* also deserves special mention: unlike *believe*, *want* and *intend*, *try* is used not only to name an attitude but also to assert that action has been undertaken. Sharvit (2003) argues that this action component of *try* renders it highly similar to modal analyses of progressive aspect; see also Grano 2011, 2017a.

It should be apparent from this brief survey that there is a wide range of semantic variation in attitude predicates, and still a lot of work to be done on the less-studied ones. The fine-grained similarities and differences that have been uncovered so far suggest that ultimately, the question is not "How many categories of attitude predicates are there?" but rather "What are the semantic parameters along which attitude predicates divide and what constraints are there on combinations of parameter settings?"

## 6.9 DISCUSSION QUESTIONS

(i) Consider the following data from Iatridou 2000: 243:

(63) I have what I want.

(64) I live in Bolivia because I want to live in Bolivia.

(65) A: You're drunk!
B: Yes, and I want to be because only this way can I forget about …

How do these examples bear on Heim's (1992) suggestion that *want*-sentences have an undefined semantics when the relevant proposition is entailed by the attitude holder's doxastic alternatives (or a superset thereof that ignores beliefs about intended actions)?

(ii) As discussed above, Heim's better-worlds semantics for *want*-sentences erroneously predicts (before adding the presuppositional component) that if *a believes p* or *a believes ¬p* is true, then *a wants p* is also true. Von Fintel's best-worlds approach also erroneously predicts an entailment from *a believes p* to *a wants p*.

But does it also predict an entailment from *a believes ¬p* to *a wants p*? Why or why not?

(iii) Whereas *want* cannot take an explicit standard of comparison unless comparative morphology is added, neighboring expressions *would rather* and *prefer* both do so, in the former case introduced by *than* (66-a) and in the latter case introduced by *to* (66-b). Can the technology discussed in this chapter be recruited to assign an appropriate semantics to sentences like these? What would an appropriate semantics look like? And do expressions like these lend credence to the idea that the grammar treats desirability as an inherently gradable notion (unlike, say, belief)?

(66)  a. John would rather visit Paris than Rome.
      b. John prefers visiting Paris to visiting Rome.

(iv) Farkas (1992) coins the term 'fiction verbs' for a class of predicates including *dream, imagine,* and *lie* which are interesting in that they can combine with finite clauses (and Romance equivalents combine with indicative complements) despite the fact that they are ordinarily used in contexts where neither the speaker nor the attitude holder seems to consider the content of the attitude true. Should these verbs be considered attitudes of acceptance in Stalnaker's (1984) sense? Why or why not? And if so, does Stalnaker's diagnostic for what counts as an attitude of acceptance need to be revised at all?

## 6.10 FURTHER READING

Three essential starting points for the semantics of *want*-sentences are: Stalnaker 1984: Chapt. 5; Heim 1992; von Fintel 1999. Subsequent work that deserves close study includes: Levinson 2003; Villalta 2008; Crnič 2011: Chapt. 3 and appendix; Lassiter 2011: Chapts. 5–6; Rubinstein 2012: Chapt. 3; Rubinstein 2017; Condoravdi and Lauer 2016; Phillips-Brown 2018. For a more philosophically oriented perspective, see Fara 2013 and Braun's (2015) reply. As for the broader typology of attitude predicates, Moltmann 1994; Asher 1987 are useful resources. The vast literature on mood choice is also an excellent point of entry; see Portner 2018; Giannakidou and Mari forthcoming for recent surveys.

# 7 Other Topics

## 7.1 INTRODUCTION

In this final chapter, we round up three additional important topics relevant to the grammar of attitude reports that have not been dealt with in the previous chapters: attitude reports and embedded TENSE (Section 7.2), NEG RAISING (Section 7.3), and INTENSIONAL TRANSITIVE VERBS (Section 7.4).

## 7.2 ATTITUDE REPORTS AND EMBEDDED TENSE

### 7.2.1 Introduction

Tenses are grammatical mechanisms for relating the time of a described event or situation to an evaluation time, which in unembedded contexts is typically the utterance time.[1] For example, (1) – by virtue of present tense *is* – is used to assert that the time of Beatrix's happiness *coincides with* the utterance time, whereas (2) – by virtue of past tense *was* – is used to assert that the time of Beatrix's happiness *precedes* the utterance time.[2]

(1)   Beatrix **is** happy.                                        *present tense*

---

[1] A more sophisticated treatment would have the relationship between event/situation time and evaluation time mediated by a so-called reference or topic time that is introduced by aspectual morphology; see e.g. Klein 1994; Kratzer 1998a. Here, and in what follows, I mostly ignore aspect, since it is largely orthogonal to the interaction between tense and attitude reports.

[2] Traditional descriptions of tense would also include the future tense as well, illustrated in (i).

   (i)   Beatrix **will be** happy.                                *future tense?*

Whether the future should be considered on a par with present and past tenses is a source of some controversy, given some of its peculiar semantic and morphosyntactic properties. See Bochnak 2019 for a recent overview.

## 7.2 Attitude Reports and Embedded Tense

(2)　Beatrix **was** happy.　　　　　　　　　　　　　　　　*past tense*

When tenses are embedded in attitude reports, they give rise to rather complicated interpretive behavior that poses challenges for simple theories of tense. My goal in what follows is to lay out the core facts and some of the main lines of theorizing that they have inspired. In order to get off the ground, we begin with some tense basics (Section 7.2.2), and then sketch a simple theory of how tense works in attitude reports that accounts for some easy cases (Section 7.2.3). Then, we turn to the two main kinds of challenges for the simple theory: the phenomena know as SEQUENCE OF TENSE (Section 7.2.4) and DOUBLE ACCESS (Section 7.2.5), respectively.

### 7.2.2 Tense Basics

To give us a concrete starting point, I'll begin by assuming a theory of tense that roughly follows what is laid out by von Fintel and Heim (2011: Chapt. 6). The key idea is that in addition to relativizing denotations to a world (and assignment function, which I will continue to suppress when not relevant), we also need to relativize denotations to a time, and accordingly, make some expressions time-sensitive.

For example, in the same way that the set of happy individuals varies from world to world, it also varies from time to time:

(3)　$[[\text{happy}]]^{w,t} = [\lambda x . x \text{ is happy in } w \text{ at } t]$

We furthermore assume that by default, just as the world parameter is set to the actual world (or the world in which the utterance is made), the time parameter is set to the time at which the utterance is made. This has as a consequence that we can treat the present tense as semantically vacuous:

(4)　$[[\text{Beatrix is happy}]]^{w,t} = \text{Beatrix is happy in } w \text{ at } t$

Past tense, by contrast, can be treated as a morpheme that induces abstraction over the time parameter of its complement and contributes existential quantification over times that are prior to the matrix evaluation time and at which the property of times denoted by its complement is true, as in (5), where $<$ is the relation of temporal precedence (I use $i$ to symbolize the type of times, so $p_{\langle i, st \rangle}$ is a variable over functions from times to functions from worlds to truth values):

(5)　$[[\text{PAST}]]^{w,t} = [\lambda p_{\langle i, st \rangle} . \exists t' < t : p(t')(w)]$
　　　　　　　　　　(adapted from von Fintel and Heim 2011: 71)

Now we define a new variant of Intensional Functional Application, which was first introduced in Section 2.2.2 above. In this new variant, it induces abstraction over both the world and the time parameter rather than over the world parameter only, as illustrated in (6):

(6) **Intensional Functional Application** (time-and-world variant): If $\alpha$ is a branching node with daughters $\beta$ and $\gamma$, then for any possible world $w$ and time $t$, if $[[\beta]]^{w,t}$ is a function whose domain contains $[\lambda t'.[\lambda w'.[[\gamma]]^{w',t'}]]$, then $[[\alpha]] = [[\beta]]^{w,t}([\lambda t'.[\lambda w'.[[\gamma]]^{w',t'}]])$.

Assuming that at the relevant level of representation in the syntax, a tense morpheme combines with the entire (pre-tensed) sentence, this setup yields outcomes like (7) for past tense sentences. In prose, 'There is some time prior to the evaluation time (utterance time) at which Beatrix is happy.'

(7) $[[\text{Beatrix was happy}]]^{w,t} = \exists t' < t\ [\text{Beatrix is happy in } w \text{ at } t']$

This simple sketch leaves many questions open. Should times be treated as instantaneous points or as intervals? How does tense interact with aspect? Is it correct to treat past tense as existentially quantifying over a past time, or should it instead introduce a contextually specified past reference time? And relatedly, is it correct to treat times as a parameter of evaluation, or should they instead be treated as pronouns in the syntax (paralleling the same question about the status of worlds discussed in Chapter 4)? See Partee 1973, Dowty 1977, and Ogihara 2007 for discussion of some of these questions. For our immediate purposes, however, the foregoing should be sufficient for appreciating how tense behaves in attitude reports, and we can leave these questions open.[3]

### 7.2.3 Tense Binding in Attitude Reports

An initial idea about how to integrate tense semantics with attitude reports (to be revised shortly) goes as follows. First, we need to relativize DOXASTIC ALTERNATIVES and other attitude alternatives not just to an individual and world, as in (8), but also to a time, as in (9), reflecting the fact that beliefs and other attitudes change over time.

---

[3] Yet another question concerns cross-linguistic applicability. Some languages are tenseless in that, while they have resources for describing the temporal location of an event or state, the grammar does not force sentences to encode a specific relation to an evaluation time. See Lin 2012 and Tonhauser 2015 for relevant cross-linguistic overviews. The relationship between tenselessness and the grammar of attitude reports is a rather understudied area, but see Bochnak et al. (2019) for a recent investigation in this vein.

## 7.2 Attitude Reports and Embedded Tense

(8) $\text{DOX}_{a,w} = \{w' \mid w'$ is compatible with $a$'s beliefs in $w\}$

(9) $\text{DOX}_{a,w,t} = \{w' \mid w'$ is compatible with $a$'s beliefs in $w$ at $t\}$

We accordingly rewrite the denotation for *believe* and other attitude verbs to reflect this update, as in (10).

(10) $[[\text{believe}]]^{w,t} = [\lambda p_{\langle s,t \rangle}.[\lambda x.\forall w' \in \text{DOX}_{x,w,t}: p(w')]]$

This in turn yields outcomes like (11) for a present-tense clause embedded under a present-tense attitude verb.

(11) $[[\text{Beatrix believes it's raining}]]^{w,t} =$
$\forall w' \in \text{DOX}_{b,w,t}$: it's raining in $w'$ at $t$

Notice that on this view, the time that figures into the content of the attitude holder's belief (here, the time at which it is raining) is identical to the time at which the attitude holder reportedly holds the belief. This turns out to be not quite right (see especially von Stechow 1995). The standard way of illustrating the problem involves reasoning about attitudes that are explicitly time-related, like (12).

(12) Beatrix believes that it's one o'clock.

Suppose I utter (12) at two o'clock. Then according to the view just sketched, Beatrix believes that at two o'clock it is one o'clock. This is a contradictory belief. And yet intuitively, if I utter (12) at two o'clock, we would say not that Beatrix believes a contradiction, but rather that Beatrix is mistaken about what time it is. The way to formalize this intuition involves rethinking tenses in attitude reports so that they are not anchored to the 'objective' utterance time of the attitude report but rather to the subjective 'now' of the attitude holder, i.e., the time at which the attitude holder locates herself. This is a flavor of *de se* semantics, discussed in Chapter 5. Whereas Chapter 5 was primarily concerned with what we might call *individual de se* (which has to do with whom the attitude holder identifies as herself), what we are now talking about is *temporal de se*, sometimes also known as DE NUNC. We modeled individual *de se* by moving away from the view that one's doxastic alternatives are a set of worlds, as in (13), and instead toward the view that one's doxastic alternatives are a set of world-individual pairs, as in (14). Now, finally, to capture temporal *de se*, we model one's doxastic alternatives as a set of world-time-individual triples, as in (15).

(13) $\text{DOX}_{x,w} = \{w' \mid w'$ is compatible with $x$'s beliefs in $w\}$

(14) $\text{DOX}_{x,w} = \{\langle w', y \rangle \mid$ it is compatible with $x$'s beliefs in $w$ for $x$ to be $y$ in $w'\}$

(15) $\text{DOX}_{x,w,t} = \{\langle w',t',y\rangle \mid$ it is compatible with $x$'s beliefs in $w$ at $t$ for $x$ to be $y$ in $w'$ at $t'\}$

We accordingly rewrite our denotation for *believe* yet again so that it induces abstraction not just over its complement's world parameter and individual argument but also over its complement's time parameter:

(16) $[[\text{believe}]]^{w,t} = [\lambda p_{\langle i,\langle s,et\rangle\rangle}.[\lambda x.\forall \langle w',t',y\rangle \in \text{DOX}_{x,w,t}: p(t')(w')(y)]]$

This yields outcomes like (17):

(17) $[[\text{Beatrix believes it's raining}]]^{w,t} =$
$\forall \langle w',t',y\rangle \in \text{DOX}_{b,w,t}$: it's raining at $t'$ in $w'$

On this setup, what Beatrix believes is not that it's raining at the objective utterance time of the attitude report but rather at her subjective 'now'.

This approach extends straightforwardly to cases in which the attitude verb is in the present tense but the embedded clause has past tense. In other words, the semantics we sketched for past tense in the previous subsection interacts correctly with the new denotation for *believe* in (16). This is illustrated in (18).

(18) $[[\text{Beatrix believes that Polly left}]]^{w,t} =$
$\forall \langle w',t',y\rangle \in \text{DOX}_{b,w,t}: \exists t'' < t'$ [Polly leaves at $t''$ in $w'$]

On this view, in a sentence like *Beatrix believes that Polly left*, the content of Beatrix's belief is not that Polly's leaving time precedes the objective utterance time of the attitude report but rather that it precedes Beatrix's subjective 'now'.

In short, 'present-under-present' and 'past-under-present' configurations are both very tractable: the desired semantics falls out automatically from a semantics for tense that works for simple sentences and a semantics for attitude reports that incorporates time-sensitivity in the appropriate way. But as soon as we turn to cases where the attitude verb is in the past tense, this simple picture is threatened: 'past under past' gives rise to the so-called sequence of tense phenomenon, and 'present under past' gives rise to the so-called 'double access' phenomenon, neither of which are as yet fully understood. In what follows, we have a look at each.

### 7.2.4 Past under Past: Sequence of Tense

The simple theory just sketched predicts what is exemplified in (19) for a 'past-under-past' attitude report.

## 7.2 Attitude Reports and Embedded Tense

(19)  $[[\text{Beatrix believed that Polly was happy}]]^{w,t} =$
$\exists t' < t \, [\forall \langle w', t'', y \rangle \in \text{DOX}_{b,w,t'} : \exists t''' < t'' \, [\text{Polly is happy at } t''' \text{ in } w']]$

According to this formula, Beatrix held a belief at some time $t'$ prior to the utterance time $t$, the content of which is that Polly is happy at some time $t'''$ prior to what Beatrix's subjective 'now' $t''$ was at the time $t'$ of the attitude being reported. The problem with this is that the relevant sentence is verifiable by two kinds of scenarios, one in which the time of Polly's hypothetical happiness coincides with Beatrix's subject 'now' at the time of the reported attitude (the 'simultaneous' or 'sequence of tense' reading, as in (20-a)), and one in which the time of Polly's hypothetical happiness precedes Beatrix's subjective 'now' at the time of the reported attitude (the 'back-shifted' reading, as in (20-b)).

(20)  Beatrix believed that Polly was happy.
   a. *simultaneous reading*: Beatrix thought: "Polly is happy."
   b. *back-shifted reading*: Beatrix thought: "Polly was happy."

Yet the formula in (19) captures only the back-shifted reading, leaving the simultaneous reading unaccounted for.

There are three main kinds of approaches on the market for accounting for the simultaneous reading of past-under-past attitude reports. One line of attack is to say that when a past tense is embedded under another past tense, it need not be interpreted as a true past tense, either because the morphosyntactic appearance of past tense in the embedded clause is a mere reflection of agreement with the higher past tense (Kratzer 1998a; Klecha 2016), or because it is deleted at LF under identity with the higher past tense (Ogihara 1989; von Stechow 1995; Anand and Hacquard 2008). Another variant of this strategy, carried out within the referential rather than the quantificational theory of tense, is to derive the simultaneous reading via coindexation of matrix and embedded tense so that they refer to the same time (Enç 1987).

A second line of attack on the simultaneous reading is to argue that embedded tenses in attitude reports can have *de re* interpretations, so that they are anchored to the utterance time rather than to the attitude holder's subjective 'now'. The main challenge facing such an approach is that it is too permissive: if the embedded past tense in a sentence like (20) is constrained only to be past with respect to utterance time, then we predict it to be compatible not only with simultaneous and back-shifted readings but also with forward-shifted readings, as in (21), provided that the time of Polly's hypothetical happiness still precedes the utterance time of the attitude report.

(21)  Beatrix thought: "Polly will be happy."

Faced with this problem, proponents of the *de re* theory of sequence of tense must impose some further constraint, what Abusch (1997) calls the Upper Limit Constraint, which stipulates that the reference time of the embedded clause cannot be later than the reference time of an embedding past tense clause. Such a constraint needs to be specific to attitude reports, as brought out by the contrast illustrated in (22-a–b), due to Ogihara (2007): whereas past-under-past in an attitude report is limited to back-shifted and simultaneous interpretations, as in (22-a) (i.e., (22-a) cannot report Marty hearing "Sam will be sick tomorrow"), a past tense embedded in a relative clause, as seen in (22-b), can have any temporal orientation with respect to the matrix time; the only restriction is that it must be past with respect to the utterance time (i.e., (22-b) can report Marty meeting a man who became sick the day after the meeting).

(22) a. Marty heard [that Sam was sick (the previous day/that day/*the next day)].
 b. Marty met the man [who was sick (the previous day/that day/the next day).] (Ogihara 2007: 410)

Finally, yet a third kind of approach is to deny that the simultaneous reading of past-under-past sentences really has the status of a distinct reading; in particular, Altshuler and Schwarzschild (2013a, b) argue that this is merely a pragmatically enriched variant of the back-shifted reading that arises when we assume that Polly's hypothetical happiness did not cease at the moment when Beatrix formed her belief.

Two other points about sequence of tense should be mentioned. First, it has been observed that not all languages behave like English in allowing past-under-past attitude reports to have simultaneous readings. In Japanese, for example, past-under-past sentences like (23) give rise to obligatory back-shifting; in order to get a simultaneous reading, an embedded present tense is employed, as in (24).

(23) Taro-wa [Hanako-ga byooki-**dat-ta** to] it-ta.
 Taro-TOP Hanako-NOM sick-be-PST that say-PST
 'Taro said that Hanako was sick.' *back-shifted reading only*

(24) Taro-wa [Hanako-ga byooki-**da** to it-ta
 Taro-TOP Hanako-NOM sick-be.PRES that say-PST
 'Taro said that Hanako was sick.' *simultaneous reading only*
 (Bochnak et al. 2019: 2)

## 7.2 Attitude Reports and Embedded Tense

This means that whatever the right approach is for English, it needs to make room for cross-linguistic variation. For relevant cross-linguistic work, see Kubota et al. 2009, Sharvit 2014, and Bochnak et al. 2019. Bochnak et al. (2019), in particular, propose to capture the variation between English and Japanese via a parameter that regulates whether a past tense can be deleted under identity with a higher past tense (as in English) or not (as in Japanese), and they go on to explore other parameters needed to extend the account to data from languages that mark tense optionally and languages that lack tense altogether.

Second, Klecha (2016) points out an interesting asymmetry between *think* and *hope* in how past-under-past sentences are interpreted:

(25)   Martina thought Carissa got pregnant.
       *Impossible reading*: Martina thought Carissa would get pregnant.

(26)   Martina hoped Carissa got pregnant.
       *Possible reading*: Martina hoped that Carissa would get pregnant.
       (Klecha 2016: 4)

In principle, (25) should be ambiguous between a simultaneous and a back-shifted interpretation, but the back-shifted interpretation is ruled out given that *get pregnant* is eventive rather than stative and eventive predicates in English need aspectual support in present-tense or simultaneous contexts (see Todorović 2015). What (25) cannot have, however, is a future-shifted interpretation, and this is unsurprising given that no theory predicts that it should. The surprise is that (26) *does* admit a future-shifted interpretation. This is unexpected on previous theories of past-under-past sentences, given that none of them predicts that different embedding verbs should give rise to different interpretive behavior in the embedded tense. (Although, as Klecha points out, parallel facts have been observed for infinitival complementation, where different embedding verbs give rise to different temporal effects: see e.g. Abusch 2004; Katz 2004; Wurmbrand 2014.) Klecha (2016) develops an account of this pattern that weaves together a number of proposals: for one thing, he adopts a version of the Upper Limit Constraint, but argues that it is not general, and instead tied to the denotations of particular verbs like *think* but not *hope*. Klecha embeds this idea within a theory in which past-under-past configurations allow the embedded past tense to be interpreted as present tense, which for Klecha is nonpast (encompassing both present and future). The proposals conspire to ensure that in (25), future-shifting is not possible, whereas in (26) it is.

### 7.2.5 Present under Past: Double Access

Consider now what our theory from Section 7.2.3 would predict about a sentence in which a past-tense attitude predicate embeds a present-tense clause. This is exemplified in (27).

(27) [[Beatrix said that Polly is pregnant]]$^{w,t}$ =
$\exists t' < t\ [\forall \langle w', t'', y \rangle \in \text{DOX}_{b,w,t'}$: Polly is pregnant at $t''$ in $w'$]

According to (27), the time of Polly's alleged pregnancy coincides with Beatrix's subjective 'now' $t''$ at the time $t'$ at which Beatrix spoke. In other words, the report is predicted to be paraphrasable as:

(28) Beatrix said: "Polly is pregnant."

The problem is that this semantics seems to be a bit too permissive, as brought out by the contrast between (29) and (30).

(29) **Yesterday**, Beatrix said that Polly is pregnant.

(30) ??**Ten years ago**, Beatrix said that Polly is pregnant.

The somewhat odd status of (30) is connected with the fact that pregnancies cannot last for ten years. This suggests that an embedded present tense conveys not only simultaneity with respect to the attitude holder's subjective now, but also with respect to the utterance time of the attitude report. In other words, the report conveys that if what Beatrix said was true, it should continue to hold true through the time of the report.

This seemingly hybrid status of the embedded tense in present-under-past attitude reports has led to the label 'double access' for this phenomenon. Relevant work on the topic includes Smith 1978; Ogihara 1989, 1995a; Heim 1994; Abusch 1997; Gennari 1999, 2003; Bar-Lev 2015; Altshuler et al. 2015; Bary and Altshuler 2015; Klecha 2016.[4] Ogihara and Abusch, for example, both adopt variants of a *de re* analysis for embedded present tense. But it remains to be seen what forces a *de re* construal and how precisely the truth conditions should be stated so as to accurately encompass both the 'simultaneous with matrix' and the 'simultaneous with utterance time' dimensions of present-under-past attitude reports. So, this is a promising area for further research.

---

[4] See also Ferreira 2017, who argues that double access obtains in Portuguese in past-under-past configurations.

## 7.3 NEG RAISING

### 7.3.1 Introduction

This section is concerned with a puzzling phenomenon known in the literature as Neg Raising, whereby some attitude reports with matrix negation seem to have the option of being interpreted as though the negation were in the embedded clause:

(31) a. Beatrix didn't think it was raining.
*Available reading:* Beatrix thought it wasn't raining.
b. Beatrix didn't want it to rain.
*Available reading:* Beatrix wanted it **not** to rain.
c. Beatrix didn't expect it to rain.
*Available reading:* Beatrix expected it **not** to rain.

Notably, not all attitude predicates give rise to such behavior; in contrast with *think*, *want*, and *expect* as seen in the above examples, *claim*, *hope*, and *figure out* do not instantiate Neg Raising, as seen in (32).

(32) a. Beatrix didn't claim it was raining.
≉ Beatrix claimed it wasn't raining.
b. Beatrix didn't hope it was raining.
≉ Beatrix hoped it wasn't raining.
c. Beatrix didn't figure out that it was raining.
≉ Beatrix figured out that it wasn't raining.

There are two main kinds of approaches to Neg Raising: one syntactic and the other semantic/pragmatic. The syntactic approach is the one that, historically speaking, gives Neg Raising its name: on this approach, negation in the embedded clause moves syntactically to the matrix clause over the course of the syntactic derivation, in such a way that its site of origin is reflected in the interpretation of the sentence, whereas its landing site is reflected in the way the words of the sentence are ultimately linearized and pronounced. This approach enjoyed support in the early generative literature (see especially Fillmore 1963; Lakoff 1969; Ross 1973; Prince 1976), and has recently been revived by Collins and Postal (2014, 2017).

The semantic/pragmatic approach to Neg Raising holds instead that the phenomenon is due to an 'excluded middle' inference associated with some attitude predicates. Consider again the sentence in (31-a). If we take it at face value as asserting that it is not the case that Beatrix thought it was raining, then it does not logically follow that Beatrix thought it was *not* raining, because it is possible that she simply had no opinion on the matter: she didn't think it *was* raining, but perhaps she also didn't think it was *not* raining. But if we instead assume that she did have an opinion on the matter, i.e., that she either thought it was raining or thought it was not raining (this is the 'excluded middle'), then upon finding out that it's not the case that she thought it was raining, it follows that she thought it was not raining. This reasoning is summarized in (33), adapted from Crowley 2019: 2, where $a$ is an arbitrary attitude holder and $p$ is an arbitrary proposition.

(33)  a. $\neg[a$ thinks $p]$           *assertion*
    b. $a$ thinks $p \vee a$ thinks $\neg p$     *excluded middle*
    c. $a$ thinks $\neg p$          *valid conclusion*

On one variant of this approach, the excluded middle arises via a presupposition associated with certain attitude predicates (Bartsch, 1973; Gajewski, 2005, 2007), and on another variant, it arises as a CONVERSATIONAL IMPLICATURE (Horn, 1978; Romoli, 2013).

The debate between the syntactic movement approach and the semantic/pragmatic 'excluded middle' approach to Neg Raising is far from settled, and Crowley (2019) goes so far as to argue that both are needed to account for all of the facts. In what follows, we discuss some of the major arguments for and against the syntactic approach, respectively.

### 7.3.2 In Favor of a Syntactic Approach

A central empirical consideration in the choice between the syntactic and the semantic/pragmatic approach to Neg Raising concerns the behavior of so-called 'strong' or 'strict' N(egative) P(olarity) I(tem)s like *in weeks* or *until Monday*. By way of background, data like (34)–(35) suggest that such NPIs must appear in the same minimal clause as an appropriate licensor (here, *not*); cf. a so-called 'weak' NPI like *ever* which, as illustrated in (36-b), can be licensed by negation in a higher clause.

(34)  a. Beatrix has **not** left home **in weeks**.
    b. Beatrix will **not** be back **until Monday**.

(35)  a. \*It's **not** the case that Beatrix has left home **in weeks**
    b. \*It's **not** the case that Beatrix will be back **until Monday**.

(36)  a. Beatrix has **not ever** left home.
    b. It's **not** the case that Beatrix has **ever** left home.

Against this backdrop, the relevant observation is that Neg Raising attitude predicates like *think* appear to allow for a strong NPI to be licensed by negation in a higher clause, as seen in (37), whereas non-Neg Raising attitude predicates like *hope* do not, as seen in (38).

## 7.3 Neg Raising

(37) a. Beatrix did**n't** think Polly had been home **in weeks**.
b. Beatrix did**n't** think Polly would be back **until Monday**.

(38) a. *Beatrix did**n't** hope Polly had been home **in weeks**.
b. *Beatrix did**n't** hope Polly would be back **until Monday**.

If we assume, in accordance with the syntactic approach to Neg Raising, that in (37), the matrix negation originates in and is interpreted in the embedded clause, then the apparent exceptionality is explained away: we can maintain the view that a strong NPI must be licensed within its minimal clause. Since *hope* is not a Neg Raising predicate, no such licensing obtains in (38), and the sentences are ungrammatical. An argument along these lines was initially proffered by Lakoff (1969). See Gajewski 2005, 2007 for an attempt to reconcile these facts with the semantic/pragmatic approach to Neg Raising via a semantically oriented approach to strong NPI licensing in conjunction with the workings of PRESUPPOSITION PROJECTION, and see Collins and Postal 2014 and Crowley 2019 for replies.

In addition, Collins and Postal (2014) offer three other arguments in favor of a syntactic treatment of Neg Raising. First, they argue that Neg Raising is subject to island constraints. For example, (39-a) is acceptable but (39-b) is not.

(39) a. I **don't believe** that the moon will vanish **until Thursday**.
b. *I **don't hold the belief** that the moon will vanish **until Thursday**.

(Collins and Postal 2014: 113)

The only difference between (39-a) and (39-b) is that (39-a) involves *believe that ...* whereas (39-b) involves *hold the belief that ...*. Insofar as these two expressions are synonymous with each other, it is unclear how a semantic/pragmatic approach to Neg Raising would account for this difference. On a syntactic approach, however, (39-a–b) involve movement of negation from the embedded clause to the matrix clause (the negation's low origin being necessary to license the strict NPI *until Thursday*), and so the unacceptability of (39-b) can be argued to fall out from an independently known constraint against movement out of a complex noun phrase (i.e., *the belief that ...*). In this way, the split between (39-a) and (39-b) parallels the split between (40-a) and (40-b):

(40) a. What does Beatrix **believe** that she will do tomorrow?
b. *What does Beatrix **hold the belief** that she will do tomorrow?

(40-a) involves licit *wh*-movement, whereas (40-b) involves illicit *wh*-movement out of a complex noun phrase.

Second, Collins and Postal (2014) offer an argument for the syntactic approach to Neg Raising based on evidence from what they call 'Horn clauses' (after Horn 1975), exemplified in (41).

(41)  I don't think that ever before have the media played such a major role in a kidnapping. (Horn 1975: 283)

The sentence in (41) instantiates so-called negative inversion, in that negation triggers subject-auxiliary inversion (*have the media* ... instead of *the media have* ...), and, as Collins and Postal (2014) argue, this is unexpected unless the matrix negation starts out in the embedded clause. As seen in (42), negative inversion ordinarily requires a clause-local negative licensor: this is provided in (42-a) (*never*) but not in (42-b).

(42)  a. Never before have the media played such a major role in a kidnapping.
      b. *It's not the case that ever before have the media played such a major role in a kidnapping.

Finally, Collins and Postal (2014) offer a third argument for the syntactic approach to Neg Raising based on the behavior of negative parenthetical structures like (43).

(43)  Sandra is not, I don't believe, having her yearly get-together.
(Collins and Postal 2014: xix)

Collins and Postal (2014) argue that negative parentheticals obey distributional restrictions that make sentences like (43) straightforward on the syntactic approach to Neg Raising but unexpected on the semantic/pragmatic approach. See Collins and Postal 2014 for the details of the argument.

### 7.3.3 Against a Syntactic Approach

Weighing against the arguments in favor of a syntactic approach to Neg Raising, there are also a number of arguments that seem to militate against a syntactic approach and therefore in favor of a semantic/pragmatic approach. Here we consider three.

The first is what Collins and Postal (2014) call the 'Composed Quantifier Argument'; versions of this argument are found, among other places, in Horn 1978, 1989 and Gajewski 2007. The relevant observation is that Neg Raising appears to be possible not just with matrix sentential negation but also with matrix negative quantifiers, as exemplified

## 7.3 Neg Raising

in (44), where embedded strong NPI *until Monday* seems to be licensed by the matrix subject *no one*.

(44) **No one** thought that Polly would be back **until Monday**.
 ≈ **Everyone** thought that Polly would **not** be back **until Monday**.

To handle cases like this, the syntactic approach would seem to be committed to the view that an embedded sentential negation raises into the matrix clause and incorporates into a quantificational subject, yielding the negative quantifier *no one*. But decompositional approaches to negative quantifiers like *no one* typically employ a negation scoping over an existential (¬∃) rather than a universal scoping over a negation (∀¬), as would be required here, and this makes such an analysis seem suspect. See, however, Collins and Postal 2014, who propose a way of making sense of (44) within the syntactic approach to Neg Raising and without such lexical decomposition. They argue that once the full facts are brought to bear, cases like (44) actually *support* the syntactic approach to Neg Raising. See Collins and Postal 2014 for the details of this argument.

Another potential argument against the syntactic approach to Neg Raising concerns VP ellipsis and is due to Crowley (2019). Crowley points out the example in (45) (where the material in the angle brackets is elided, i.e., not pronounced):

(45) John didn't think it would snow but Sue did ⟨think it would snow⟩.

(Crowley 2019: 3)

It is well documented that VP ellipsis is licensed by semantic identity of the elided VP and some antecedent VP. So on a syntactic approach to Neg Raising, the expectation is that the elided VP would be interpreted as *think it wouldn't snow*, matching the putative pre-movement interpretation of the antecedent VP. But this is contrary to fact: the elided VP is interpreted as *think it would snow*. Thus it is not clear how to reconcile (45) with the syntactic approach to Neg Raising. For more on the relationship between ellipsis and the debate over Neg Raising, see Jacobson 2018, 2020.

Finally, a third argument against the syntactic approach to Neg Raising, also due to Crowley (2019), concerns so-called antecedent-contained deletion structures. The relevant example is given in (46) (where, again, the material in the angle brackets is elided).

(46)　John doesn't expect to pass [a single exam that Mary does ⟨expect to pass⟩]. (Crowley 2019: 4)

In (46), an elided VP (the missing material after *does*) is embedded in its antecedent VP (i.e., *expect to pass a single exam that Mary does*). In order to avoid an infinite regress problem in the recovery of the missing VP, the bracketed object must move covertly out of the matrix VP. But it must also remain below negation to license the NPI *single*. On the semantic/pragmatic approach to Neg Raising, this is not a problem, because the negation is in the matrix clause, and can therefore take wide scope over everything else in the sentence, including the moved object. But on the syntactic approach to Neg Raising, the negation is in the embedded clause, and hence there is no way the object can move out of the matrix VP while still remaining within the scope of negation. Therefore, this seems to be another case where the semantic/pragmatic approach fares better than the syntactic approach.

## 7.4 INTENSIONAL TRANSITIVE VERBS

### 7.4.1 Introduction

Alongside attitude reports that involve embedded finite or nonfinite clauses, we also find attitude reports that involve what look like ordinary direct objects, as in (47).

(47)　Beatrix **wanted/looked for/imagined/admired/feared** the frisbee.

Sentences like (47) exhibit three properties that set them apart from ordinary transitive clauses and that are instead characteristic of propositional attitude reports; for this reason, verbs like those in (47) are known as intensional transitive verbs. In what follows, we first lay out these three properties, and then have a look at the two major kinds of analyses that such verbs have inspired. According to one analysis, sentences like (47) instantiate hidden embedded clausal material; in its strong form, this analysis is associated with PROPOSITIONALISM: the thesis that embedded clauses are the only source of intensionality in natural language. According to the other analysis, there are no hidden clauses in sentences like (47). Instead, intensional transitive verbs select for intensional quantifiers or (on another variant of this analysis) properties. This analysis is associated with INTENSIONALISM: the thesis that any expression (whether it embeds a clause or not) can trigger an intensional context. In this way, intensional transitive verbs bear

## 7.4 Intensional Transitive Verbs

on a foundational question about the organization of natural language grammar: what does it take to trigger an intensional environment?

### 7.4.2 Diagnosing Intensionality

The first crucial property of intensional transitive verbs is that they give rise to what looks like a *de dicto/de re* ambiguity. (When indefinites are involved, this is often called a specific/nonspecific ambiguity.) For example, (48) is ambiguous between the two readings paraphrased in (48-a) and (48-b), respectively.[5] By way of contrast, an ordinary transitive clause like (49) has no such ambiguity: (49), on any way of reading it, entails that there was a frisbee that Beatrix caught.

(48) Beatrix {**wanted/was looking for**} a frisbee.
 a. *De dicto*/Non-specific reading: Beatrix wanted/was looking for a frisbee, without necessarily having any particular one in mind.
 b. *De re*/Specific reading: There was a frisbee that Beatrix wanted/was looking for.

(49) Beatrix **caught** a frisbee.
 = There was a frisbee that Beatrix caught.

Second, on their *de dicto* reading, sentences with intensional transitive verbs lack existential entailments with respect to indefinite direct objects, as seen in (50) (compare the ordinary transitive clause in (51)).

(50) Beatrix {**wanted/was looking for**} a frisbee, but unfortunately for Beatrix, there was no frisbee.

(51) #Beatrix **caught** a frisbee, but unfortunately for Beatrix, there was no frisbee.

Third and finally, on their *de dicto* reading, sentences with intensional transitive verbs do not admit substitution of extensionally equivalent expressions. For example, supposing that all creatures that have hearts also have kidneys, and vice versa, there is no entailment relation (in either direction) between (52-a) and (52-b), though there is an entailment relation (in both directions) between (53-a) and (53-b).

---

[5] Here, and in what follows, I will mostly focus on *want* and *look (for)* as paradigm examples of intensional transitive verbs. See Moltmann 1997, Forbes 2013, and Schwarz forthcoming for discussion of other intensional transitive verbs and their fine-grained similarities and differences. Probably, not all three of the properties discussed here hold for every item that we would want to call an intensional transitive verb (see especially Forbes 2013), though they probably hold for most of them (see especially Schwarz forthcoming).

(52) a. Beatrix {wanted/was looking for} a creature with a heart.
 b. ↮ Beatrix {wanted/was looking for} a creature with a kidney.

(53) a. Beatrix **caught** a creature with a heart.
 b. ↔ Beatrix caught a creature with a kidney.

These three properties all militate against the treatment of transitive *want* or *look (for)* as ordinary type $\langle e, \langle e, t \rangle \rangle$ extensional transitive verbs as illustrated in (54) for *catch*.

(54) $[[\text{catch}]]^w = [\lambda x.[\lambda y.y \text{ catches } x \text{ in } w]]$

Instead, in order to account for the above properties, intensional transitive verbs need an analysis in which their internal argument has some intensional type. But what intensional type? Here there is debate in the literature, and no consensus as yet. Various scholars have analyzed intensional transitive verbs as denoting relations to propositions (type $\langle st, et \rangle$), to intensions of quantifiers (type $\langle \langle s, \langle et, t \rangle \rangle, et \rangle$, or to properties (type $\langle \langle s, et \rangle, et \rangle$). In what follows, we have a look at each of these options and some of the issues at stake in deciding between them.

### 7.4.3 Propositionalism

First we consider the hypothesis that intensional transitive verbs denote relations to propositions. This is particularly attractive in the case of *want* because we know independently that *want* acts as a relation to a proposition, when it combines with a (nonfinite) clause. Hence, such an analysis would pave the way for having just one denotation for *want* across its different syntactic appearances. But if *want* in (for example) (55) denotes a relation to a proposition, what exactly is that proposition? And how do we square this with the fact that *a frisbee* is ordinarily not proposition-denoting?

(55) Beatrix wants a frisbee.

One proposal in the literature for answering these questions is that sentences like (55) contain a silent verb meaning *have*, as in (56). On this view, the analysis of (55) parallels the analysis of (57), and we make sense of the three intensionality diagnostics outlined above.

(56) Beatrix wants $\emptyset_{have}$ a frisbee.

(57) Beatrix wants to have a frisbee.

Proponents of this view include Quine 1956, 1960; McCawley 1974; Ross 1976; den Dikken et al. 1996; Larson et al. 1997, and critics include

## 7.4 Intensional Transitive Verbs

Merchant 1999; Wechsler 2008. Also relevant is Harley 2004, who argues that transitive *want* sentences do not involve a silent *have*, but instead a silent abstract preposition that underlies the verbs *have*, *get*, and *give*.

Perhaps the strongest piece of independent evidence for the hidden clause analysis comes from the behavior of temporal modifiers, first pointed out by McCawley (1974). Observe that (58) is ambiguous between one reading in which *on Tuesday* names the day when the wanting took place, as in (58-a), and another reading in which it is part of the content of the desire, as in (58-b). Compare (59), which does not have any comparable ambiguity.

(58)  Beatrix wanted a frisbee on Tuesday.
   a. *Reading 1:* Beatrix wanted on Tuesday for it to be the case that she would have a frisbee.
   b. *Reading 2:* Beatrix wanted it to be the case that on Tuesday, she would have a frisbee.

(59)  Beatrix caught a frisbee on Tuesday.

On the silent *have* analysis, the facts in (58) fall out as a simple attachment ambiguity: *on Tuesday* can associate either with the embedded clause or the matrix clause. (And Schwarz 2006 documents similar attachment ambiguities with *too* and *again*.)

In a similar vein, observe the contrast between (60) and (61).

(60)  #Beatrix caught a frisbee tomorrow.

(61)  Beatrix wanted a frisbee tomorrow.

(60) has no coherent interpretation (except maybe in time travel contexts, if we're being charitable), because of the semantic incompatibility between past tense and *tomorrow*. Nonetheless, (61) has a coherent interpretation, namely that Beatrix held a desire sometime before the utterance time to the effect that she would have a frisbee the day after the utterance time. On the hidden clausal analysis, there is an embedded clause in (61) for *tomorrow* to attach to, and because that clause can be temporally forward-shifted from the time of the wanting, there is no semantic incompatibility.

Another potential piece of support for the hidden clausal analysis, also due to McCawley (1974), comes from sentences like (62), exhibiting so-called propositional anaphora.

(62)  Joe wants a wife, but his mother won't allow it/*her.

(McCawley 1974)

In (62), it would be problematic to assume that *it* takes *a wife* as its antecedent, since in that case the form of the anaphor should be *her*, but this choice sounds quite odd in this context. Instead, the antecedent seems to be the proposition that Joe have a wife. On the hidden clausal analysis, this is straightforward: *it* is anteceded by the hidden embedded clause.

Finally, a third potential piece of support for the hidden clausal analysis, from Larson et al. (1997), concerns comparative sentences like (63). Of note is the ambiguity that they give rise to, articulated in (63-a–b).

(63)    Jonathan wants more toys than Benjamin.    (Larson et al. 1997)
   a. *Reading 1:* Jonathan wants to have more toys than Benjamin **has**.
   b. *Reading 2:* Jonathan wants to have more toys than Benjamin **wants to have**.

On the hidden clausal analysis, the ambiguity has a straightforward account: there are two antecedent verb phrases in the structure (*have* ... and *want to have* ...) and therefore two ways of recovering the missing material in the standard of comparison.

Unfortunately for the hidden clausal analysis, however, not all intensional transitive verbs pattern like *want* in exhibiting independent evidence for a hidden clause. This is a point first made by Partee (1974). Consider *look (for)*. It does not give rise to attachment ambiguities with temporal modifiers: (64) has one reading only, according to which Tuesday is the day that the reported search took place. And (65) has no coherent interpretation. (See also Schwarz 2006, who shows that, unlike *want*, *look (for)* does not give rise to attachment ambiguities with *too* or *again*.)

(64)    Beatrix looked for a frisbee on Tuesday.

(65)    #Beatrix looked for a frisbee tomorrow.

Propositional anaphora also sound somewhat odd in connection with *look (for)*, as seen in (66). While perhaps not entirely unacceptable, there is something a bit awkward about (66), presumably owing to the fact that it takes some work to concoct an appropriate value for *it*.

(66)    ?Joe is looking for a wife, but his mother won't allow it.

Finally, there is no ambiguity in comparative sentences like (67): (67) can only mean that Beatrix looked for more frisbees than Polly looked for. It does not have any other reading, such as 'Beatrix looked for more frisbees than Polly had/found.'

## 7.4 Intensional Transitive Verbs

(67)  Beatrix looked for more frisbees than Polly.

To be sure, none of these observations prove that the hidden clausal analysis is wrong for *look (for)*. For example, as pointed out by Larson et al. (1997), even among overt clausal complements, there is variation with respect to whether the embedded clause allows for independent temporal modification, as witnessed by the contrast between (68) and (69).

(68)  Beatrix **hoped** to eat hot dogs tomorrow.

(69)  #Beatrix **tried** to eat hot dogs tomorrow.

So it is conceivable that *look (for)* has a hidden clausal analysis, but the hidden clause is simply more difficult to detect. But once we go down this path, something quite important is at stake: if the hidden clausal analysis turns out to be correct even for *look (for)*, where the evidence for a hidden clause is scant, it suggests that intensionality may be triggered solely by embedded *clauses*. This imposes a rather powerful limitation on the interface between syntax and semantics. Larson (2002) develops such a view. If, by contrast, the hidden clausal analysis is wrong for *look (for)* and/or at least some other intensional transitive verbs, then it suggests that intensionality has a freer rein in the grammar. We now take a brief look at some work in this latter vein.

### 7.4.4  Intensionalism

If at least some intensional transitive verbs do not select for propositions, what do they select for? One approach holds that they select for intensional quantifiers (Montague 1974) and the other holds that they select for properties (Zimmerman 1993).

At stake in the choice between these two approaches are some rather delicate questions about the interpretive behavior of certain kinds of quantifiers when they are embedded under intensional transitive verbs. Consider the data in (70)–(71). (70) instantiates an overtly biclausal structure and gives rise to the expected *de re*/*de dicto* ambiguity paraphrased in (70-a) and (70-b), respectively. By contrast, the intensional transitive verb structure in (71) seems to allow only the *de re* reading.

(70)  Beatrix is trying to find most of the frisbees.
    a.  *Reading 1*: For most of the frisbees $x$, Beatrix is trying to find $x$.
    b.  *Reading 2*: Beatrix's goal is: find most of the frisbees.

(71)  Beatrix is looking for most of the frisbees.

    a. *Reading 1:* For most of the frisbees *x*, Beatrix is trying to find *x*.
    b. #*Reading 2:* Beatrix's goal is: find most of the frisbees.

More generally, Zimmerman (1993) argues that *de dicto* readings with intensional transitive verbs are possible only with weak quantifiers. Following Milsark (1974), *weak quantifiers* are defined as quantifiers that sit comfortably in existential *there*-sentences, as in (72-a), and they stand in contrast with so-called *strong quantifiers*, as in (72-b).

(72)   a.   There are **several frisbees** in the backyard.   *weak quantifier*
       b.   ??There are **most frisbees** in the backyard.   *strong quantifier*

If intensional transitive verbs select for intensional quantifiers, then there would be no reason to expect *de dicto* readings to be restricted to weak quantifiers only. But, Zimmerman argues, the restriction is expected if intensional transitive verbs instead select instead for properties, because it is independently known that only weak quantifiers can be type-shifted into properties. Strong quantifiers, not having this option, are forced to scope out, triggering an obligatory *de re* semantics.

It is not clear, though, that the property analysis makes all the right predictions. For example, as Zimmerman (1993) points out, (73) has a *de dicto/de re* ambiguity, even though *every* is not a weak quantifier.

(73)   I have looked for every typo in the manuscript.
                                                           (Zimmerman 1993: 177)
       a.   *Reading 1:* For every typo in the manuscript *x*, I have looked for *x*.
       b.   *Reading 2:* My goal was: find every typo in the manuscript.

But perhaps not all hope is lost for the property analysis: Geenhoven and McNally (2005) attempt to solve the problem in (73) via a non-quantificational analysis for *every*.

The choice between the hidden clausal analysis and the two variants of the alternative approach considered here is far from settled. And it is quite possible that both kinds of analyses will ultimately be needed to account for all of the data. If this is so, then not all sources of intensionality in natural language grammar have an underlyingly clausal source.

## 7.5 DISCUSSION QUESTIONS

(i) As discussed above, attitude reports with matrix present tense are easily tractable, whereas attitude reports with matrix past tense give rise to difficult puzzles. How about attitude reports with matrix future tense? Assuming we analyze *will* as the mirror image of past tense (contributing existential quantification over times that *follow* the evaluation time), do sentences like (74)–(76) have the semantics predicted by the theory of tense binding sketched in Section 7.2.3 above? Or do any of them require a special treatment? (E.g. does (74) give rise to double access? Does (76) have a simultaneous reading?)

(74)   Beatrix **will** say that Polly **is** happy.

(75)   Beatrix **will** say that Polly **was** happy.

(76)   Beatrix **will** say that Polly **will be** happy.

(ii) A crucial question facing any approach to Neg Raising is why the phenomenon is manifest with some attitude predicates but not others. Try coming up with two lists of attitude predicates, one for those that instantiate Neg Raising and one for those that do not. Is there any independently detectable syntactic difference between the predicates in each set that might be used to motivate the idea that movement of a negative element should be licit from one type but not the other? Alternatively, is there any independently detectable semantico-pragmatic difference between the predicates in each set that might be used to motivate the idea that one type supports excluded middle inferences but the other does not?

(iii) As discussed above, proponents of propositionalism would analyze intensional transitive verbs like those in (77) as selecting for propositions underlyingly.

(77)   Beatrix {**wanted/looked for/imagined/admired/feared**} the frisbee.

In the case of *want*, the putative proposition can be articulated in a fairly satisfying way as *to have the frisbee*. Is this the case for the other intensional transitive verbs listed here? To what extent do they afford satisfying paraphrases that have overtly propositional objects?

## 7.6 FURTHER READING

Good starting points for investigating tense in attitude reports include: Enç 1987; Heim 1994; Abusch 1997; Ogihara 1995b; von Stechow 1995; Klecha 2016.

For a representative range of approaches to Neg Raising, see Horn 1978; Gajewski 2005, 2007; Romoli 2013; Collins and Postal 2014, 2017. Additionally, Crowley 2019 serves as a good recent overview, especially when paired with Jacobson's (2020) response. See also Frazier et al. 2018 for relevant experimental work arguing in favor a semantic/pragmatic account to Neg Raising.

Finally, for intensional transitive verbs, see Moltmann 1997; Forbes 2013; Schwarz forthcoming for useful surveys. For additional work on intensional transitive verbs, aside from those works already cited in the body of this chapter, see also Richard 2001; Forbes 2006; Montague 2007; Zimmerman 2006; Moltmann 2008, 2013a.

# Glossary

**belief set** The set of worlds compatible with an individual's beliefs. See Section 2.3.2.
**bouletic alternatives** The set of worlds compatible with an individual's desires. See Chapter 6.
**centered worlds** World-individual pairs. On the Hintikkan approach, attitude reports quantify over sets of worlds (such as the attitude holder's BELIEF SET in the case of belief reports), whereas, in the tradition of Lewis, to model DE SE ATTITUDE REPORTS, attitude reports quantify over sets of world-individual pairs. See Section 5.3.
**choice function** Function that inputs a set and returns some member of that set, involved in some approaches to the DE DICTO/DE RE AMBIGUITY as it pertains to indefinites. See Section 4.3.
**compositionality** A foundational principle of formal semantics, according to which the meaning of a complex expression is a function of the meanings of its parts and how those parts are arranged syntactically.
**concept generator** Function from individuals to INDIVIDUAL CONCEPTS, in Percus and Sauerland's (2003a) approach to *de re* attitude reports. See Section 4.5.5.
**control** A grammatical configuration in which the (typically unexpressed) subject of an embedded clause depends on the embedding clause for its interpretation. For example, the sentence *Beatrix wants to go outside* cannot report that Beatrix wants someone else to go outside – it can only report that Beatrix wants *herself* to go outside (or to be pedantic, that Beatrix wants *the individual who she takes herself to be* to go outside – see DE SE ATTITUDE REPORT).
**conversational implicature** A cancellable, invited inference that an utterance gives rise to as a result of its meaning interacting with the context and with general conversational principles. Involved in one potential solution to FREGE'S PUZZLE. See Section 3.3.
***de dicto/de re* ambiguity** The multiplicity of readings that many attitude reports give rise to depending on whether an expression in the complement clause is interpreted as part of the content of the attitude (the *de dicto* reading) or as an attitude-external means of referring to or quantifying over some aspect of the content of the attitude. For example, *Beatrix wants to marry a plumber* can report either that Beatrix wants her eventual spouse to be a plumber (*de dicto*) or that there is a particular plumber that Beatrix wants to marry (*de re*). See Chapter 4.

*de nunc* The interpretation that a tense in the complement clause of an attitude report has when it is anchored to the subjective 'now' of the attitude holder (the time at which s/he self-locates at the time of the attitude) rather than to the actual utterance time. See Section 7.2.3.

*de se* **attitude report** An attitude report that meets two conditions: (i) the content of the attitude is *about* the attitude holder and (ii) the attitude holder is *aware* that the content of the attitude is about herself. See Chapter 5.

*de te* **attitude report** An attitude report (or more properly an INDIRECT SPEECH REPORT that involves an addressee) that meets two conditions: (i) the content of the attitude is *about* the addressee and (ii) the attitude-holder is *aware* that the content of the attitude is about the addressee. See Section 5.4.

**double access** Phenomenon in which a present tense embedded under a past tense attitude verb is in some way indexical to the utterance time. See Section 7.2.5.

**double vision** Term coined by Klein (1978) for Quine's (1956) puzzle about *de re* attitude reports in mistaken identity contexts. In Quine's original example, Ralph sees Ortcutt wearing a brown hat and forms the belief that Ortcutt is a spy. Later Ralph sees Ortcutt at the beach, and not realizing it's the same person, believes the individual at the beach is not a spy. So it seems that Ralph holds the contradictory beliefs that Ortcutt is a spy and that Ortcutt is not a spy, even though Ralph is not guilty of any error in logical reasoning. See Section 4.5.

**doxastic alternatives** See BELIEF SET.

**extension** In this book's background theory, the semantic value of an expression at a particular world. Compare: INTENSION.

**focus** An information-structural category often accompanied by intonational emphasis, which some kinds of operators are sensitive to. For example, *only* is focus-sensitive, as witnessed by the fact that *Beatrix only introduced Polly to MAGGIE* has truth conditions that are different from those of *Beatrix only introduced POLLY to Maggie* (where all caps is meant to signal intonational emphasis). The former means that the only individual Beatrix introduced Polly to is Maggie, whereas the latter means that the only individual Beatrix introduced to Maggie is Polly. Some attitude verbs display focus-sensitivity as well. See Section 6.6.

**Fodor's third reading** A reading of an indefinite in an attitude report that is non-specific but TRANSPARENT. This challenges the traditional dichotomy of the DE DICTO/DE RE AMBIGUITY, wherein non-specific indefinites in attitude reports should always be OPAQUE. See Section 4.3.3.

**Frege's puzzle** The fact that sometimes two attitude reports that differ only in the choice between two co-referring proper names seem to be able to differ in truth value. For example, it might be true to say that 'Lois Lane thinks that Superman is strong', but nonetheless seem false to say that 'Lois Lane thinks that Clark Kent is strong'. This fact stands in tension with otherwise strong reasons for thinking that co-referential proper names make identical semantic contributions to the sentences they appear in. See Chapter 3.

**gradability** A semantic property of some linguistic expressions, associated with the ability to support comparison and other scalar concepts. For example, the adjective *tall* is gradable, as witnessed by its participation in structures like *very tall* or *taller than Maggie*. Some attitude verbs are gradable as well. See Section 6.5.

**hidden indexicals** An approach to FREGE'S PUZZLE, according to which semantic representations of attitude reports contain covert context-sensitive variables that encode information about how the attitude holder conceives of the referents in the content of the attitude. See Section 3.4.

**hyperintensionality** That property of any linguistic phenomenon, or theory thereof, that involves semantic distinctions that are more finely grained than INTENSIONS. See Section 2.5.

**indexical** A linguistic expression that depends on some aspect of the utterance context for its value, such as the utterance time, location, or participants. Typical examples include TENSES and expressions like *today* and *yesterday*, indexical locatives like *here*, and first- and second-person pronouns. Compare: SHIFTED INDEXICAL.

**indirect speech report** A sentence used to report something that was said, without using direct quotation.

**individual concept** Function from possible worlds to individuals.

**intension** In this book's background theory, a function from possible worlds to EXTENSIONS. See Section 2.2.2.

**intensional transitive verb** A transitive verb like *want* or *seek* whose direct object displays intensional properties. For example, *Beatrix wanted a unicorn* or *Beatrix sought a unicorn* does not entail the existence of any unicorns; cf. *Beatrix kicked a unicorn*, which does. See Section 7.4.

**intensionalism** The thesis that, in principle, any kind of expression (whether it embeds a clause or not) can trigger an INTENSIOnal context. See Section 7.4.4. Compare: PROPOSITIONALISM.

**intentionality** Philosophical term for the capacity of the mind to represent mind-external objects.

**Interpreted Logical Forms** In Larson and Ludlow's (1993) theory of attitude reports, syntactic structures whose terminal and nonterminal nodes are paired with the semantic values of the expressions at those nodes. See Section 2.5.7.

**Kripke's puzzle** In its original formulation, Kripke's puzzle is that – in a context where Pierre has two distinct conceptions of London, not realizing they are the same city, and thinking one is pretty and the other not pretty – there seems to be no satisfying way to judge the truth value of the sentence *Pierre thinks that London is pretty*. See Section 3.5. Compare: FREGE'S PUZZLE.

**logophor** A special kind of pronoun found in some languages such as Ewe (a Niger-Congo language spoken in Togo and Ghana), which generally occurs only in attitude reports and INDIRECT SPEECH REPORTS, and is restricted to picking out the attitude-holder or speaker. See Section 5.7.1.

**modal base** In Kratzer's (1981) semantics for modals, the contextually supplied set of accessible worlds over which a modal expression quantifies. The two most important kinds of modal bases are *epistemic* (worlds compatible with the relevant evidence in the actual world) and *circumstantial* (worlds compatible with the relevant circumstances of the actual world). See also: ORDERING SOURCE.

**modality** Broadly construed, any linguistic phenomenon that has to do with possibility or necessity; narrowly construed, the semantic category associated with modal auxiliaries like *must*, *can*, and *should*.

**mood** A grammatical opposition found in embedded clauses in some languages, such as the indicative/subjunctive contrast in Romance languages, whose regulation is tied to factors that sometimes include the choice of the embedding verb. (This is sometimes more precisely called *verbal mood*, as opposed to *sentential mood*, which has to do with clause type distinctions closely associated with different types of speech acts, most centrally declarative, interrogative, and imperative).

**Neg Raising** Phenomenon in which a negated attitude report is interpreted as though the negation were embedded in the complement clause. For example, the prominent reading of *Beatrix doesn't think it's raining* can be paraphrased as *Beatrix thinks that it's not raining*. See Section 7.3.

**opaque** Of a linguistic expression in an intensional context, evaluated relative to the local evaluation world rather than the actual world. Compare: TRANSPARENT.

**ordering source** In Kratzer's (1981) semantics for modals, a mechanism that ranks the worlds in the MODAL BASE along some dimension and then picks out only those worlds that are highest ranking. The most important kind of ordering source is *deontic*, which ranks worlds according to how closely they match some set of ideals (e.g. rules, goals, or desires).

**perceptual report** A sentence used to report a sensory experience like hearing or seeing, as in *Beatrix saw Polly cross the street*.

**presupposition projection** Phenomenon whereby a presupposition triggered in an embedded context persists in the embedding context. For example, *Maggie left again* presupposes that Maggie left before, and this persists even when the sentence is embedded in a sentence like *If Maggie left again, I won't be surprised*. See Sections 4.4.3 and 6.7.

**problem of logical equivalence** The foundational problem for propositional attitude reports in possible worlds semantics: possible worlds are not sufficiently fine-grained to distinguish distinct sentences that have the same truth conditions, even though the semantics of propositional attitude reports seems to require sensitivity to such distinctions. See Section 2.5.

**problem of logical omniscience** A problem affecting the Hintikkan possible worlds approach to attitude reports, whereby belief reports validate inferences that, taken together, portray the attitude-holder as being omniscient with respect to all of the logical consequences of her beliefs. See Section 2.4.

**proposition** The meaning of a declarative sentence (theories of which vary); something that can be true or false.

**propositional attitude** A mental state directed at a PROPOSITION.

**propositional attitude report** A sentence used to report a PROPOSITIONAL ATTITUDE.

**propositional concept** Function from possible worlds to propositions, used in Stalnaker's (1984, 1987) approach to the PROBLEM OF LOGICAL EQUIVALENCE. See Section 2.5.2.

**propositionalism** The thesis that only expressions that embed *clauses* can trigger an INTENSIONal context. See Section 7.4.3. Compare: INTENSIONALISM.

***res* movement** A syntactic operation posited by Heim (1994) that moves a *de re*-interpreted constituent to a position adjoining the attitude predicate, proposed as a way of compositionally implementing a Kaplan 1968-style approach to *de re* attitude reports. See Section 4.5.4.

**rigid designator** An expression whose semantic value does not vary from one world to the next. Kripke (1980) (from whom the term originates) argues that proper names fall into this category. See Section 3.2.

**self-ascribe** To attribute a property to oneself.

**sententialism** Thesis that rejects the need for propositions as part of a semantics for attitude reports and instead proposes that complement clauses in attitude reports simply denote sentences. See Section 2.5.6.

**sequence of tense** Broadly construed, rules concerning the relationship between tenses in multi-clausal contexts; narrowly construed, a phenomenon found in some languages but not others whereby a past tense embedded under a past tense attitude verb is interpreted as simultaneous to the attitude time. See Section 7.2.4.

**shifted indexical** A linguistic expression that behaves like an INDEXICAL in unembedded sentences but in complements to attitude reports may receive an interpretation that is relative to the reported context rather than the actual utterance context. See Section 5.7.2.

**situation semantics** A framework for semantic analysis, developed by Barwise (1981) and Barwise and Perry (1983), that replaces possible worlds with finer-grained entities called situations. Unlike possible worlds, situations are not necessarily temporally and spatially all-inclusive. See Section 2.5.4.

**split intensionality** A proposal by Keshet (2011) within the scope theory of intensionality, according to which there is a syntactic device for converting an expression's EXTENSION into its corresponding INTENSION, rather than letting that conversion happen through a semantic composition rule. See Section 4.4.2.

**structured intensions** Intensions enriched with information about how they are encoded. A kind of HYPERINTENSIONALITY designed to avoid the PROBLEM OF LOGICAL EQUIVALENCE. See Section 2.5.5.

**tense** A grammatical category used for relating the time of a described event or situation to an evaluation time, typically the utterance time (making tense typically INDEXICAL). See Section 7.2.

**transparent** Of a linguistic expression, evaluated relative to the actual world. Compare: OPAQUE.

**truth conditions** The conditions under which a sentence is true, used as a principle for individuating sentence meanings.

**use-conditional meaning** Any dimension of an expression's meaning characterizable in terms of the conditions under which it is appropriate to use that expression (often considered in opposition to TRUTH CONDITIONAL meaning).

# Bibliography

Abbott, Barbara. 2010. *Reference*. Oxford: Oxford University Press.
Abusch, Dorit. 1994. The scope of indefinites. *Natural Language Semantics*, 2, 83–135.
   1997. Sequence of tense and temporal de re. *Linguistics and Philosophy*, 20, 1–50.
   2004. On the temporal composition of infinitives. Pages 1–34 of: Guéron, Jacqueline, and Lecarme, Jacqueline (eds.), *The Syntax of Time*. Cambridge, MA: MIT Press.
Aloni, Maria. 2005. Individual concepts in modal predicate logic. *Journal of Philosophical Logic*, 34, 1–64.
Altshuler, Daniel, and Schwarzschild, Roger. 2013a. Correlating cessation with double access. Pages 43–50 of: Aloni, Maria, Franke, Michael, and Roelofsen, Floris (eds.), *19th Amsterdam Colloquium*. semanticsarchive.
   2013b. Moment of change, cessation implicatures and simultaneous readings. Pages 45–62 of: D'Antonio, Sarah, Moroney, Mary, and Little, Carol Rose (eds.), *Proceedings of Sinn und Bedeutung 17*. semanticsarchive.
Altshuler, Daniel, Hacquard, Valentine, Roberts, Thomas, and White, Aaron Steven. 2015. On double access, cessation and parentheticality. Pages 18–37 of: Chemla, Emmanuel, Homer, Vincent, and Winterstein, Grégoire (eds.), *Proceedings of Semantics and Linguistic Theory 25*. eLanguage.
Anand, Pranav. 2006. *De De Se*. Ph.D. dissertation, Massachusetts Institute of Technology.
Anand, Pranav, and Hacquard, Valentine. 2008. When the present is all in the past. Pages 209–228 of: de Saussure, Louis, Moeschler, Jacques, and Puskás, Genoveva (eds.), *Recent Advances in the Syntax and Semantics of Tense, Mood and Aspect*. Berlin and New York, NY: Mouton de Gruyter.
   2009. Epistemics with attitudes. Pages 37–54 of: Friedman, Tova, and Ito, Satoshi (eds.), *Proceedings of SALT 18*. Ithaca, NY: Cornell University Press.
   2013. Epistemics and attitudes. *Semantics & Pragmatics*, 6, 1–59.
Anand, Pranav, and Nevins, Andrew. 2004. Shifty operators in changing contexts. Pages 20–37 of: Young, Robert B. (ed.), *Proceedings of SALT 14*. Ithaca, NY: Cornell University Press.

Asher, Nicholas. 1987. A typology for attitude verbs and their anaphoric properties. *Linguistics and Philosophy*, **10**, 125–197.
Austin, J. L. 1962. *How to Do Things with Words*. Cambridge, MA: Harvard University Press.
Bach, Kent. 1997. Do belief reports report beliefs? *Pacific Philosophical Quarterly*, **78**, 215–241.
Baglini, Rebekah. 2015. *Stative Predication and Semantic Ontology: A Crosslinguistic Study*. PhD Dissertation, University of Chicago.
Ball, Brian. 2019. Attitudes and ascriptions in Stalnaker models. *Linguistics and Philosophy*, **42**, 517–539.
Bar-Lev, Moshe E. 2015. *De re* tenses and trace conversion. Pages 184–203 of: Chemla, Emmanuel, Homer, Vincent, and Winterstein, Grégoire (eds.), *Proceedings of Semantics and Linguistic Theory 25*. eLanguage.
Baron, Christopher. 2016. Generalized concept generators. Pages 59–68 of: Hammerly, Christopher, and Prickett, Brandon (eds.), *Proceedings of NELS 46*. CreateSpace Independent Publishing Platform.
Bartsch, Renate. 1973. 'Negative transportation' gibt es nicht. *Linguistische Berichte*, **27**, 1–7.
Barwise, Jon. 1981. Scenes and other situations. *Journal of Philosophy*, **78**, 369–397.
Barwise, Jon, and Cooper, Robin. 1981. Generalized quantifiers and natural language. *Linguistics and Philosophy*, **4**, 159–219.
Barwise, Jon, and Perry, John. 1983. *Situations and Attitudes*. Cambridge, MA: MIT Press.
  1985. Shifting situations and shaken attitudes. *Linguistics and Philosophy*, **8**, 399–452.
Bary, Corien, and Altshuler, Daniel. 2015. Double access. Pages 89–106 of: Csipak, Eva, and Zeijlstra, Hedde (eds.), *Proceedings of Sinn und Bedeutung 19*. semanticsarchive.
Bäuerle, Rainer. 1983. Pragmatisch-semantische Aspekte der NP-Interpretation. Pages 121–131 of: Faust, Manfred, Harweg, Roland, Lehfeldt, Werner, and Wienold, Götz (eds.), *Allgemeine Sprachwissenschaft, Sprachtypologie und Textlinguistik: Festschrift für Peter Hartmann*. Tübingen: Gunter Narr.
Berg, Jonathan. 1988. The pragmatics of substitutivity. *Linguistics and Philosophy*, **11**, 355–370.
Berto, Francesco. 2010. Impossible worlds and propositions: Against the parity thesis. *The Philosophical Quarterly*, **40**, 471–486.
  2013. Impossible worlds. In: Zalta, Edward N. (ed.), *The Stanford Encyclopedia of Philosophy*, winter 2013 edn. Metaphysics Research Lab, Stanford University.
  2017. Impossible worlds and the logic of imagination. *Erkenntnis*, **82**, 1277–1297.
Bigelow, John. 1978. Believing in semantics. *Linguistics and Philosophy*, **2**, 101–144.

Bjerring, Jens Christian. 2013. Impossible worlds and logical omniscience. *Synthese*, **190**, 2505–2524.
Blumberg, Kyle, and Holguín, Ben. 2019. Embedded attitudes. *Journal of Semantics*, **36**, https://doi.org/10.1093/jos/ffz004, 377–406.
Bochnak, M. Ryan. 2019. Future reference with and without future marking. *Language and Linguistics Compass*, **13**, 1–22.
Bochnak, M. Ryan, Hohaus, Vera, and Mucha, Anne. 2019. Variation in tense and aspect, and the temporal interpretation of complement clauses. *Journal of Semantics*, **36**, doi:10.1093/jos/ffz008, 407–452.
Bogal-Allbritten, Elizabeth. 2016. *Building Meaning in Navajo*. PhD Dissertation, University of Massachusetts.
Bolinger, Dwight. 1968. Post-posed main phrases: An English rule for the Romance subjunctive. *Canadian Journal of Linguistics*, **14**, 3–30.
Bonardi, Paolo. 2019. Manifest validity and beyond: An inquiry into the nature of coordination and the identity of guises and propositional-attitude states. *Linguistics and Philosophy*, **42**, 475–515.
Bonomi, Andrea. 1983. *Eventi mentali*. Milano: Il Saggiatore.
  1995. Transparency and specificity in intensional contexts. Pages 164–185 of: Leonardi, P., and Santambrogio, M. (eds.), *On Quine, New Essays*. Cambridge, MA: Cambridge University Press.
Braddon-Mitchell, David, and Jackson, Frank. 2007. *The Philosophy of Mind and Cognition: An Introduction*. Milan: Blackwell Publishers.
Bratman, Michael E. 1987. *Intentions, Plans, and Practical Reason*. Cambridge, MA: Harvard University Press.
Braun, David. 1998. Understanding belief reports. *Philosophical Review*, **107**, 555–595.
  2015. Desiring, desires, and desire ascriptions. *Philosophical Studies*, **172**, 141–162.
Bresnan, Joan. 1972. *Theory of Complementation in English Syntax*. PhD Dissertation, Massachusetts Institute of Technology.
Burge, Tyler. 1977. Belief de re. *Journal of Philosophy*, **74**, 338–362.
  1978. Self-reference and translation. Pages 137–153 of: Guenthner, F., and Guenthner-Reutter, M. (eds.), *Meaning and Translation*. London: Duckworth.
  1979. Individualism and the mental. *Midwest Studies in Philosophy*, **4**, 73–122.
Büring, Daniel. 2003. To want it is to want to be there. Paper for workshop on Division of Linguistic Labor at the Château de la Bretesche near Nantes, France.
Cable, Seth. 2011. A new argument for lexical decomposition. *Linguistic Inquiry*, **42**, 131–138.
Carnap, Rudolf. 1947. *Meaning and Necessity: A Study in Semantics and Modal Logic*. Chicago, IL: University of Chicago Press.
Castañeda, Hector-Neir. 1966. 'He': A study in the logic of self-consciousness. *Ratio*, **7**, 130–157.

1967. Omniscience and indexical reference. *Journal of Philosophy*, **64**, 203–210.

1968. On the logic of attributions of self-knowledge to others. *Journal of Philosophy*, **65**, 439–456.

Charlow, Simon, and Sharvit, Yael. 2014. Bound 'de re' pronouns and the LFs of attitude reports. *Semantics & Pragmatics*, **7**, 1–43.

Chierchia, Gennaro. 1984. *Topics in the Syntax and Semantics of Infinitives and Gerunds*. PhD Dissertation, University of Massachusetts.

1989. Anaphora and attitudes *de se*. Pages 1–32 of: Bartsch, Renate, van Benthem, Joham, and van Emde Boas, Peter (eds.), *Semantics and Contextual Expression*. Dordrecht: Foris.

Chomsky, Noam, and Lasnik, Howard. 1993. The theory of principles and parameters. Pages 506–569 of: Jacobs, Joachim, von Stechow, Arnim, Sternefeld, Wolfgang, and Vennemann, Theo (eds.), *Syntax: An International Handbook of Contemporary Research*. Berlin: Mouton de Gruyter.

Church, Alonzo. 1950. On Carnap's analysis of statements of assertion and belief. *Analysis*, **10**, 97–99.

1954. Intensional isomorphism and identity of belief. *Philosophical Studies*, **5**, 65–73.

Clapp, Lenny. 2002. Davidson's program and interpreted logical forms. *Linguistics and Philosophy*, **25**, 261–297.

Clements, George N. 1975. The logophoric pronoun in Ewe: Its role in discourse. *Journal of West African Languages*, **10**, 141–177.

Collins, Chris, and Postal, Paul M. 2014. *Classical NEG Raising: An Essay on the Syntax of Negation*. Cambridge, MA: MIT Press.

Collins, Chris, and Postal, Paul M. 2017. Interclausal NEG Raising and the scope of negation. *Glossa: A Journal of General Linguistics*, **2**, 1–29.

Condoravdi, Cleo. 2002. Temporal interpretation of modals: Modals for the present and for the past. Pages 59–88 of: Beaver, David, Kaufmann, Stefan, Clark, Brady, and Casillas, Luis (eds.), *The Construction of Meaning*. Stanford, CA: CSLI Publications.

Condoravdi, Cleo, and Lauer, Sven. 2011. Performative verbs and performative acts. Pages 149–164 of: Reich, Ingo, Horch, Eva, and Pauly, Dennis (eds.), *Sinn und Bedeutung 15*. Saarbrüken: Universaar.

2016. Anankastic conditionals are just conditionals. *Semantics & Pragmatics*, **9**, 1–61.

Cooper, Robin, and Ginzburg, Jonathan. 1996. A Compositional Situation Semantics for Attitude Reports. Pages 1–15 of: Seligman, Jerry, and Westerståhl, Dag (eds.), *Logic, Language and Computation*. Stanford, CA: CSLI Publications.

Cresswell, Maxwell J. 1973. *Logics and Languages*. London: Methuen and Co.

1980. Quotational theories of propositional attitudes. *Journal of Philosophical Logic*, **9**, 17–40.

1985. *Structured Meanings: The Semantics of Propositional Attitudes*. Cambridge, MA: MIT Press.

1990. *Entities and Indices*. Boston, MA: Kluwer Academic Publishers.

2002. Why propositions have no structure. *Noûs*, **36**, 643–662.

Cresswell, Maxwell J., and von Stechow, Arnim. 1982. De re belief generalized. *Linguistics and Philosophy*, **5**, 503–535.

Crimmins, Mark. 1992. *Talk about Belief*. Cambridge, MA: MIT Press.

Crimmins, Mark, and Perry, John. 1989. The prince and the phone booth: Reporting puzzling beliefs. *Journal of Philosophy*, **86**, 685–711.

Crnič, Luka. 2011. *Getting Even*. PhD Dissertation, Massachusetts Institute of Technology.

Crowley, Paul. 2019. Neg-Raising and Neg movement. *Natural Language Semantics*, **27**, 1–17.

Davidson, Donald. 1967. The logical form of action sentences. In: Rescher, N. (ed.), *The Logic of Decision and Action*. Pittsburgh, PA: University of Pittsburgh Press.

1968. On saying that. *Synthese*, **19**, 130–146.

Davis, Wayne A. 1984. The two senses of desire. *Philosophical Studies*, **45**, 181–195.

Dawson, Virginia, and Deal, Amy Rose. 2019. Third readings by semantic scope lowering: Prolepsis in Tiwa. Pages 329–346 of: Espinal, M. Teresa, Castroviejo, Elena, Leonetti, Manuel, McNally, Louise, and Real-Puigdollers, Cristina (eds.), *Proceedings of Sinn und Bedeutung 23*. semanticsarchive.

Deal, Amy Rose. 2018. Compositional paths to *de re*. Pages 622–648 of: Maspong, Sireemas, Stefánsdóttir, Brynhildur, Blake, Katherine, and Davis, Forrest (eds.), *Proceedings of SALT 28*. Ithaca, NY: Cornell University.

den Dikken, Marcel, Larson, Richard, and Ludlow, Peter. 1996. Intensional 'transitive' verbs and concealed complement clauses. *Rivista di Linguistica*, **8**, 331–348.

Donnellan, Keith S. 1970. Proper names and identifying descriptions. *Synthese*, **21**, 335–358.

Dowty, David. 1977. Toward a semantic analysis of verb aspect and the English 'imperfective progressive'. *Linguistics and Philosophy*, **1**, 45–78.

1985. On recent analyses of the semantics of control. *Linguistics and Philosophy*, **8**, 291–331.

Dresner, Eli. 2010. Language and the measure of mind. *Mind & Language*, **25**, 418–439.

Dretske, Fred. 1972. Contrastive statements. *Philosophical Review*, **81**, 411–437.

1975. The content of knowledge. Pages 77–93 of: Freed, Bruce, Marras, A., and Maynard, P. (eds.), *Forms of Representation*. Amsterdam: North Holland Publishing Company.

Dusche, M. 1995. Interpreted logical forms as objects of the attitudes. *Journal of Logic, Language, and Information*, **4**, 301–315.

Enç, Mürvet. 1987. Anchoring conditions for tense. *Linguistic Inquiry*, **18**, 633–657.

Fara, Delia Graff. 2013. Specifying desires. *Noûs*, **47**, 250–272.

Farkas, Donka. 1992. On the semantics of subjunctive complements. Pages 69–104 of: Hirschbueler, P., and Koerner, K. (eds.), *Romance Languages and Modern Linguistic Theory*. Amsterdam and Philadelphia, PA: Benjamins.

  1988. On obligatory control. *Linguistics and Philosophy*, **11**, 27–58.

Felappi, Giulia. 2014. In defence of sententialism. *dialectica*, **68**, 581–603.

Ferreira, Marcelo. 2017. On the indexicality of Portuguese past tenses. *Journal of Semantics*, **34**, 633–657.

Fiengo, Robert, and May, Robert. 1996. Interpreted logical forms: A critique. *Rivista di Linguistica*, **8**, 349–373.

Fillmore, Charles J. 1963. The position of embedding transformations in a grammar. *Word*, **19**, 208–231.

Fine, Kit. 2003. The role of variables. *Journal of Philosophy*, **100**, 605–631.

  2007. *Semantic relationism*. Blackwell Publishing.

  2017. Truthmaker semantics. Pages 556–557 of: Hale, B., Wright, C., and Miller, A. (eds.), *Companion to the Philosophy of Language*. Chichester, UK: John Wiley & Sons, Ltd.

von Fintel, Kai. 1999. NPI-licensing, Strawson-entailment, and context-dependency. *Journal of Semantics*, **16**, 97–148.

  2012. The best we can (expect to) get? Challenges to the classic semantics for deontic modals. Paper for a session on Deontic Modals at the Central APA, February 17, 2012.

von Fintel, Kai, and Heim, Irene. 2011. Intensional semantics. Unpublished lecture notes, MIT.

Fodor, Janet Dean. 1970. *The Linguistic Description of Opaque Contexts*. PhD Dissertation, Massachusetts Institute of Technology.

Fodor, Jerry. 1977. *Language of Thought*. Hassocks: Harvester Press.

  1978. Propositional attitudes. *The Monist*, **61**, 501–523.

Forbes, Graeme. 2006. *Attitude Problems: An Essay on Linguistic Intensionality*. Oxford: Oxford University Press.

  2013. Intensional transitive verbs. In: Zalta, Edward N. (ed.), *The Stanford Encyclopedia of Philosophy*, fall 2013 edn. Metaphysics Research Lab, Stanford University.

Frazier, Lyn, Clifton Jr., Charles, Rich, Stephanie, and Duff, John. 2018. Anticipating negation: The *dos* and *don'ts* of Neg Raising. *Syntax*, **21**, 160–194.

Frege, Gottlob. 1892. Über Sinn und Bedeutung. *Zeitschrift für Philosophie und philosophische Kritik*, 100, 25–50.

Gajewski, Jon. 2005. *Neg-Raising: Polarity and Presupposition*. PhD dissertation, Massachusetts Institute of Technology.

  2007. Neg-raising and polarity. *Linguistics and Philosophy*, **30**, 289–328.

García-Carpintero, Manuel, and Torre, Stephan. 2016. *About Oneself: De Se Thought and Communication*. Oxford: Oxford University Press.

Geach, P. T. 1967. Intentional identity. *Journal of Philosophy*, **64**, 627–632.

Geenhoven, Veerle Van, and McNally, Louise. 2005. On the property analysis of opaque complements. *Lingua*, **115**, 885–914.

Gennari, Silvia. 1999. Embedded present tense and attitude reports. Pages 91–108 of: Matthews, Tanya, and Strolovitch, Devon (eds.), *Semantics and Linguistic Theory 9*. Ithaca, NY: Cornell University.

  2003. Tense meanings and temporal interpretation. *Journal of Semantics*, **20**, 35–71.

Geurts, Bart. 1998. Presuppositions and anaphors in attitude contexts. *Linguistics and Philosophy*, **21**, 545–601.

Geurts, Bart, Beaver, David I., and Maier, Emar. 2016. Discourse representation theory. In: Zalta, Edward N. (ed.), *The Stanford Encyclopedia of Philosophy*, spring 2016 edn. Metaphysics Research Lab, Stanford University.

Giannakidou, Anastasia. 1998. *Polarity Sensitivity as (Non)Veridical Dependency*. Amsterdam: John Benjamins Publishing Company.

  1999. Affective dependencies. *Linguistics and Philosophy*, **22**, 367–421.

Giannakidou, Anastasia, and Mari, Alda. Forthcoming. *Veridicality in Grammar and Thought: Modality, Propositional Attitudes and Negation*. Chicago, IL: University of Chicago Press.

Giorgi, Alessandra, and Pianesi, Fabio. 1997. *Tense and Aspect*. New York, NY: Oxford University Press.

Gluer, Kathrin, and Pagin, Peter. 2006. Proper names and relational modality. *Linguistics and Philosophy*, **29**, 507–535.

Graff, Delia. 2003. Desires, scope and tense. *Philosophical Perspectives*, **17**, 141–163.

Grano, Thomas. 2011. Mental action and event structure in the semantics of *try*. Pages 426–443 of: Ashton, Neil, Chereches, Anca, and Lutz, David (eds.), *Proceedings of SALT 21*. eLanguage.

  2015. Getting your to-do list under control: Imperative semantics and the grammar of intending. Pages 241–252 of: Bui, Thuy, and Özyildiz, Deniz (eds.), *Proceedings of NELS 45, Vol. 1*. Amherst, MA: GLSA Publications.

  2016a. A coercion-free semantics for intention reports. Pages 213–223 of: Ershova, Ksenia, Falk, Joshua, Geiger, Jeffrey, Hebert, Zachary, Jr., Robert E. Lewis, Munoz, Patrick, Phillips, Jacob B., and Pillion, Betsy (eds.), *Proceedings of the Fifty-First Annual Meeting of the Chicago Linguistic Society*. Chicago, IL: Chicago Linguistic Society.

  2016b. Semantic consequences of syntactic subject licensing: Aspectual predicates and concealed modality. Pages 306–322 of: Bade, Nadine, Berezovskaya, Polina, and Schöller, Anthea (eds.), *Proceedings of Sinn und Bedeutung 20*. semanticsarchive.

  2017a. Control, temporal orientation, and the cross-linguistic grammar of *trying*. *Glossa*, **2(1)**, 94.

  2017b. The logic of intention reports. *Journal of Semantics*, **34**, 587–632.

2019a. Belief, intention, and the grammar of persuasion. Pages 125–136 of: Ronai, E., Stigliano, L., and Sun, Y. (eds.), *Proceedings of the 54th Annual Meeting of the Chicago Linguistic Society*. Chicago, IL: Chicago Linguistic Society.

2019b. Choice functions in intensional contexts: Rehabilitating Bäuerle's challenge to the scope theory of intensionality. Pages 159–164 of: Stockwell, Richard, O'Leary, Maura, Xu, Zhongshi, and Zhou, Z.L. (eds.), *Proceedings of the 36th West Coast Conference on Formal Linguistics*. Somerville, MA: Cascadilla Proceedings Project.

Grano, Thomas, and Lasnik, Howard. 2018. How to neutralize a finite clause boundary: Phase theory and the grammar of bound pronouns. *Linguistic Inquiry*, **49**, 465–499.

Grice, Paul. 1967. *Logic and Conversation*. Unpublished ms. of the William James Lectures, Harvard University.

Gupta, Anil, and Savion, Leah. 1987. Semantics of propositional attitudes: A critical study of Cresswell's "Structured Meanings." *Journal of Philosophical Logic*, **16**, 395–410.

Gutzmann, Daniel. 2015. *Use-Conditional Meaning: Studies in Multidimensional Semantics*. Oxford: Oxford University Press.

Hacquard, Valentine. 2006. *Aspects of Modality*. PhD Dissertation, Massachusetts Institute of Technology.

2010. On the event relativity of modal auxiliaries. *Natural Language Semantics*, **18**, 79–114.

2014. Bootstrapping attitudes. Pages 330–352 of: Snider, Todd, D'Antonio, Sarah, and Weigand, Mia (eds.), *Proceedings of SALT 24*. LSA and CLC Publications.

Hacquard, Valentine, and Lidz, Jeff. 2019. Children's attitude problems: Bootstrapping verb meaning from syntax and pragmatics. *Mind & Language*, **34**, 73–96.

Haida, Andreas. 2009. *(Proto-)logophoricity in Tangale*. Handout of talk given at NELS 40, MIT.

Hanks, Peter. 2011. Structured propositions as types. *Mind*, **120**, 11–53.

2015. *Propositional Content*. Oxford: Oxford University Press.

Harley, Heidi. 2004. Wanting, having, and getting: A note on Fodor and Lepore 1998. *Linguistic Inquiry*, **35**, 255–267.

Harman, Gilbert. 1972. Logical form. *Foundations of Language*, **9**, 38–65.

Hegarty, Michael. 2016. *Modality and Propositional Attitudes*. Cambridge: Cambridge University Press.

Heim, Irene. 1982. *The Semantics of Definite and Indefinite Noun Phrases*. PhD Dissertation, University of Massachusetts.

1992. Presupposition projection and the semantics of attitude verbs. *Journal of Semantics*, **9**, 183–221.

1994. Comments on Abusch's theory of tense. Pages 143–170 of: Kamp, Hans (ed.), *Ellipsis, Tense and Questions*. Amsterdam: University of Amsterdam.

2002. Features of pronouns in semantics and morphology. Handout of talk given at USC.

Heim, Irene, and Kratzer, Angelika. 1998. *Semantics in Generative Grammar*. Malden, MA: Blackwell Publishing.

Higginbotham, James. 1983. The logic of perceptual reports: An extensional alternative to situation semantics. *Journal of Philosophy*, **80**, 100–127.

1986. Linguistic theory and Davidson's program. Pages 29–48 of: Lepore, E., and MacLaughlin, B. (eds.), *Truth and Interpretation: Perspectives on the Philosophy of Donald Davidson*. Oxford: Blackwell.

1991. Belief and logical form. *Mind and Language*, **6**, 344–369.

2003. Remembering, imagining, and the first person. Pages 496–533 of: Barber, Alex (ed.), *Epistemology of Language*. Oxford: Oxford University Press.

2006. Sententialism: The thesis that complement clauses refer to themselves. *Philosophical Issues: Philosophy of Language*, **16**, 101–119.

2009. Review of *The Nature and Structure of Content* (King 2007). *Philosophical Books*, **50**, 29–37.

Hintikka, Jaakko. 1969. Semantics for propositional attitudes. Pages 21–45 of: Davis, J. W., Hockney, D. J., and Wilson, W. K. (eds.), *Philosophical Logic*. Dordrecht: Reidel.

1975. Impossible possible worlds vindicated. *Journal of Philosophical Logic*, **4**, 475–484.

Horn, Laurence R. 1975. Neg-raising predicates: Toward an explanation. Pages 280–294 of: Grossman, Robin E., San, L. James, and Vance, Timothy J. (eds.), *Papers from the Eleventh Regional Meeting of the Chicago Linguistic Society*. Chicago, IL: Chicago Linguistic Society.

1978. Remarks on Neg-Raising. Pages 129–220 of: Cole, Peter (ed.), *Syntax and Semantics 9: Pragmatics*. New York, NY: Academic Press.

1989. *A Natural History of Negation*. Chicago, IL: University of Chicago Press.

Hornstein, Norbert, and Pietroski, Paul. 2010. Obligatory control and local reflexives: Copies as vehicles for *de se* readings. Pages 67–87 of: Hornstein, Norbert, and Polinsky, Maria (eds.), *Movement Theory of Control*. Amsterdam: John Benjamins.

Huang, C.-T. James, and Liu, C.-S. Luther. 2001. Logophoricity, attitudes and *ziji* at the interface. Pages 141–195 of: Cole, Peter, Huang, C.-T. James, and Hermon, Gabrielle (eds.), *Syntax and Semantics, Vol. 33: Long-Distance Reflexives*. New York, NY: Academic Press.

Huang, C.-T. James, Li, Y.-H. Audrey, and Li, Yafei. 2009. *The Syntax of Chinese*. Cambridge: Cambridge University Press.

Iatridou, Sabine. 2000. The grammatical ingredients of counterfactuality. *Linguistic Inquiry*, **31**, 231–270.

Ioup, Georgette. 1975. Some universals for quantifier scope. *Syntax and Semantics*, **4**, 37–58.

Jacobson, Pauline. 2018. Some people think there is Neg Raising and some don't: Neg Raising meets ellipsis. *Linguistic Inquiry*, **49**, 559–576.

2020. Neg Raising and ellipsis (and related issues) revisited. *Natural Language Semantics*, **28**, 111–140.

Jago, Mark. 2007. Hintikka and Cresswell on logical omniscience. *Logic and Logical Philosophy*, **15**, 325–354.

2015. Hyperintensional propositions. *Synthese*, **192**, 585–601.

Jerzak, Ethan. 2019. Two ways to want? *Journal of Philosophy*, **116**, 65–98.

Kamp, Hans. 1990. Prolegomena to a structural account of belief and other attitudes. Pages 27–90 of: Anderson, C. A., and Owens, J. (eds.), *Propositional Attitudes: The Role of Content in Logic, language, and Mind*. Stanford, CA: CSLI Publications.

Kamp, Hans, van Genabith, Josef, and Reyle, Uwe. 2011. Discourse representation theory. Pages 125–394 of: Gabbay, Dov M., and Guenthner, Franz (eds.), *Handbook of Philosophical Logic, 2nd Edition, Volume 15*. Dordrecht: Springer.

Kaplan, David. 1968. Quantifying in. *Synthese*, **19**, 178–214.

1989. Demonstratives. Pages 481–563 of: Almog, Joseph, Perry, John, and Wetttstein, Howard (eds.), *Themes from Kaplan*. Oxford: Oxford University Press.

Karttunen, Lauri. 1974. Presupposition and linguistic context. *Theoretical Linguistics*, **1**, 181–194.

Katz, Graham. 2004. The temporal interpretation of finite and non-finite complement clauses of attitude verbs. Ms., University of Osnabrück.

Kennedy, Christopher. 1999. *Projecting the Adjective: The Syntax and Semantics of Gradability and Comparison*. New York, NY: Garland.

2007. Vagueness and grammar: The semantics of relative and absolute gradable adjectives. *Linguistics and Philosophy*, **30**, 1–45.

Keshet, Ezra. 2008. *Good Intensions: Paving Two Roads to a Theory of the De re / De dicto Distinction*. PhD Dissertation, Massachusetts Institute of Technology.

2010a. Possible worlds and wide scope indefinites: A reply to Baüerle 1983. *Linguistic Inquiry*, **41**, 692–701.

2010b. Situation economy. *Natural Language Semantics*, **18**, 385–434.

2011. Split intensionality: A new scope theory of *de re* and *de dicto*. *Linguistics and Philosophy*, **33**, 251–283.

Keshet, Ezra, and Schwarz, Florian. 2019. De re / de dicto. In: Gundel, Jeanette, and Abbott, Barbara (eds.), *The Oxford Handbook of Reference*. Oxford: Oxford University Press.

King, Jeffrey C. 1995. Structured propositions and complex predicates. *Noûs*, **29**, 516–535.

1996. Structured propositions and sentence structure. *Journal of Philosophical Logic*, **25**, 495–521.

2007. *The Nature and Structure of Content*. Oxford: Oxford University Press.

Klecha, Peter. 2016. Modality and embedded temporal operators. *Semantics and Pragmatics*, **9**, 1–49.

Klein, Ewan. 1978. *On Sentences Which Report Beliefs, Desires, and Other Mental States*. PhD Dissertation, University of Cambridge.

Klein, Wolfgang. 1994. *Time in Language*. Cambridge: Cambridge University Press.

Kratzer, Angelika. 1981. The notional category of modality. Pages 38–74 of: Eikmeyer, J., and Riesner, H. (eds.), *Words, Worlds, and Contexts*. Berlin: Walter de Gruyter.

    1996. Severing the external argument from the verb. Pages 109–137 of: Rooryck, J., and Zaring, L. (eds.), *Phrase Structure and the Lexicon*. Dordrecht: Kluwer.

    1998a. More structural analogies between pronouns and tenses. Pages 92–109 of: Strolovitch, Devron, and Lawson, Aaron (eds.), *Proceedings of Semantics and Linguistic Theory VIII*. Cornell University: CLC Publications.

    1998b. Scope or pseudoscope? Are there wide-scope indefinites? Pages 163–196 of: Rothstein, Susan (ed.), *Events and Grammar*. Berlin: Springer.

    2006. Decomposing attitude verbs. Talk given in honor of Anita Mittwoch. The Hebrew University Jerusalem. Handout available at http://semanticsarchive.net/Archive/DcwY2JkM/attitude verbs2006.pdf.

    2019. Situations in natural language semantics. In: Zalta, Edward N. (ed.), *The Stanford Encyclopedia of Philosophy*, summer 2019 edn. Metaphysics Research Lab, Stanford University.

Kripke, Saul. 1979. A puzzle about belief. Pages 239–283 of: Margalit, Avishai (ed.), *Meaning and Use*. Dordrecht: Reidel.

    1980. *Naming and Necessity*. Oxford: Blackwell.

Kubota, Yusuke, Lee, Jungmee, Smirnova, Anastasia, and Tonhauser, Judith. 2009. On the cross-linguistic interpretation of embedded tenses. Pages 307–320 of: Riester, Arndt, and Solstad, Torgrim (eds.), *Sinn un Bedeutung 13*. Online Publikationsverbund der Universität Stuttgart.

Kuno, Susumu, and Kaburaki, Etsuko. 1977. Empathy and syntax. *Linguistic Inquiry*, **8**, 625–672.

Kusumoto, Kiyomi. 1998. Tenses as logophoric pronouns. Handout of talk given at the MIT/UConn/UMass Semantics Workshop.

Lakoff, Robin. 1969. A syntactic argument for negative transportation. Pages 140–147 of: Binnick, Robert, Davison, Alice, Green, Georgia M., and Morgan, Jerry L. (eds.), *Papers from the Fifth Regional Meeting of the Chicago Linguistic Society*. Chicago, IL: Chicago Linguistic Society.

Landau, Idan. 2013. *Control in Generative Grammar: A Research Companion*. Cambridge: Cambridge University Press.

    2015. *A Two-Tiered Theory of Control*. Cambridge: MIT Press.

    2018. Direct variable binding and agreement in obligatory control. Pages 1–41 of: Patel-Grosz, P., Grosz, P., and Zobel, S. (eds.), *Pronouns in Embedded Contexts at the Syntax-Semantics Interface*. Cham: Springer.

Larson, Richard. 2002. The grammar of intensionality. Pages 228–262 of: Preyer, Gerhard, and Peter, Georg (eds.), *Logical Form and Language*. Oxford: Oxford University Press.

Larson, Richard, and Ludlow, Peter. 1993. Interpreted logical forms. *Synthese*, **95**, 305–356.

Larson, Richard, and Segal, Gabriel. 1995. *Knowledge of Meaning*. Cambridge, MA: MIT Press.

Larson, Richard, den Dikken, Marcel, and Ludlow, Peter. 1997. Intensional transitive verbs and abstract clausal complementation. Available at http://semlab5.sbs.sunysb.edu/~rlarson/itv.pdf.

Lasersohn, Peter. 2005. Context dependence, disagreement, and predicates of personal taste. *Linguistics and Philosophy*, **28**, 643–686.

Lassiter, Daniel. 2011. *Measurement and Modality*. PhD dissertation, New York University.

Lepore, Ernie, and Loewer, Barry. 1989. You can say that again. *Midwest Studies in Philosophy*, **14**, 338–356.

Levinson, Dmitry. 2003. Probabilistic model-theoretic semantics for *want*. Pages 222–239 of: Young, R., and Zhou, Y. (eds.), *Proceedings of SALT 13*. Ithaca, NY: Cornell University.

Lewis, David. 1970. General semantics. *Synthese*, **22**, 18–67.

  1973. *Counterfactuals*. Cambridge, MA: Harvard University Press.

  1979. Attitudes *de dicto* and *de se*. *The Philosophical Review*, **88**, 513–543.

  1986. *On the Plurality of Worlds*. Oxford: Basic Blackwell.

Lin, Jo-Wang. 2012. Tenselessness. Pages 669–695 of: Binnick, Robert I. (ed.), *The Oxford Handbook of Tense and Aspect*. New York, NY: Oxford University Press.

Ludlow, Peter. 1997. Introduction to Part IV: Attitude reports. Pages 771–778 of: Ludlow, Peter (ed.), *Readings in the Philosophy of Language*. Cambridge, MA: MIT Press.

  2000. Interpreted logical forms, belief attribution, and the dynamic lexicon. Pages 31–42 of: Jaszczolt, K. M. (ed.), *Pragmatics and Propositional Attitude Reports*. Oxford: Elsevier.

Ludwig, Kirk. 1992. Impossible doings. *Philosophical Studies*, **65**, 257–281.

  2014. Propositions and higher-order attitude attributions. *Canadian Journal of Philosophy*, **43**, 741–765.

Ludwig, Kirk, and Ray, Greg. 1998. Semantics for opaque contexts. *Philosophical Perspectives*, **12**, 141–166.

Lycan, William G. 2012. Desire considered as a propositional attitude. *Philosophical Perspectives*, **26**, 201–215.

Maier, Emar. 2006. *Belief in Context: Toward a Unified Semantics of De Re and De Se Attitude Reports*. PhD Dissertation, Radbound Universiteit Nijmegen.

  2009. Presupposing acquaintance: a unified semantic for *de dicto*, *de re*, and *de se* belief reports. *Linguistics and Philosophy*, **32**, 429–474.

  2011. On the roads to *de se*. Pages 393–412 of: Ashton, Neil, Chereches, Anca, and Lutz, David (eds.), *Proceedings of SALT 21*. eLanguage.

Maier, Ernst. 2015. Parasitic attitudes. *Linguistics and Philosophy*, **38**, 205–236.
Malamud, Sophia Alexandra. 2006. *Semantics and Pragmatics of Arbitrariness*. PhD dissertation, University of Pennsylvania.
Mates, Benson. 1952. Synonymity. Pages 111–138 of: Linsky, Leonard (ed.), *Semantics and the Philosophy of Language*. Urbana, IL: University of Illinois Press.
Matthews, Robert. 2007. *The Measure of Mind*. Oxford: Oxford University Press.
Matthewson, Lisa. 1999. On the interpretation of wide-scope indefinites. *Natural Language Semantics*, **7**, 79–134.
May, Robert. 1977. *The Grammar of Quantification*. PhD Dissertation, Massachusetts Institute of Technology.
Mayr, Clemens. 2019. Triviality and interrogative embedding: Context sensitivity, factivity, and neg-raising. *Natural Language Semantics*, **27**, 227–278.
McCawley, James D. 1974. On identifying the remains of deceased clauses. *Language Research*, **9**, 73–85.
McKay, Thomas, and Nelson, Michael. 2014. Propositional attitude reports. In: Zalta, Edward N. (ed.), *The Stanford Encyclopedia of Philosophy*, spring 2014 edn. Metaphysics Research Lab, Stanford University.
Merchant, Jason. 1999. Book notice of Peter Ludlow (ed.) (1997) *Readings in the Philosophy of Language*, MIT Press. *Language*, **75**, 862–863.
Mill, John Stuart. 1843. *A System of Logic, Ratiocinative and Inductive, Being a Connected View of the Principles of Evidence, and the Methods of Scientific Investigation*. London: John W. Parker.
Milsark, Gary. 1974. *Existential Sentences in English*. PhD Dissertation, Massachusetts Institute of Technology.
Moltmann, Friederike. 1994. Attitude reports, events, and partial models. Ms., CUNY Graduate Center.
  1997. Intensional transitive verbs and quantifiers. *Natural Language Semantics*, **5**, 1–52.
  2003. Propositional attitudes without propositions. *Synthese*, **135**, 70–118.
  2008. Intensional verbs and their intentional objects. *Natural Language Semantics*, **16**, 239–270.
  2013a. *Abstract Objects and the Semantics of Natural Language*. Oxford: Oxford University Press.
  2013b. Propositions, attitudinal objects, and the distinction between actions and products. *Canadian Journal of Philosophy*, **43**, 679–701.
  2017. Cognitive products and the semantics of attitude verbs and deontic modals. Pages 254–290 of: Moltmann, F., and Textor, M. (eds.), *Act-Based Conceptions of Propositional Content*. New York, NY: Oxford University Press.
  Forthcoming. Outline of an object-based truthmaker semantics for modals and attitude reports. In: Egan, A., van Elswyck, P., and Kinderman, D. (eds.), *Unstructured Content*. New York, NY: Oxford University Press.
Montague, Michelle. 2007. Against propositonalism. *Noûs*, **41**, 503–518.

Montague, Richard. 1974. *Formal Philosophy*. New Haven, CT: Yale University Press.

Moore, Joseph. 1999. Propositions without identity. *Noûs*, 33, 1–29.

Morgan, Jerry. 1970. On the criterion of identity for noun phrase deletion. Pages 380–389 of: *Proceedings of CLS 6*. Chicago, IL: CLS.

Morzycki, Marcin. 2016. *Modification*. Cambridge: Cambridge University Press.

Moulton, Keir. 2009. *Natural Selection and the Syntax of Clausal Complementation*. PhD dissertation, University of Massachusetts.

Musan, Renate. 1995. *On the Temporal Interpretation of Noun Phrases*. PhD Dissertation, Massachusetts Institute of Technology.

Ninan, Dilip. 2008. *Imagination, Content, and the Self*. PhD Dissertation, Massachusetts Institute of Technology.

  2010. De se attitudes: Ascription and communication. *Philosophy Compass*, 5/7, 551–567.

  2012. Counterfactual attitudes and multi-centered worlds. *Semantics & Pragmatics*, 5, 1–57.

Nolan, Daniel P. 2013. Impossible worlds. *Philosophy Compass*, 8/4, 360–372.

Ogihara, Toshiyuki. 1989. *Temporal Reference in English and Japanese*. PhD Dissertation, University of Texas at Austin.

  1995a. Double-access sentences and reference to states. *Natural Language Semantics*, 3, 177–210.

  1995b. The semantics of tense in embedded clauses. *Linguistic Inquiry*, 26, 663–679.

  2007. Tense and aspect in truth-conditional semantics. *Lingua*, 117, 392–418.

Pagin, Peter. 2019. Belief sentences and compositionality. *Journal of Semantics*, 36, 241–284.

Pan, Haihua. 1995. *Locality, Self-Ascription, Discourse Prominence, and Mandarin Reflexives*. PhD Dissertation, University of Texas at Austin.

Partee, Barbara. 1973. Some structural analogies between tenses and pronouns. *Journal of Philosophy*, 70(18), 601–609.

  1974. Opacity and scope. Pages 81–101 of: Munitz, and Unger (eds.), *Semantics and Philosophy*. New York, NY: NYU Press.

  1982. Belief-sentences and the limits of semantics. Pages 87–106 of: Peters, Stanley, and Saarinen, Esa (eds.), *Processes, Beliefs, and Questions*. Dordrecht: D. Reidel Publishing Company.

Partee, Barbara H., ter Meulen, Alice, and Wall, Robert E. 1990. *Mathematical Methods in Linguistics*. Dordrecht: Kluwer Academic Publishers.

Pasternak, Robert. 2019. A lot of hatred and a ton of desire: intensity in the mereology of mental states. *Linguistics and Philosophy*, 42, https://doi.org/10.1007/s10988-018-9247-x, 267–316.

Patel-Grosz, Pritty. 2020. Pronominal typology and the *de se*/*de re* distinction. *Linguistics and Philosophy*, 43, 537–587.

Pearson, Hazel. 2013. *The Sense of Self: Topics in the Semantics of de se Expressions*. PhD dissertation, Harvard University.

2015. The interpretation of the logophoric pronoun in Ewe. *Natural Language Semantics*, **23**, 77–118.

2016. The semantics of partial control. *Natural Language & Linguistic Theory*, **34**, 691–738.

2017. *He himself* and *I. Snippets*, **31**, 20–21.

2018. Counterfactual de se. *Semantics & Pragmatics*, **11**, 1–41.

Forthcoming. Attitude verbs. In: Gutzmann, Daniel, Matthewson, Lisa, Meier, Cécile, Rullmann, Hotze, and Zimmerman, Thomas Ede (eds.), *The Wiley-Blackwell Companion to Semantics*. Oxford: John Wiley & Sons.

Pearson, Hazel, and Dery, Jeruen. 2014. Dreaming de re and de se: Experimental evidence for the Oneiric Reference Constraint. Pages 322–339 of: Etxeberria, Urtzi, Fălăuș, Anamaria, Irurtzun, Aritz, and Leferman, Bryan (eds.), *Proceedings of Sinn und Bedeutung 18*. Bayonne and Vitoria-Gasteiz: semanticsarchive.

Percus, Orin. 2000. Constraints on some other variables in syntax. *Natural Language Semantics*, **8**, 173–229.

Forthcoming. Index-dependence and embedding. In: Gutzmann, Daniel, Matthewson, Lisa, Meier, Cécile, Rullmann, Hotze, and Zimmerman, Thomas Ede (eds.), *The Wiley-Blackwell Companion to Semantics*. Oxford: John Wiley & Sons.

Percus, Orin, and Sauerland, Uli. 2003a. On the LFs of attitude reports. Pages 228–242 of: Weisberger, Matthias (ed.), *Proceedings of Sinn und Bedeutung 7*. Konstanz: Universität Konstanz.

2003b. Pronoun movement in dream reports. Pages 347–366 of: Kadowaki, Makoto, and Kawahara, Shigeto (eds.), *Proceedings of NELS 33*. Amherst: GLSA.

Perry, John. 1979. The problem of the essential indexical. *Noûs*, **13**, 3–21.

Pesetsky, David. 1992. Zero Syntax, Vol. II. Ms, Massachusetts Institute of Technology.

Phillips-Brown, Milo. 2018. I want to, but …. Pages 951–968 of: Truswell, Robert, Cummins, Chris, Heycock, Caroline, Rabern, Brian, and Rohde, Hannah (eds.), *Proceedings of Sinn und Bedeutung 21*. semanticsarchive.net.

Pickel, Bryan. 2017. Structured propositions in a generative grammar. *Mind*, **128**, 329–366.

Pickel, Bryan, and Rabern, Brian. 2017. Does semantic relationism solve Frege's puzzle? *Journal of Philosophical Logic*, **46**, 97–118.

Pollard, Carl. 2008. Hyperintensions. *Journal of Logic and Computation*, **18**, 257–282.

2015. Agnostic hyperintensional semantics. *Synthese*, **192**, 535–562.

Portner, Paul. 1997. The semantics of mood, complementation, and conversational force. *Natural Language Semantics*, **5**, 167–212.

2005. *What is Meaning? Fundamentals of Formal Semantics*. Malden, MA: Blackwell Publishing.

2007. Imperatives and modals. *Natural Language Semantics*, **15**, 351–383.

2018. *Mood*. New York, NY: Oxford University Press.

Portner, Paul, and Rubinstein, Aynat. 2012. Mood and contextual commitment. Pages 461–487 of: Chereches, Anca (ed.), *The Proceedings of SALT 22*. Ithaca, NY: CLC Publications.

Prince, Ellen. 1976. The syntax and semantics of Neg-Raising, with evidence from French. *Language*, **52**, 404–426.

Prior, Arthur. 1958. Escapism: The logical basis of ethics. Pages 135–146 of: Melden, A. I. (ed.), *Essays in Moral Philosophy*. Seattle, WA: University of Washington Press.

Putnam, Hilary. 1954. Synonymity, and the analysis of belief sentences. *Analysis*, **14**, 114–122.

Quine, Willard van Orman. 1951. Two dogmas of empiricism. *The Philosophical Review*, **60**, 20–43.

1956. Quantifiers and propositional attitudes. *Journal of Philosophy*, **53**, 177–187.

1960. *Word and Object*. Cambridge, MA: MIT Press.

1969. Propositional objects. Pages 139–160 of: Quine, Willard van Orman (ed.), *Ontological Relativity and Other Essays*. New York, NY: Columbia University Press.

Rantala, Veikko. 1982. Impossible worlds semantics and logical omniscience. *Acta Philosophica Fennica*, **35**, 106–115.

Reinhart, Tanya. 1990. Self-representation. Ms. based on lecture delivered at Princeton conference on anaphora, October 1990.

1997. Quantifier scope: How labor is divided between QR and choice functions. *Linguistics and Philosophy*, **20**, 335–397.

Richard, Mark. 1990. *Propositional Attitudes: An Essay on Thoughts and How We Ascribe Them*. Cambridge: Cambridge University Press.

2001. Seeking a centaur, adoring Adonis: Intensional transitives and empty terms. Pages 103–127 of: French, P., and Wettstein, H. (eds.), *Figurative Language, Vol. 25. Midwest Studies in Philosophy*. Oxford and New York, MA: Basic Blackwell.

Ripley, David. 2012. Structures and circumstances: Two ways to fine-grain. *Synthese*, **189**, 97–118.

Romoli, Jacopo. 2013. A scalar implicature-based approach to Neg-Raising. *Linguistics and Philosophy*, **36**, 291–353.

Romoli, Jacopo, and Sudo, Yasutada. 2009. De re/de dicto ambiguity and presupposition projection. Pages 425–438 of: Riester, Arndt, and Solstad, Torgrim (eds.), *Proceedings of Sinn und Bedeutung 13*. University of Stuttgart.

Rooth, Mats. 1982. *Association with Focus*. PhD dissertation, University of Massachusetts, Amherst.

1992. A theory of focus interpretation. *Natural Language Semantics*, **1**, 75–116.

Ross, Alf. 1941. Imperatives and logic. *Theoria*, **7**, 53–71.

Ross, John R. 1973. Slifting. Pages 133–169 of: Schutzenburger, M. P., Gross, M., and Halle, M. (eds.), *The Formal Analysis of Natural Languages: Proceedings of the First International Conference*. The Hague: Mouton.

Ross, John R. 1976. To 'have' and to not have 'have'. Pages 263–270 of: Jazayery, Mohammad Ali, Polomé, Edgar C., and Winter, Werner (eds.), *Linguistic and Literary Studies in Honor of Archibald A. Hill*. The Hague: Mouton.

Rubinstein, Aynat. 2012. *Root Modalities and Attitude Predicates*. PhD Dissertation, University of Massachusetts Amherst.

  2017. Straddling the line between attitude verbs and necessity modals. Pages 109–131 of: Arregui, Ana, Rivero, María Luisa, and Salanova, Andrés (eds.), *Modality across Syntactic Categories*. Oxford: Oxford University Press.

Russell, Bertrand. 1903. *Principles of Mathematics*. New York, NY: Norton.

  1905. On denoting. *Mind*, **14(56)**, 479–493.

  1940. *An Inquiry into Meaning and Truth*. London: George Allen and Unwin.

Sag, Ivan, and Pollard, Carl. 1991. An integrated theory of complement control. *Language*, **67**, 63–113.

Salmon, Nathan. 1986. *Frege's Puzzle*. Cambridge, MA: MIT Press.

  2010. Three perspectives on quantifying in. Pages 64–76 of: Jeshion, Robin (ed.), *New Perspectives on Singular Thought*. Oxford: Oxford University Press.

Saul, Jeniffer M. 1998. The pragmatics of attitude ascription. *Philosophical Studies*, **92**, 363–389.

  1993. Still an attitude problem. *Linguistics and Philosophy*, **16**, 423–435.

  1997. Substitution and simple sentences. *Analysis*, **57**, 102–108.

  2007. *Simple Sentences, Substitution, and Intuitions*. Oxford: Oxford University Press.

Scheffler, Israel. 1955. On synonymy and indirect discourse. *Philosophy of Science*, **22**, 39–44.

  1977. Naming and knowing. *Midwest Studies in Philosophy*, **2**, 28–41.

  1987. *Remnants of Meaning*. Cambridge, MA: MIT Press.

  1992. Belief ascription. *Journal of Philosophy*, **89**, 499–521.

  2003. *The Things We Mean*. Oxford: Clarendon.

Schlenker, Philippe. 1999. *Propositional Attitudes and Indexicality: A Cross-Categorial Approach*. PhD Dissertation, Massachusetts Institute of Technology. Revised version 2000.

  2003. A plea for monsters. *Linguistics and Philosophy*, **26**, 29–120.

  2011. Indexicality and *de se* reports. Pages 1561–1604 of: Maienborn, Claudia, von Heusinger, Klaus, and Portner, Paul (eds.), *Semantics: An International Handbook of Natural Language Meaning*. Berlin: Mouton de Gruyter.

Schwager, Magdalena. 2011. Speaking of qualities. Pages 395–412 of: Cormany, Ed, Ito, Satoshi, and Lutz, David (eds.), *Proceedings of SALT 19*. eLanguage.

Schwarz, Florian. 2006. On *needing* Propositions and *looking for* Properties. Pages 259–276 of: Gibson, M., and Howell, J. (eds.), *Proceedings of SALT XVI*. Ithaca, NY: Cornell University.

Forthcoming. Intensional transitive verbs: I owe you a horse. In: Gutzmann, Daniel, Matthewson, Lisa, Meier, Cécile, Rullmann, Hotze, and Zimmerman, Thomas Ede (eds.), *The Wiley-Blackwell Companion to Semantics*. Oxford: John Wiley & Sons.

Schwarzschild, Roger. 2002. Singleton indefinites. *Journal of Semantics*, **19**, 289–314.

Searle, John. 1958. Proper names. *Mind*, **67**, 166–173.

Segal, Gabriel. 1989. A preference for sense and reference. *Journal of Philosophy*, **86**, 73–89.

Seymour, Michel. 1992. A sentential theory of propositional attitudes. *Journal of Philosophy*, **89**, 181–201.

Sharvit, Yael. 2003. Trying to be progressive: The extensionality of *try*. *Journal of Semantics*, **20**, 403–445.

2011. Covaluation and unexpected BT effects. *Journal of Semantics*, **28**, 55–106.

2014. On the universal principles of tense embedding. *Journal of Semantics*, **31**, 263–313.

Shier, David. 2012. Propositional attitude reports. Pages 795–808 of: Russell, G., and Fara, D. Graff (eds.), *The Routledge Companion to Philosophy of Language*. New York, NY: Routledge.

Sider, Theodore. 1995. Three problems for Richard's theory of belief ascriptions. *Canadian Journal of Philosophy*, **25**, 487–514.

Sim, Kwang Mong. 1997. Epistemic logic and logical omniscience: A survey. *International Journal of Intelligent Systems*, **12**, 57–81.

Smith, Carlota. 1978. The syntax and interpretation of temporal expressions in English. *Linguistics and Philosophy*, **2**, 43–99.

Soames, Scott. 1985. Lost innocence. *Linguistics and Philosophy*, **8**, 59–71.

1987. Direct reference, propositional attitudes and semantic content. *Philosophical Topics*, **15**, 47–87.

1995. Beyond singular propositions. *Canadian Journal of Philosophy*, **25**, 515–549.

2002. *Beyond Rigidity: The Unfinished Semantic Agenda of Naming and Necessity*. Oxford: Oxford University Press.

2010. *Philosophy of Language*. Princeton, NJ: Princeton University Press.

2014. Cognitive propositions. Pages 91–124 of: King, Jeffrey C., Soames, Scott, and Speaks, Jeff (eds.), *New Thinking about Propositions*. Oxford: Oxford University Press.

2015. *Rethinking Language, Mind, and Meaning*. Princeton, NJ: Princeton University Press.

2019. Propositions as cognitive acts. *Synthese*, **196**, 1369–1383.

Stalnaker, Robert. 1968. A theory of conditionals. Pages 98–112 of: Resher, N. (ed.), *Studies in Logical Theory*. Oxford: Blackwell.

1984. *Inquiry*. Cambridge, MA: MIT Press.

1987. Semantics for belief. *Philosophical Topics*, **15**, 177–190.

2004. Assertion revisited. *Philosophical Studies*, **118**, 299–322.

von Stechow, Arnim. 1995. On the proper treatment of tense. Pages 362–386 of: Galloway, Teresa, and Simons, Mandy (eds.), *SALT V*. Cornell University.

2002. Binding by verbs: Tense, person and mood under attitudes. Ms., University of Tübingen.

2003. Feature deletion under semantic binding. Pages 133–157 of: Kadowaki, M., and Kawahara, S. (eds.), *Proceedings of NELS 33*. Amherst, MA: GLSA Publications.

von Stechow, Arnim, and Zimmerman, Thomas Ede. 2005. A problem for a compositional account of *de re* attitudes. Pages 207–228 of: Carlson, G. N., and Pelletier, F. J. (eds.), *Reference and Quantification: The Partee Effect*. Stanford, CA: CSLI.

Stephenson, Tamina. 2007a. Judge dependence, epistemic modals, and predicates of personal taste. *Linguistics and Philosophy*, **30**, 487–525.

2007b. *Towards a Theory of Subjective Meaning*. PhD Dissertation, MIT.

2010. Control in centred worlds. *Journal of Semantics*, **27**, 409–436.

Sudo, Yasutada. 2014. On *de re* predicates. Pages 447–456 of: Santana-LaBarge, Robert E. (ed.), *West Coast Conference on Formal Linguistics 31*. Somerville, MA: Cascadilla Press.

Swanson, Eric. 2011. Propositional atittudes. Pages 1538–1561 of: Maienborn, Claudia, von Heusinger, Klaus, and Portner, Paul (eds.), *Semantics: An International Handbook of Natural Language Meaning*. Berlin: Mouton de Gruyter.

Szabó, Zoltán Gendler. 2010. Specific, yet opaque. Pages 32–41 of: Aloni, Maria, Bastiaanse, Harald, de Jager, Tikitu, and Schulz, Katrin (eds.), *Logic, Language, and Meaning: Proceedings of the Seventeenth Amsterdam Colloquium*. Berlin: Springer.

2011. Bare quantifiers. *Philosophical Review*, **120**, 247–283.

Tancredi, Christopher. 2010. Rigid designation and Frege's puzzle. *CARLS series of Advanced Study of Logic and Sensibility*, 4, 185–196.

Thomason, Richmond H. 1980. A model theory for propositional attitudes. *Linguistics and Philosophy*, **4**, 47–70.

Todorović, Neda. 2015. Tense and aspect (in)compatibility in Serbian matrix and subordinate clauses. *Lingua*, **167**, 82–111.

Tonhauser, Judith. 2015. Cross-linguistic temporal reference. *Annual Review of Linguistics*, **1**, 129–154.

Uegaki, Wataru. 2016. Content nouns and the semantics of question-embedding. *Journal of Semantics*, **33**, 623–660.

2019. The semantics of question-embedding predicates. *Language and Linguistics Compass*, **13**, 1–17.

van Rooij, Robert. 1999. Some analyses of pro-attitudes. Pages 534–548 of: de Swart, Henriëtte (ed.), *Logic, Game Theory and Social Choice*. Tilburg: Tilburg University Press.

Villalta, Elisabeth. 2008. Mood and gradability: An investigation of the subjunctive mood in Spanish. *Linguistics and Philosophy*, **31**, 467–522.

Wang, Yingying, and Pan, Haihua. 2014. A note on the non-de se interpretation of attitude reports. *Language*, **90**, 746–754.
Wechsler, Stephen. 2008. Dualist syntax. In: Müller, Stefan (ed.), *Proceedings of the 15th International Conference on Head-Driven Phrase Structure Grammar*. CSLI On-line Publications.
  2010. What 'you' and 'I' mean to each other: Person indexicals, self-ascription, and theory of mind. *Language*, **86**, 332–365.
White, Aaron Steven, and Rawlins, Kyle. 2018. Question agnosticism and change of state. Pages 1325–1342 of: Truswell, Rob, Cummins, Chris, Heycock, Caroline, Rabern, Brian, and Rohde, Hannah (eds.), *Proceedings of Sinn und Bedeutung 21*. Independently published.
Williams, Alexander. 2015. *Arguments in Syntax and Semantics*. Cambridge: Cambridge University Press.
Winter, Yoad. 1997. Choice functions and the scopal semantics of indefinites. *Linguistics and Philosophy*, **20**, 399–467.
Wurmbrand, Susi. 2014. Tense and aspect in English infinitives. *Linguistic Inquiry*, **45**, 403–447.
Yalcin, Seth. 2018. Belief as question-sensitive. *Philosophy and Phenomenological Research*, **97**, 23–47.
Yanovich, Igor. 2011. The problem of counterfactual *de re* attitudes. Pages 56–75 of: Ashton, Neil, Chereches, Anca, and Lutz, David (eds.), *Proceedings of SALT 21*. eLanguage.
Zimmerman, Thomas Ede. 1993. On the proper treatment of opacity in certain verbs. *Natural Language Semantics*, **1**, 149–179.
  2006. Monotonicity in opaque verbs. *Linguistics and Philosophy*, **29**, 715–761.

# Index

acquaintance relations, 109–20, 138, 140–2
agreement, 141–2, 189
Amharic, 150–1

binding, 18, 100, 119, 125–6, 141–3, 145, 186

centered worlds, 128–9, 132, 135, 136, 139, 141, 153
Chinese, *see* Mandarin Chinese
choice functions, 91, 93–4, 96, 97, 99
*claim*, 129–31, 133, 136, 137, 143, 193
closure (logical), 33–6, 39–42, 44, 63
compartmentalization, 39, 41
complementizer, 25, 59
compositionality, 16, 66, 75
concept generators, 117–19, 121
conditionals, 21, 50, 69, 71, 80, 92, 105, 156, 157
conflicting desires, 168–72
conjunction introduction, 168–72
context parameter, 132, 146, 149
control, 123–5, 128–30, 132–4, 136, 137, 141, 145, 152, 179
conversational implicature, 6, 45, 64, 72–4, 194
counterfactual attitude reports, 112, 142–3, 157, 162, 181

*de dicto/de re* ambiguity, 26, 73, 82–121, 199, 203
*de nunc*, *see* temporal *de se*
*de re* blocking effect, 137–40
*de se* attitude reports, 122–53, 187
*de te* attitude reports, 133–4
decomposition, 59–63
degrees, 173–4

Discourse Representation Theory, 52, 121
double access, 192, 205
double vision, 106–20
*doubt*, 63, 180
*dream*, 138–40, 142, 152, 183

ellipsis, 126, 197
event semantics, 57
Ewe, 144–5
extensional semantics, 16–22

fiction verbs, 183
focus, 174–6
Fodor's third reading, 94–6, 103, 121
Frege's puzzle, 7, 54, 66–81, 108

gradability, 172–4, 180, 183

hidden indexicals, 68, 75–6, 78, 81, 107
Hintikka, Jaakko, 29–42
*hope*, 60, 62, 122, 123, 163, 181, 191, 193, 194, 203
hyperintensionality, 42–55, 64, 70

implicit belief, 37, 42
impossible worlds, 49–52, 65
indexicals, 132, 146–51
indirect speech reports, 2, 54, 133
infinitives, 1, 3, 59–63, 123, 125, 179, 191
*intend*, 2, 60, 163, 181
Intensional Functional Application, 26, 33, 59, 98, 102, 129, 136, 186
intensional semantics, 22–6
intensional transitive verbs, 3, 198–206
intensionalism, 198, 203–4

233

intentionality, 2
Interpreted Logical Forms, 54–5, 65, 78

Japanese, 190
judge parameter, 135

Kaplan, David, 49, 107, 110–14, 116, 118, 146
Kripke, Saul, 24, 70–1, 76–9, 107, 108
Kripke's puzzle, 76–9, 107

Lewis, David, 23, 54, 110, 124, 126–7, 138, 153, 156
logical closure, see closure (logical)
logophors, 144–6
long-distance reflexives, 151–2

Mandarin Chinese, 151–2
mathematical beliefs, 46–7
modal base, 56, 159, 165, 170
modals, 21, 31, 56, 59, 63, 80, 87, 105, 159, 165, 180
monotonicity, 164–7, 171
Montague–Scott approach, 41–2, 171, 176
mood, 179–81, 183

Navajo, 61, 151
Neg Raising, 193–8, 205, 206
negative polarity items, 147, 177, 194–5, 197, 198
Nez Perce, 119

opaque, 95, 103
ordering source, 56, 159, 169–72, 180

perceptual reports, 3, 59–60
*persuade*, 61, 134, 141, 181
possible worlds, 22–3
predicates of personal taste, 135–7
presupposition projection, 105–6, 176–7, 195
problem of logical equivalence, 5, 7, 47, 52, 55
problem of logical omniscience, 36–42

proper names, 6–7, 16, 19, 24, 42, 54, 66–81, 107–8, 110, 120
propositional concepts, 47–9
propositionalism, 198, 200–3, 205

question-sensitivity, 40, 170
Quine, Willard Van Orman, 19, 107–10, 128, 200

*res* movement, 115–19, 121
rigid designators, 24, 54, 70, 76, 80, 88, 108, 120

scope, 84–105, 166, 198, 204
self-ascription, 127, 147
sententialism, 53–4, 65, 74
sequence of tense, 188–91
shifted indexicals, 132, 146–51
shortest spy, 112–15
situation semantics, 51–2, 65
Spanish, 180, 181
specific indefinites, 95, 199
Split Intensionality, 102–5
Stalnaker, Robert, 38–40, 46–9, 155, 156, 164, 178, 179
structured propositions, 52–4, 65

temporal *de se*, 187–8
tense, 184–92, 204, 205
third reading, see Fodor's third reading
transparent, 95, 96, 103
truth conditionality, 4, 16, 22
*try*, 182, 203
type-shifting, 131, 173

Upper Limit Constraint, 190, 191

veridicality, 180
vividness, 113–15

*want*, 60, 62, 82, 94, 109, 113, 152, 154–83, 193, 198–202
*wish*, 60, 157
world pronouns, 97–102, 104, 105, 117

Zazaki, 146–9